ECONOMIC DEVELOPMENT AND
THE DYNAMICS OF CLASS

STUDIES OF DEVELOPING COUNTRIES (formerly *Non European Societies*)

edited by

prof. dr. L. H. Janssen S.J. (Tilburg), dr. P. Kloos (Leiden), prof. dr. R. A. J. van Lier (Wageningen) and prof. dr. J. D. Speckmann (Leiden).

1 dr. Annemarie de Waal Malefijt, *The Javanese of Surinam. Segment of a plural society*
2 prof. dr. A. J. F. Köbben, *Van primitieven tot medeburgers*
3 V. F. P. M. van Amelsvoort M.D., *Culture, stone age and modern medicine. The early introduction of integrated rural health in a non-literate society. A New Guinea case study in medical anthropology*
4 dr. J. D. Speckman, *Marriage and kinship among the Indians in Surinam*
5. dr. L. M. Serpenti, *Cultivators in the Swamps, Social structure and horticulture in a New Guinea society (Frederik-Hendrik Island, West New Guinea)*
6 dr. D. G. Jongmans, *Anthropologists in the Field*
7 dr. R. A M. van Zantwijk, *Servants of the Saints. The social and cultural identity of a Tarascan community in Mexico*
8 dr. Cora Vreede-de Stuers, *Parda, A study of Moslim Women's Life in Northern India*
9 dr. Cora Vreede-de Stuers, *Girl Students in Jaipur*
10 dr. J. Tennekes, *Anthropology, Relativism and Method. An inquiry into the methodological principles of a science of culture*
11 prof. dr. J. van Baal, *'Symbols for communication'*
12 dr. P. Kloos, *'The Maroni River Caribs of Surinam'*
13 dr. K. W. van der Veen, *'I give thee my daughter'*
14 dr. G. Jansen, *The doctor-patient relationship in an African tribal society*
15 prof. Peter C. W. Gutkind, *Urban anthropology.* Perspectives on 'Third World' urbanization and urbanism
16 *The neglected factor.* 'Family planning: perception and reaction at the base.' Edited by D. G. Jongmans and H. J. M. Claessen
17 dr. P. Kloos, *Culturele antropologie.* Een inleiding. 2e druk
18 dr. G. M. van Etten, *Rural health development in Tanzania.* A case-study of medical sociology in a developing country
19 prof. dr. B. F. Galjart, *Peasant mobilization and solidarity*
20 dr. B. G. Grijpstra, *Common efforts in the development of rural Sarawak, Malaysia*
21 Thomas K. Fitzgerald, editor, *Nutrition and anthropology in action*
22 Gary Brana-Shute, *On the Corner.* Male social life in a Paramaribo Creole neighborhood
23 dr. P. H. Streefland, *The Sweepers of Slaughterhouse.* Conflict and Survival in a Karachi Neighborhood
24 dr. M. Vellinga, *Economic Development and the Dynamics of Class.* Industrialization, Power and Control in Monterrey, Mexico

PREFACE

This study has explored the relationship between the Mexican process of economic development and the dynamics of its sociopolitical process, with an emphasis on the major growthpole of the country: the industrial city of Monterrey. It has focussed on the period of the 1960's and the beginning of the 1970's when the economic growth through industrialization took on spectacular proportions on a national level and in particular in Monterrey.

In the debate on external dependency and industrial development in Latin America, Monterrey takes a special position. It represents one of the few areas in Latin America where an autonomous large-scale process of industrial development has come about, "carried" by local entrepreneurs who, moreover, have developed into one of the most powerful pressure groups on the national level.

The study is based on research in Mexico in 1968, 1970 and 1971, and visits to the area in 1973 and 1976. The first version was written in 1974 and has been substantially revised since then.

I am indebted to a number of people and institutions who have helped me in one way or another in the writing of this book. I owe a great deal to the encouragement and advice I have received throughout from Gerald R. Leslie. Benjamin Gorman, Dirk Kruijt, L. N. McAlister, T. Lynn Smith, Glaucio A. D. Soares, J. S. Vandiver and Hernán Vera Godoy read various sections of the book and made a number of valuable suggestions. The quality of the analysis owes much to Sugiyama Iutaka.

I gratefully acknowledge the help of the University of Florida and the University of Utrecht Computing Centers. The Center for Latin American Studies at the University of Florida gave me financial assistance during my research in Mexico, for which I would like to express my gratitude.

I am indebted to Jorge Balán who helped me to establish contact in the Monterrey area. In Monterrey, the staff of the *Centro de Investigaciones Económicas* at the Universidad de Nuevo León has given invaluable assistance during the actual fieldwork stage. I am grateful to Jesús Marcos, Ernesto Bolaños, Alejandro Martínez, Andrés Montemayor and Ramiro García. Lic. Martinez assisted me in the selection and training of the interviewers. Lic. Montemayor arranged a number of interviews with Monterrey prominents. Lic. García assisted me in sampling.

It is impossible to mention here all the people in Monterrey who have helped me in one way or another in the completion of the research. I would like to make an exception for Ernesto Leal Flores, publisher of the weeklies *Oigame* and *El Ciudadano* who made available to me a complete copy of the volumes 1970 and 1971, for which I am very grateful.

The major share of the typing was carried out by Corrie van Wijngaarden and Pat Whitehearst. I am grateful to them for their assistance.

Yvon Vellinga has helped me in the many tedious tasks of producing the manuscript and with a show of solidarity for which I am deeply grateful.

TABLE OF CONTENTS

X

LIST OF TABLES

LIST OF FIGURES

CHAPTER I
INTRODUCTION

Since the government of populist president Lazaro Cárdenas in the 1930's, the Mexican economy has been characterized by rather spectacular growth rates. Notably in the 1960's, before the Brazilian "miracle" came in the forefront of attention, Mexico's rapid rate of economic growth and the reasons behind it drew the attention of the international economist community (cf. Goldsmith, 1966; Freithaler, 1967; Fernandez Hurtado, 1967; King, 1970).

The various studies focus on different aspects of this growth process, but they concur in their emphasis on the leading role of the government, or rather the state apparatus in the economic and political sphere. Especially its initiative in this latter area has been pronounced.

Parallel to the dynamics in the economic structure, a political apparatus has been created that has served the goal of economic expansion. The equilibrium between the economic and the political process, however, has been delicate from the start. In the course of the 1960's, the growing tension between the dynamics of economic development and stagnating political structures, which became manifest in the increasing demand for autonomous popular participation in the political process, emphasized the repressive tendencies of the system. The general unrest among the popular strata in this period, culminating in the student-worker revolt of 1968 and its subsequent brutal repression, should be viewed in this context.

The present study concentrates on this area of tensions between economic and political development in a period of rapid industrialization. The main questions directing it, concern not only the general characteristics of each of the two processes and the way they are interrelated. More particularly they focus on the mechanisms by which the political system is maintained, on the problem of how these function and in whose interests, and how again social and political forces are related to economic interests.

The study of these questions utilizes class analysis. The application of this theoretical perspective to Latin American societies has, as is well known, not been without debate. This discussion has been carried mainly by foreign scholars, dedicating themselves to the study of Latin American problems. Among Latin American scholars themselves, class analysis is much less an issue and is generally accepted as a useful key to understanding their social and economic reality.

The debate has centered around the status of horizontal versus vertical

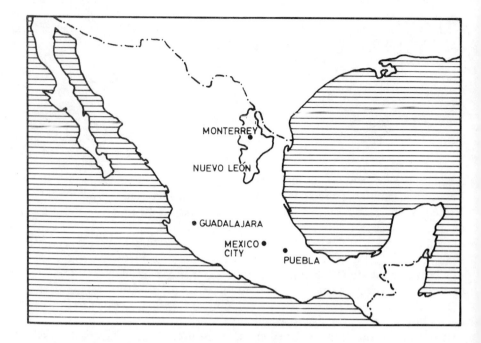

structure mechanisms as the central principles which explain the functioning of the sociopolitical system (cf. Williams, 1969; Hutchinson, 1966: Jaguaribe, 1968; Leff, 1968). The vertical chains obviously cut through horizontal class interest groupings and interfere with class mobilization. Their importance has been emphasized through a clientelist model of society[1] that filed an exclusive claim to the valid interpretation of Latin American political reality, condemning class analysis to the category of irrelevant approaches.

This discussion pro and contra clientelism or class analysis has become quite voluminous and cannot be reproduced here (for an excellent reference: Flynn, 1973) We would like however to make a few general remarks on the issue.

It is clear that the validity of many of the findings on the functioning of Latin American political systems, inspired by the clientelist model, cannot be denied. After all, patron-client ties figure among these systems' most conspicuous characteristics. The objections against the model that was used then, primarily concern its pretension of exclusivity and its incapacity to provide an explanation of the political process in which more justice is done to the elements of coercion and manipulation, part of the power relationship ex-

---

[1] This model has been defined most adequately by Lemarchand and Legg (1972). Clientelism, according to them, corresponds to "a more or less personalized relationship between actors or sets of actors commanding unequal wealth, status or influence, based on conditional loyalties, and involving mutually beneficient transactions." (151-152)

pressed in political clientelism. Most studies taking the clientelist approach (cf. Lemarchand and Legg, 1972; Powell, 1970) almost automatically assume a spontaneous appearance of these patron-client patterns from below, and bypass the issue of their deliberate organization and maintenance for political purposes from above (Flynn, 1973: 26), an issue which in Mexico is very acute (González Casanova, 1965, 1968; Anderson and Cockcroft, 1972; Cockcroft, 1972). This emphasis on the alleged voluntaristic aspects of these vertically oriented structures further assumes consensus and harmony in mechanisms that, in our opinion, should be interpreted as instances of class control in a situation where the alternatives at the lower levels of society are severely limited.

These points summarize the reasons why, in this study, we have opted for class analysis without however negating the heuristic value of clientelism which can make us understand better the workings of some of the mechanisms of class control. This class analysis follows the classical perspective and operates on the macrolevel al well as on the microlevel. On these levels, the problem of maintenance and change in the political system is studied against the background of the dynamics of the process of economic development.

The research problem, and the specific approach taken, suggest an emphasis on the position of urban workers, and in particular the industrial proletariat, which in Marxian theory is the source of the dynamics of the system. This status cannot always be claimed by this segment of the working class in Latin America (Touraine and Pécaut, 1967-1968; Landsberger, 1967). In fact, research indicates them to form a basis for status quo oriented politics. These observations, however, concern primarily the leanings of urban organized labour, reflect the position of the labor leadership, their firm integration in government-manipulated patronage networks, and the effective functioning of the instruments of manipulation and control at their disposal. The rank and file themselves, and this applies in particular to Mexico, have not been heard and have been projected into the role of passive subjects of these instruments[2]

This study of industrial workers and their potential as a dynamic factor with regard to socioeconomic change will be realized through an analysis of their alienation and class consciousness. In the next chapter, the theoretical perspective that has directed the study will be further elaborated.

[2] González Casanova (1968) laments the general absence of research in the area. The only study at the time which has been published on the subject was Kahl (1965).

3

CHAPTER II
THE THEORETICAL CONTEXT*

1. INTRODUCTION

In this study a general theoretical perspective has been adopted that has drawn its basic inspiration from the Marxian theses on the source and nature of societal dynamics. Before defining the main elements of this framework, we will make a few remarks on the scientific status of the Marxian approach.

One of the most characteristic features of Marxian analysis is its synthetic character. It attempts to grasp society in its totality[1], rather than to deal with any specific aspect in isolation. At the same time it is historical. It does not analyze societies in terms of their structures at one given moment, but it attempts to arrive at an understanding of their structure and functioning within the context of processes of historical change.

These synthetic-analytic and historical-dynamic characteristics are among the most attractive elements of the Marxian approach. Rather than presenting ready made, universally valid theories, this approach provides assumptions, principles and building blocks that can be utilized in the development of paradigms for the analysis of processes of societal change (cf. Zeitlin, 1967; 152). In addition the definition is being emphasized of "general laws", propositions explaining changes between the phases of development of a mode of production and the change from one mode of production to another. These paradigms and "general laws" move primarily on a metatheoretical level. Here their heuristic qualities serve in the generation of the general hypotheses that guide and direct the study of concrete situations. They do, however, not define directly any specific concrete social reality. These are theoretical instruments, tools that serve us in the process of obtaining knowledge of this reality. The key concepts used by us to study the dynamics of class, alienation and class consciousness, should be seen in this light.

---

* Parts of this chapter were taken from a study written together with Dirk Kruijt (cf. Kruijt and Vellinga, 1977).

[1] This totality has a structure, through which Marx means to indicate that the various elements are distributed according to an organization of the whole. This organization determines the function of each element within the totality (cf. Bottomore, 1966; 13 ff). These structures of elements, and subelements, are constantly subject to change and their mutual interaction account for a complex series of feedback mechanisms. The Althusserian systematization of Marx's writings (cf. Althusser, 1965; Poulantzas, 1969; Harnecker, 1969), distinguishes three main substructures in a societal system: the economic structure, the idiological structure, and the legal-political structure. We will adhere to the original Marxian distiction between the economic (production), social (classes) and political (organization of the State) orders (cf. letter by Marx to Annenkow, 28-XII-1846).

4

It is obvious that the economic structure of the capitalist mode of production was most intensively studied bij Marx and here the theoretical framework has been elaborated most systematically. For other societal spheres it has been less developed and provides general reference points for investigation. The problem areas in which the Marxian approach presents definite advantages over other theoretical perspectives are especially those of power, coercion and control. Here, and in other areas, however, no exclusive validity is claimed. In practice the metatheoretical nature of the Marxian perspective facilitates the assimilation of lower-order hypotheses within the general framework through theoretical synthesis.

Within the Marxian model of analysis the basic dynamics is defined by a number of rather general statements of tendency. The structure of the "essential" economic process, production, and its results depend upon the interaction between two conditions: the level of development of the productive forces and the nature of the relations of production. The productive forces initially fulfill here the role of dynamic agent with regard to the structure of the relations of production, which in turn feed back on the development of the productive forces. A similar relationship of a dialectical nature is proposed between the economic order as a whole ("substructure") and the processes of change in the political order and value sphere ("superstructure"). The economic conditions do play the role of "ultimate determinants", but, once developed, the institutions (military, bureaucratic, legal, religious) that form part of the "superstructure" acquire a certain autonomy in functioning and development and feed back upon the "substructure".[2] These mechanisms can be presented as follows:

Figure 1: The basic dynamics of the Marxian scheme

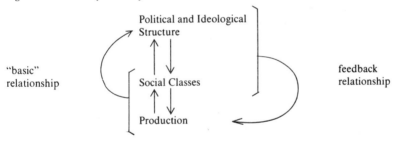

[2] The theses on "ultimate determination of economic conditions" and "relative autonomy of superstructural institutions" have been worked out most clearly in Marx and Engels' historical and political analyses (see in particular: *The Eighteenth Brumaire of Louis Bonaparte* and *The Peasant War in Germany*). In these writings the dynamics of historical change indeed finds its ultimate explanation in changes in the economic structure. The "ultimate determination" of the superstructure bij the substructure is a recurrent theme, emphasized also because of the constant polemic with the 19th century idealistic tradition (cf. letter from Engels to Mehring, 14-VI-1893). However, structure and process within the superstructure, once institutionalized, in some instances are being analyzed rather autonomously. Here the substructure is presented not als a "cause" but as a "motor" of processes of change in society, functioning through impulses and mutual feedback mechanisms. Similar phenomena are being specified for the superstructure (cf. also letter from Marx to Engels, 10-IX-1862).

The concept of social classes fits in the model between the "sub"-structure and the "superstructure".

As a historical category, social classes result from processes of exploitation in the economic order. They stand in an osmotic relationship to the politico-ideological order. As an analytical category the concept has been used by the classical Marxists in various ways. Despite its important role in the analysis of processes of social change, Marx himself postponed a systematic exposition of his theory of class and devoted most of his time to a continuous refinement of the model in *Capital*. The manuscript of the third and last volume of *Capital* breaks off after little more than one page of what should have been a systematic discussion of the problem. From Marx's writings, however, and especially those in which he applied his theoretical framework and methodology to the study of the problems of his time, an adequate definition can be inferred of the essentials of the theory of class (cf. Marx, 1967b; Marx, 1964; also Ollman, 1968).

2. CLASS AND CLASS CONSCIOUSNESS

2.1. *Marx's Class Analysis*

The two-class conflict model is the most wellknown and at the same time the most abstract model of a class society Marx and Engels have used. The conflict results from differences in ownership and control of the means of production. These differences go back to the development of a social division of labor, with the growing separation of capital and labor as its core process. The result is an order of unequal functions, gradually institutionalizing and maintaining itself, through the unequal distribution of power and economic surplus. The "capitalists" expropriate surplus value produced by "those who own nothing but their labor time" (*exploitation*)[3]. These processes of accumulation and expropriation of capital skew the power relations in society and create a "dominated" class controlled by a "dominant" class determined to preserve its privilege (*power*). In fact both classes complement each other as mutually antagonistic parts of the same exploitation system.

Ossowski (1963) has pointed to the fact that in Marx and Engels' more concrete historical studies more classes are mentioned than the two figuring in the more abstract model.[4] He attributes this phenomenon to inconsistencies due to problems with the conceptual operations of class analysis. The study of

---

[3] "Exploitation" in this way had a rather precise, quantitative meaning (cf. Harnecker, 1971) and lacked the vagueness we find in more recent analyses. González Casanova (1969) offers an attempt to reestablish the status of exploitation in modern social science.

[4] In *The Eighteenth Brumaire of Louis Bonaparte*, for example, figure no less than nineteen groupings that are defined as "classes".

[5] See Israel (1970: 282) and Dos Santos (1970: 175 ff) for an effort to combine class models and specific levels of analysis.

these operations, however, provides arguments other than those mentioned by Ossowski, and bring forward a more systematic definition of the use of the bipolar class model.

Marx and Engels use the class model in various definitions, depending on the specific problem that was studied and the level of abstraction on which the analysis moved.[5] The number and type of classes are determined by a number of criteria that ultimately go back to the basic discriminating criterion (the relationship to the means of production). Among these so-called "secondary criteria" are stratification factors (income, education, occupation, life style) and the location in the structure of interestgroups in society. The multidimensional multiple-class model will be used in more specific and concrete analyses. The bipolar two-class model here serves primarily an important heuristic purpose and does not directly define a specific empirical reality. The use of various levels of analysis and class models can be systematized as follows:

Figure 2: Class analysis

level of analysis	objective of the analysis	additional criterion	examples
mode of production	basic tendencies of social change (f.e. from feudalism to capitalism)	consciousness power	organization of bourgeoisie and proletariat; dominating and dominated classes
phase	changes within a mode of production (f.e. monopoly capitalism, dependent incorporation within world economy)	power stratification surplus distribution	international vs. national bourgeoisie; worker aristocracy; middle classes
cycles	changes within a phase (f.e. Mexico under Cárdenas)	political; in principle as many criteria as distinct interest groups can be defined	coalitions between segments of the working class

(a)   The level of the mode of production (present in *Capital* and the other more abstract analytical writings): the processes analyzed on this level concern qualitative changes in the expropriation of the economic surplus, the criteria being exploitation and domination. The bipolar two-class conflict model is used here.

(b)   The level of the phasic changes within a mode of production: the processes analyzed concern the rise and consolidation of sectors within the class

7

structure and their relationship to more specific forms of surplus expropriation and participation in the political power structure. This requires the use of a multiple-class model. In his analyses of English industrial capitalism, Marx himself uses a model containing three classes (industrial and rural bourgeoisie, proletariat) and a number of "residual" categories ("middle classes"). The neomarxist *dependentistas* like Sunkel (1972), Dos Santos (1970, 1971) and Szentes (1976) follow a similar procedure distinguishing between the "international" and the "local consular" bourgeoisie, the latter one being subdivided in a number of sectors. In addition the "middle class" is explicitly recognized as a category having its societal base in the political and military institutions.

(c) the level of the (political) cycles within a particular phase: in their concrete historical studies Marx and Engels (Marx, 1964; 1967b; 1969; Engels, 1966) include in their class models in principle any interest group that has organized and entered the political arena. Stratification factors and short-term economic and political interests serve here as discriminating criteria. The analysis concerns primarily the formation of class coalitions and the short-term struggle of interests during concrete processes of economic and social change. The class structure than, is a multiple and multidimensional one.

It is clear, now, why the presence of various different class models does not represent a theoretical inconsistency in Marx's work. It does relate to the use of different levels of analysis and discriminating criteria while adapting class analysis to the specific requirements of the study of concrete situations.

2.2. The Concept of Class Consciousness

In the previous paragraph social classes have been analyzed in relation to other classes as part of the dynamics of class structures. Class consciousness conceptualizes a dimension of the process of class formation. This process has two components:

(a) The "objective" component of class formation: the changes in the structure of production and the technical division of labor from which develop classes or class segments in correlation with a form of exploitation, accumulation and power. This process results in the formation of a "Klasse an sich".

(b) The "subjective" component: the formation of a "Klasse für sich". The concepts of "Klasse an sich" and "Klasse für sich"[6] function as poles of a continuum describing the process of class formation. "Klasse an sich" denotes the outcome of the objective process of formation: the (internal) equivalence of positions of those belonging to a class resulting from a shared location in society's structure. This location ultimately depends on the relations of ownership and control of the means of production. "Klasse für sich" presup-

---

[6] The terms were Bukharin's.

poses the growth of an awareness of class position and shared interests as a consequence of the participation in social and political conflict. During this process organizations for the defense of these interests (social movements, unions, parties) are formed. In addition, the development of an ideology takes place on the basis of this awareness of a community of interests, the interpretation of the existing structure of society and the strategy and tactics of action. The development of organization and ideology will result in forms of organized action (bargaining, strikes, uprisings), as indications of a class struggle directed towards the radical change of the economic, social and political order.

Figure 3: The process of class formation

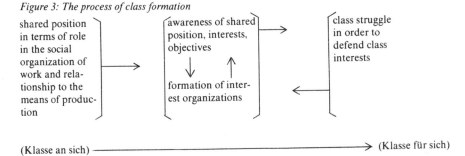

(Klasse an sich) ⟶ (Klasse für sich)

The concept of class consciousness, as the concept of social class, moves on various levels of analysis. On the level of the mode of production it functions as a pure, abstract theoretical concept, without *direct* empirical referent. Here it conceptualizes the systematic expression of the interests of a class. This requires a unity of perspective of the functioning of society, the own class position also in relation to the other class. Within a particular phase of development of a mode of production, the analysis takes on a less abstract tone. Here idealtypical constructs can be made of "possible" forms of consciousness, given the specific objective conditions of a given society. These constructs provide reference points in the study of concrete situations and serve as a background against which actual states of consciousness can be interpreted (Dos Santos, 1970; Lukács, 1970).

Next to class consciousness two other concepts, class psychology and ideology, have to be introduced in the conceptual analysis. All three relate to different dimensions of the "subjective" component of the process of class formation: the analysis of the system as a whole (*class consciousness*), the (individual) definition of the situation (*class psychology*) and the action programs (*ideology*).

The concept of class consciousness referes to class interests which also can be viewed on different levels of analysis. On a high level of abstraction they refer to collective aspirations that form part of the value system of a class and concern privilege maximation within zero-sum situations (cf. Israel, 1970; 288). The interests are antagonistic: realization of the aspirations by one class

9

will prevent the others from doing the same. At this stage, however, a hierarchy of interests has to be introduced as an additional variable which defines "long-term objectives", that concern the creation of an alternative society, and provide the criteria for the evaluation of the "short-term goals" as effective means towards the realization of these objectives.[7]

Class psychology and ideology refer to phenomena generated by the class situation of concrete social groupings or individuals. Class psychology is meant to conceptualize those phenomena on the empirical level that concern the perception of the individuals of their class position, the definition of their adversary as members of a class or other type of intersts grouping, and awareness of the conflict of interests; in addition, the manifestation of their willingness to participate in a class organization. On this level, however, these elements constitute a rather fragmentary and sometimes chaotic conglomerate of thoughts and feeling states, often containing "alien" elements, and lacking the systematization and the macroperspective that prevail on the level of class consciousness (Lenin, 1969; Lukács, 1970).

A first systematization and ordering of these phenomena can be promoted by an ideology that defines the concrete situation, indicates the long and short-term class interests, and suggests the objectives and means for action. This ideology is, in first instance, not necessarily identical with a body of ideas that fulfills merely rationalizing and justifying functions with regard to the enterprise of a social class. At this stage, an ideology may represent a conscious expression of class interests, while at the same time suggesting a strategy and an action program for the realization of these interests. The rationalizing and justifying element may come in only at a later stage when, for example, the defense of their interests would force certain classes to conceal the structural conflict in society, to negate the existence of class cleavages, to emphasize the common good, etc. But, even then, this element may correspond to an effective representation of basic class interests (cf. Dos Santos, 1970; 182).

Lenin (1969) has conceptualized the development of class consciousness within his theory of revolutionary organization through the definition of a number of idealtypical constructs that serve the analysis of concrete instances of class conflict. The following scheme systematizes the "types" of consciousness together with the differences in ideology, organization, interests and action.

---

[7] This appears to be a normative operation, although the "orthodox" Marxist methodology claims scientific objectivity, under reference to the proceedings of a dialectical analysis of reality (cf. Goldmann, 1969; for a discussion of this point, see: Aron, 1968: 190 ff and Israel, 1971: 86 ff). The idea of "false" or "incomplete" consciousness (Lukács, 1970) also has to be viewed within this context and concerns the negation of class interests by the members of a class, through the realization of (deviant) short-term goals and the rejection of the (possibility of realization of) long-term objectives (Israel, 1970; 288). Futher conceptual analysis is needed, however, to define for this idea a meaning within a general sociological context.

Figure 4: Lenin's types of consciousness

type	interests	action	organization	ideology
sponta-neistic I	improvement in working conditions, "bread and butter" issues	destruction/sabotage, work stoppages, strikes	mutual-aid funds, cooperatives, unions of short duration	expressions of solidarity in defense of immediate interests
economistic II	improvement in levels of living wages, emancipation of the working class	planned strikes and other planned action, collective bargaining and (labor) legislation	union organizations and parliamentary representation through working. class parties	defense of working class interests in legality and through parliamentarism, "gradual improvement"
political-revolutionary III	proletarian revolution as long-term objective, short-term goals as II	as II with agitation in preparation for revolutionary action	unions and revolutionary party	anti-capitalist and anti imperialist action program

Lenin conceives of a development from spontaneistic to more planned programs and actions in the course of the process of formation of the proletariat. This process of institutionalization is accompanied by a strenghtening of the labor organizations that replace the ad-hoc commitees of concrete conflict situations and by the establishment of relations with political parties. This development can take two forms:

(a) a more "economistic" one, which emphasizes the (economic) emancipation of the proletariat and the formulation of action programs within an "official" legal context. Eventually organized labor will gradually be integrated into official bargaining structures (called "trade unionism" and "reformism" by Marx and Lenin).

(b) a more "political-revolutionary" one, which emphasizes the internal division of labor within the working-class movement between the unions which take care of the immediate working-class interests and the revolutionary party, led by professional revolutionaries. These "revolutionary cadres" whose political consciousness is based on a scientific analysis of society, together with the "masses of workers" and the "workers' vanguard", form the actors within this Leninist scheme. The "masses of workers" primarily act on the basis of a "spontaneous consciousness and "class psychology". They are only active in periods of concrete action and return to their matters afterwards. The "workers' vanguard" guarantees the element of continuity in the class struggle through their daily activities in organizing, strike funds, worker press and other "mass" organizations.

These elements from Lenin's position on the development of class consciousness show a generality and concern with broad macrolevel processes similar to the one we noted earlier in our discussion of the Marxian framework. Their usefulness resides primarily in the leads for research they offer and in the factors they suggest to be included in the paradigm for investigation.

3. ALIENATION

3.1 The Concept of Alienation

While class consciousness focuses on the process of class formation, alienation concentrates on the working situation, and emphasizes the working conditions themselves under an organization of production following capitalist patterns. In this, it is a basic factor conceptualizing a work experience that, within the Marxian framework, is hypothesized to have a wide range of consequences for attitude and behavior in other spheres, notably in those of labor action. The nature of these consequences which form part of the so-called "generalization hypothesis" will be discussed later on (cf. Marx, 1963; also Seeman, 1967).

This approach toward alienation and its status in an explanation of the dynamics of class under a capitalist mode of production is not universally accepted. This even among Marxists, although in our opinion it does have deep roots in the works of Marx himself. Let us clarify this issue shortly, before proceeding to a more detailed exposition on the concept of alienation.

Especially in modern sociological studies, the concept of alienation has caused considerable confusion and ultimately came to stand for the thousand and one conditions of tension and strain in industrial societies. Over the last few decades it has been used as:

(a)   A sociophilosophical notion, denoting *das Unbehagen* in "Western" culture (Feuer, 1963).

(b)   A concept describing a primarily psychological or sociopsychological condition (Davids, 1955; Goffman, 1967). Some authors, like Erich Fromm, Erik H. Erikson and Norman D. Brown, combine the Marxist concept of alienation with psychoanalysis in a conceptual *marriage de convenance* which will arouse man to the dangers of a life without love (Simpson, 1968).

(c)   A concept denoting problems of social integration, often equated with anomie and utilized as part of a theoretical perspective that conflicts with the Marxian approach (Mizruchi, 1965; Scott, 1965; Dean, 1961; Taviss, 1969; Hajda, 1961 a.o.).

(d)   A concept covering macroprocesses like the decline of primary group relationships, the trend toward bureaucratization in various realms of life, based on discussions going back to Tönnies and Weber (Pappenheim, 1959).

(e)   Most of the empirical studies on the subject of alienation were inspired by Seeman (1959), who was the first to put alienation on sociological footing.

12

The dimensions of alienation defined by him represent an *ad hoc* listing of many of the previously discussed uses of the concept.

Common elements in these uses of the concept of alienation are: lack of unity of meaning, its application to a series of societal processes that do not directly reflect on the experience in the immediate working situation, utilization outside the theoretical context within which it had a very specific meaning.

Also within Marxian social science, alienation has caused some debate. The central issue was the status of Marx's Economic and Philosophical Manuscripts, containing the exposition on alienation, and the question of continuity in Marx's thought. Althusser is the main representative of the orientation within that tradition rejecting alienation as a "pre-Marxist" notion, rooted in youthful undigested Hegelian influences. He maintains that with the mature Marx, e.g. the writer of *Capital*, an entirely new approach was born which represents a radical break with the Marx of the early writings (Althusser, 1965). This position, in our opinion, cannot be maintained and certainly not, as Petrovic (1967) and Israel (1971) have shown, on the basis of Marx's analysis in *Capital*. Despite some reformulation, primarily due to the necessity to fit the alienation theme into the newly elaborated theoretical framework, also in this study the idea of alienation is still very much a part of his model (compare f.e. Marx, 1967a, volume I: 71 ff).

Alienation conceptualizes a process that within the Marxian approach has four dimensions. The well-known definition of these dimensions is contained in his *Economic and Philosophical Manuscripts* (Marx, 1963: 121 ff) and they all relate to processes that arise under the regime of capitalist production:

(a) The separation of the worker from the product he creates in the course of the production process in which he participates. The worker involves himself in the making of this product which, however, after its completion is appropriated by his employer and becomes part of a world by which he is dominated and exploited.

(b) The separation of the worker from the act of production within his work activity. Given the complete absence of any control over his immediate working situation, and the general lack of alternatives, work assumes a forced character lacking opportunities for development and selffulfillment. Work becomes a means for earning a living, and no more than that.

(c) The separation of man "from himself". Labor is such a fundamental process for human self-realization that man "dehumanizes" when he has to work under exploitative conditions that deny creative productive work, destroy any autonomy of the worker over the act of production, and change work for him to a mere instrumental activity that serves only to maintain his subsistence.

(d) The separation of the worker from other men and notably from those who control the production process, own his labor and appropriate the products he creates. The situation of the worker is paradoxical in the sense that, through his own production activity, he produces the power of his master.

The multidimensional concept of aliementation forms part of the Marxian theory of class exploitation and directs itself towards this exploitation as it manifests itself in the direct production process. In doing so, however, the concept moves on a high level of abstraction. It embodies a macroperspective forming part of a metatheoretical framework. As such, its utility resides with its heuristic, rather than with its formal explanatory functions. Obviously, the concept lacks a *direct* reference to the concrete behavior and feelings of individuals.

Obviously, the use of this concept involves a few assumptions concerning human nature. Marx conceived of man, as is well known, as a dynamic factor in the social process. This dynamics resides in the mutually related potentialities to change his environment and to achieve individual self-realization, obviously through work: "the basic existential activity of man" (Marcuse, 1968: 275). Especially this latter idea involves normative notions. When Marx writes about the full expression of the talents and capacities of the individual and the satisfaction of his needs, he clearly has a certain selection out of the potential scale of talents, capacities, and needs in mind (cf. Israel, 1971; 67). The idea of alienation ties in with this perspective of the dynamic potentialities of man that the conditions of capitalist production attempt to cut short.

3.2. The Process of Alienation and Conditioning Factors

Alienation as an objective process knows a development and can present itself in varying degrees of intensity. These variations are rooted, according to Marx, primarily in a complex of three interrelated factors: division of labor, private property – e.g. private ownership of the means of production – , and the process of commodification.

Alienation intensifies under hte conditions of capitalist production where this factor complex has been most strongly expressed. Marx viewed the process, however, as historically transient (cf. Petrovic, 1967). With the elimination of the specific economic and social conditions that had brought it about under capitalism, alienation would also disappear. The alternative model of society, in which the production sector would be reorganized on the basis of selfmanagement and absolute control over the working situation by the immediate producers, did however, as we all know, never get off the drawing table.

Schematically, the relationship of this objective process of alienation to its conditioning factors can be presented as follows:

Figure 5: Alienation and Conditioning Factors

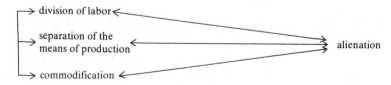

Let us specify the workings of these factors.

(a) The division of labor represents the basic conditioning factor. On a societal level this phenomenon has led to a separation of the worker from the means of production, and to his ultimate exploitation by the capitalist. On the level of the actual process of commodity production, the division of labor resulted in a separation between manual and intellectual skills, and in the subordination of these manual skills to the machine in the course of the process of mechanization. In response to these changes in technological structure, the production process itself, was subdivided into various successive steps. Formerly, the worker was responsible for the entire series of operations that is required for the production of the commodity but, more and more, he has become preoccupied with the execution of very partial operations which have become his exclusive function (Marx, 1967a, vol. I: 359).

This separation between manual and intellectual aspects of work and the subdivision of the production process into an endless series of small monotonous routine tasks prevents the worker, according to Marx, from realizing his human potentialities. It further limits his alternatives by atomizing the work force into small powerless parts in the machine, and increases the objective possibilities of his exploitation by those who own the means of production.

(b) Private property; the relationship between private property (private ownership of the means of production) and alienation follows a dialectical pattern. Historically, the separation in relationship to the means of production emerged in the course of the process of the division of labor. In this process, private property can be said to be the result of alienated labor. Once having achieved a certain objective reality, private property becomes the mechanism which deepens existing and promotes further alienation (Marx, 1963: 156 ff). Its abolition was viewed by Marx as a precondition for the elimination of alienation.

(c) Commodification: the exploitative relationship which is at the core of the process of alienation is further conditioned by commodification, a process which forms part of Marx's theory of value (Marx, 1967a, vol. I: 35 ff).

Any product, according to this theory, has two value dimensions: first, the *use value*, which is an instrumental value determined by the capacity of the product to satisfy persistent needs, and second, the *exchange value*, which equals the value a product acquires when changed into a commodity. A commodity, by definition, relates to other commodities for which it can be exchanged. This exchange relationship is expressed in the exchange value of the product which in modern society is stated in money terms.

Thus, in the case of a commodity, use value and exchange value have been separated, the second one being determined by the mechanisms of the capitalist market system. In the exchange of commodities, a network of power relations emerges between the independent producers participating in the system.

The capitalist market covers social relations by commodity relations. Ownership of commodities means power that, in turn, is dedicated to a further transformation to a commodity structure. Ultimately, not only products but also human labor comes to acquire exchange value and is sold as a commodity (Marx, 1963: 138 ff). The worker has no alternative but to sell his labor power in the market in order to subsist. Because of the skewed power relations that limit his alternatives, work increasingly becomes experienced as imposed, forced labor. The worker is subject to processes of alienation because the work he is doing is not *his* work, but work for someone else. During this labor process, the worker does not belong to himself but to another person. He lacks completely control over his own working situation (Marx, 1963: 122 ff). The more organized and advanced the system of production, the more unfree he will be. The greater his productivity, the greater his poverty.[8] The commodity is the economic expression of man's self-alienation.

4. CLASS CONSCIOUSNESS AND ALIENATION
SOME CONCLUDING REMARKS AND A PARADIGM

Reviewing the discussion in this theoretical introduction, in reference to:
— general theoretical perspectives that form points of departure for the analysis,
— the analysis of the components and correlates of each of the two core concepts, and
— the taxonomy of their theoretical relationships,
The elements of a paradigm can be identified that will guide the analysis and specify the factors to be included.
(a) *The production sector*, with respect to:
— its main structural changes specified by subsectors;
— the generation of the economic surplus, its distribution and ultimate uses.
(b) *The class situation*, with respect to:
— the segmentation of society in classes, subclasses and related groupings;
— patterns, regularities or trends in the change within and among the classes;
— the role of each class in production, distribution and exchange;
— the degree of proletarization of the sectors of the working class.
(c) *The class relations*, with respect to:
— the economic surplus and the exploitation of the labor sector;
— the political structure and the use of control and coercion;
— the relationship between politically and economically dominant classes: the decision making with regard to economic and financial policies;
— legal and ideological structures;
— the state apparatus and its relation to the class structure.
(d) *The working class*, with respect to:
d.l. its relevant categories:

[8] Marx refers here to poverty in a relative and not in an absolute sense. Moreover the term has a wider than strictly economic meaning and denotes also social and psychological aspects.

- masses of workers: recruitment, internal segmentation, level of participation in workers organizations and political parties;
- vanguard: recruitment, internal segmentation, functioning, relations with the masses of workers and with political parties;
- political parties: membership, internal structure, functioning, relation with vanguard and with masses of workers.

d.2. its alienation and its manifestation on:
- the level of commodity production: technological structure, property structure, distribution of economic surplus, division of labor, social organization and control in the working environment.

d.3. its class consciousness and the manifestations on:
- the ideological level, with respect to:
  - the analysis of society as a whole and the role attributed to the working class;
  - the analysis of the common adversary: the employers, sectors of the bourgeoisie, the classist structure itself, the State, foreign economic interests;
  - the analysis of the working class itself: interests, programs for action, to be characterized as either spontaneous or planned (tradeunionist or political revolutionary).
  - the counterideology of the bourgeoisie: the role attributed to the working class, efforts at class reconciliation, and the negation of class schisms.
- the organization level:
  - degree of union organization, organizational strength (strike funds, press, etc.), internal differentiation, the organizations and their history.
  - degree of political participation: the party structure and the history of the parties, their influence in the working class, action programs (short term and long term).
- the level of political practice:
  - forms of struggle and history of struggle: strikes, meetings, bargaining, legal processes, uprisings, and other forms of collective action.
  - intersectorial coalitions, interclass coalitions, political pacts, etc.

It is clear that in a study like ours, necessarily some sacrifices have been made with regard to the general paradigm, due to the shortcomings of the available data and to the decision to narrow the actual research down to the Monterrey industrial proletariat.

The investigation of the concrete situation, which deals with individual attitudes and behavior, obviously cannot study these as *direct* indicators of either alienation or class consciousness. The relationship between the metatheoretical level, on which these concepts move, and the empirical theoretical level is, as we stated before, not a straight deductive one. Metatheory has with regard to the lower theoretical levels primarily heuristic and hypotheses-generating functions that do not lend themselves to an evaluation through criteria of measurement and verification, but should be reviewed in terms of their fruitfulness with regard to more specific empirical-theoretical propositions. In our investigation, then, work experience and working class psychology will conceptualize a discussion that, afterwards, should be inserted into a more abstract theoretical picture.

(a) *Work experience* focuses on the immediate working situation and, in particular, on a series of conditions and subjective feeling states emerging from the interaction between workers and the sociotechnical dimensions of the working environment. It has a multidimensional structure. The individual dimensions are:

— *domination*: degree of control over the daily work process;
— *fractionization*: degree of decomposition of the production process;
— *isolation*: degree of development of a community of workmates;
— *distanciation*: degree of identification with the job as such.

The first and second dimension refer to the subjective consequences with the individual workers of technological structure and division of labor. The third dimension refers to the potentially atomizing effects of both, posing barriers to the development of a work community that would stimulate labor unity. The last dimension reflects the evaluation of the job in its totality, its possibilities for self-realization and the preference for free time.[9]

These dimensions do not pretend to measure the earlier discussed alienation phenomenon in all its aspects and nuances. Our intentions are of a more modest kind. The subjective reflection of the *objective* process of alienation has been emphasized together with the variations in its occurrence and their determinants.

(b) *Working class psychology*, as has been explained before, focuses on the perception of the individual's class position, the definition of his adversary and the conflict of interests, and his membership of a class organization with interst group characteristics. The individual dimensions are.

— *class identification*
— *awareness*
— *quantitative union participation*
— *qualitative union participation*

The dimensions of both phenomena, work experience and working-class psychology, know a process of development. The classical writings, themselves, suggest a series of explanatory variables that are hypothesized to relate to variations in this development, and several have already been mentioned before. They will be discussed further in Chapter V, together with those suggested by the modern sociological literature.

[9] cf. " . . . (alienated labor) . . . is not the satisfaction of a need, but only a means for satisfying other needs. Its alien character is clearly shown by the fact that, as soon as there is no physical or other compulsion, it is avoided like the plague." (Marx, 1963: 125).

CHAPTER III
THE MEXICAN SITUATION

Any effort to define the general tendencies of the Mexican process of economic and sociopolitical change will have to handle the basic questions concerning the accumulation, distribution and utilization of the economic surplus. This chapter will deal with these processes and some of their more important consequences and correlates in the sphere of social classes and in the political system. The analysis will emphasize the general characterizing features and thus be limited to the main lines. Together with the meso level analysis, this definition of macro determinants and conditioning factors will serve to place the results of the empirical research into context, enable their interpretation and establish their significance against the background of the general dynamics of Mexican society.

1. THE HISTORICAL CONTEXT

The economic and sociopolitical situation in Mexico has a number of historical antecedents, the knowledge of which is a precondition for a proper understanding of present-day reality. Some of these elements show a remarkable degree of historical continuity. One of them, which runs as a thread of consistency through the history of Mexican socioeconomic development, has been the important role of foreign economic penetration from the colonial period up till the present dependent process of industrialization.

During almost three centuries of colonial rule, the resources of the country were exploited to the benefit of the metropolis. In 1821 a formal political independence was achieved that ended the colonial relationship but changed it for a new situation of dependence from foreign capital (British, French, German), that structurally exhibited characteristics analogous to the colonial system (Solís, 1970: 14 ff). A long period followed characterized by political instability, economic stagnation and repeated interventions by foreign powers.

The Porfirio Díaz regime (1880-1910) ended this situation, bringing political stability and economic growth. It pursued national integration with force, economic expansion was promoted at all cost. All barriers against foreign investment were lifted without any coordination of the investments or other government implemented restrictions. Railways, mines and oilfields passed into foreign hands. The same happened with the domains that were acquired by foreign landholding companies. According to various estimates, a fifth to a quarter of the nation's landed property passed under foreign control (González Navarro, 1969: 207). In addition, also the incipient industry and the trade sector were largely in foreign hands. Around 71 percent of the capital invested in industry between 1886 and 1910 was foreign owned (Solís, 1970: 65). This foreign domination of the economy was largely established by U.S. capital. During the *Porfiriato* the strong dependency relationship was established which by and large has characterized Mexican-U.S. relations up until present times.

The 1910 Revolution ended the Porfirio Díaz regime. It meant to improve the situation of the urban middle sector, the urban workers and the landless laboreres in the countryside. This was to be done without completely remodeling the economic system and preserving ample space for private initiative, next to the activities of the public sector. The country's dependence on foreign investment was not basically changed. On the contrary, from 1910 to 1926 the number of industrial, commercial and mining enterprises in the hands of foreign capitalists increased sharply (Solís, 1970: 96). During the revolutionary period many of the smaller Mexican enterprises had sold their interests to U.S. investors. Under Cárdenas a first effort was made to "Mexicanize" a substantial part of the economic sector through straight nationalization (railroads, oil), expansion of the direct government investment and a limit to foreign investment in those sectors considered vital to the national interest. This trend towards "Mexicanization", however, weakened under the following governments.

In the mid-1930's finally the process of economic growth began on the basis of institutional and legal foundations that had been laid at the end of the Revolution and through the 1920's and subsequent years had developed into an elaborate infrastructure promoting industrialization, culminating with the foundation of the *Nacional Financiera* in 1934. In the period from 1940 on, rapid change in the urban and industrial sphere changed the face of Mexico. During the Second World War, as in the rest of Latin America, the process of economic growth got a strong additional stimulus. The temporary interruption of the ties with the world market promoted the formation of an import-substituting industry and the utilization of previously unused capacity of the existing industries. Agricultural production expanded continously until the mid 1950's and the economic growth depended heavily on the export of agricultural products in addition to those of the mining sector.

In the second half of the 1950's the process of economic development has been directed to a greater degree on the internal market and its course has been determined even more by the growth of industrial production. This process has followed a pattern characterized by extreme inequalities in income distribution, a high concentration of income and ownership of the means of production, accompanied by a continuous expansion of the foreign investment in the Mexican economy.

20

2. SOME NOTES ON THE ECONOMIC STRUCTURE

These characteristics and correlates of the process of economic growth in the last few decades require a more precise definition. This will clarify at the same time the main lines of the development strategy that was followed and indicate the structural changes that constitute the material basis for the sociopolitical processes that will be analyzed later on.

2.1. *Economic Growth Through Industrialization*

The strategy of industrialization, which in Mexico has been promoted as *the* means to end underdevelopment, has resulted in a process of economic growth that especially in the 1960's reached spectacular proportions. In this period official publications glowingly reported on the expansion of Mexico's production and proudly pointed to the accompanying improvements in economic, social and educational opportunities that would put the nation on a certain road to equality and social justice for all. Looking back, it can rather easily be concluded that his position was far too optimistic. It is understandable that the process of growth as such generated a certain feeling of euphoria especially in government circles, but a more critical analysis shows us that this feeling had little or no basis in the characteristics of the process of development in a wider sense. Indeed, the growth of the G.N.P. all through the 1960's fluctuated between 6 to 7 percent (in 1964 even 10 percent), which was unparalleled among Latin American nations. Part of this growth, however, was offset by the increase in population (3.4 to 3.6 percent) which left a net growth of little more than 3 percent (Wionczek, 1971: 11). This economic "boom" was mainly the result of industrial expansion. The production has been directed primarily towards the internal market. Mexican exports consist mainly of raw materials. These suffer from lack of stability as a result of price fluctuations on the world market. The volume of imports, however, has been dictated by the needs of the industrializing expanding economy with the resulting balance of payments problems, a familiar pattern among Third World nations

TABLE 1: ECONOMIC GROWTH RATES OF SELECTED LATIN AMERICAN COUNTRIES 1960-1969 (PER-CENTAGES)

countries	growth of G.N.P.			per capita G.N.P. growth
	1960-1966	1967	1968	1961-1969
Mexico	6.3	6.5	7.3	3.3
Argentina	2.9	1.9	4.8	1.9
Brazil	4.1	5.0	8.3	2.6
Chile	5.4	2.0	2.7	2.0
Venezuela	5.1	6.0	5.7	1.3
Latin America	4.6	4.5	6.4	2.2

Source: Labastida, 1972: 102

TABLE 2: THE SECTORAL DISTRIBUTION OF THE MEXICAN G.N.P. IN 1936, 1953 AND 1967 (PERCEN-TAGES)

economic sectors	G.N.P.		
	1936	1953	1967
agriculture	27.7	20.6	15.9
mining	6.0	2.9	1.5
oil	3.0	2.9	3.2
manufacturing	16.4	21.2	26.5
construction	2.5	3.2	3.9
electric energy	1.0	1.0	1.6
services	43.4	48.2	47.4
Total G.N.P.	100.0	100.0	100.0

Source: Solís, 1970: 220

The distribution of the economic growth over the various sectors of the economy is specified in table 2. Striking is the strong decline of the traditional workhorses of the economy: agriculture and mining. The economic growth has been carried by the manufacturing industry. The dynamics of this sector itself have been determined to a great extent by the expansion of "modern" capital intensive industries (metallurgy, chemicals). Those containing most of the "traditional" enterprises and artisanshops (foodstuffs, textiles, etc.) did stagnate and decline in relative importance from 54.8 percent in 1950 to 42.8 percent in 1965. The relative importance of the production goods industry (chemicals, metallurgy, machinery, etc.) increased from 16.5 to 30.6 percent (Solís, 1970: 222). Mexican industrial production has emphasized more and more the fabrication of these capital goods and half products, a development very similar to the Brazilian pattern (Leff, 1968).

TABLE 3: THE STRUCTURE OF THE CONTRIBUTION TO THE MEXICAN G.N.P. BY MANUFACTURING IN 1950, 1960 AND 1965 (PERCENTAGES)

industry	contribution to G.N.P. by manufacturing		
	1950	1960	1965
food, drinks, tobacco	30.1	28.9	27.2
textilles, shoes, apparel and fabrics	24.7	17.4	15.6
wood, paper and paper products	8.2	4.9	4.4
chemicals	8.8	14.6	16.6
nonmetallic minerals	4.4	4.5	4.3
metallurgy and metal products	7.7	13.5	14.0
other	16.1	16.2	16.9
total	100.0	100.0	100.0

Source: Solís, 1970: 221

22

The slow pace at which the demand on the internal market is expanding, however, threatens to pose sharp limits to further industrial growth. This applies in particular to those industrial sectors directly or indirectly dependent on the institutionalization of patterns of mass consumption. In this respect Padilla (1969: 14), Singer (1969: 168) and Wionczek (1971: 19) point to the phenomenon of industries, mostly import-substituting monopolies producing far below top capacity. A major stumbling block forms the lack of an institutional framework (in the sphere of taxation, monetary policy, etc.) which would redistribute the income concentrated in the hands of those relatively small sectors of the population which have been the main beneficiaries of the process of economic growth, give to the great majority of the Mexican population a proportional share of the pie and enable the government to accumulate the financial resources that would permit a more extensive participation in the struggle against underdevelopment. This problem of course leads us directly to the issues of class relations and political power.

2.2. The Generation and Distribution of Income

In Mexico, the process of accumulation of capital has been aided by the depression of popular consumption. Again, a large scale expansion of the domestic market through a substantial redistribution of income and wealth and other redistributive mechanisms, has not been contemplated as part of national policy. The volume of demand instead has expanded slowly by areas and sectors. Industrialization and related processes have generated an intermediate level of demand, too weak, however, to produce full employment for all productive resources. External factors, like tourism, the border transactions with the U.S., and foreign capital, have filled the gap and made economic growth possible. A further analysis of the process of accumulation reveals the exploitative nature of the Mexican economy and the extreme inequalities in the distribution of income which go with it.

In the period between 1940 to 1970, the size of the total Mexican labor force grew from 6 to approximately 16.5 million (Aquilar, 1970a: 144). The size of the salaried segment increased in the same period from 40 to 60 percent. Despite the increase in employment, the phenomenon of unemployment and underemployment have taken on massive proportions. Together they are estimated to affect around 40 percent of the labor force (Dominguez, 1974: 3). In the countryside the situation is particularly critical as a result of chronic underemployment and seasonal unemployment. Against the background of these phenomena, the generally low levels of income are not surprising. The legal minimum income is notoriously difficult to enforce. According to Domínguez (1974: 4) over 40 percent of the salaried population is not receiving the minimum wages. Further, in practice the periodic revisions of the collactive contracts stay behind the rise in the cost of living, fed by inflation. The real wages of the lower income strata have shown a descending trend (Singer, 1969: 129 ff). In the second half of the 1960's, the lower third of the total economically active population suffered a loss in real wages; the next 50 percent remained virtually stagnant (La Cascia, 1969: 62; also Cockcroft 1972: 248). These phenomena had direct consequences for the process of accumulation of capital. In combination with inflation they represented "forced savings," primarily benefitting profit recipients while hampering wage earners and fixed income groups (Singer, 1969: 190). The industrialists among these profit recipients, were greatly aided by the policy of industrialization through import substitution which operated behind high tariff walls. The share in wages and salaries of the N.N.P. dropped from 30.5 percent in 1939 to 24 percent in 1950, increased slowly in the subsequent decade, reaching 32 percent in 1967 (Solís, 1970: 317). This meant that it took almost 30 years to parallel the rather modest achievements of the Cárdenas administration. The result, however, remained an income distribution that was highly unequal: in 1969, the lower 50 percent of the national distribution of family incomes, received 15 percent of the total income, the upper 10 percent received 51.0 percent (De Navarrete, 1970: 40 ff). Corrective action by the government has remained weak. Formerly the government programs stressed public welfare as one of their important goals. However, the rural programs and the urban welfare policies as low cost housing, food subsidies, enforcement of minimum wages, etc. have been weakly organized,[1] not in the least because of the institutionalized corruption (cf. Carrión, 1969: 122 ff).

Behind this general picture of the Mexican distribution of income, stand substantial intersectoral inequalities, notably between agriculture, industry and commerce,[2] while within each of these sectors also great disparities exist as a consequence of the high concentration of income and ownership of the means of production. These inter- and intrasectoral inequalities with regard to the distribution of income coincide with substantial regional inequalities.

Especially the agricultural sector as a whole scores very badly. It only accounted for 15.9 percent of the G.N.P. (1967) while still employing almost 50 percent of the nation's workforce (Wionczek, 1971: 36). The Mexican Revolution, which had agrarian reform written in its banner, sacrificed agriculture to industry and the countryside to the city. The strategy of economic growth through import-substituting industrialization assigned to agriculture a subordinate role. Besides supplying the internal demand, where it suffered from the increasing price differential between agricultural and industrial products, it had to earn the foreign exchange needed to finance the industrialization process. Agricultural exports in fact represented in the 1960's over 50 percent of the value of total exports. This emphasis on production for the world market had great consequences for the structure of the sector itself.

[1] The agrarian sector has received since the 1940's, less and less public money. An absolute low was reached during the administration of López Mateos (1959-1964) when only 10.4 percent of total government investment went to the rural sector (Puenta Leyva, 1969: xvi).
[2] The productivity of the agricultural sector as a whole stays far behind compared with industry and commerce. The per capita productivity is only 13.1 and 18.7 percent, respectively, of the productivity in these other two sectors (Puenta Leyva, 1969: xiv).

After the distribution of lands in the 1920's and 1930's an infrastructure, especially in roads and irrigation works, was constructed that brought considerable changes. On the irrigated lands the commercial crops gained importance. In the 1940's heavy investments were made in the mechanization of this type of agriculture. The production per hectare increased rapidly, also as a result of the use of new methods of seed selection, fertilizers and insecticides. This development benefitted almost exclusively the owners of the large estates who had escaped division of their lands and had transformed their *latifundios* into big agroindustrial enterprises (Solís, 1970: 148). It also benefitted the small holders, owning from 100 to 300 hectares (depending on type of land and crop) and the *ejidos* on the rich irrigated lands, as f.e. in the north Pacific area (González Navarro, 1969: 217). The *ejiditarios* on the lands lacking irrigation and the subsistence farmers remained the weaker and neglected elements of the agricultural sector.[3] More and more the gap was widened between the advanced rural regions and those with a predominance of subsistence agriculture. (cf. Dumont, 1961: 86 ff).

The national industry traditionally has been concentrated in Mexico and the Federal District, Nuevo León and Vera Cruz. In the 1960's the so-called *maquiladores* (border industry) in the states of Chihuahua, Coahuila, Tamaulipas and Baja California gained importance. The gap between these industrializing, urbanizing regions and the backward rural areas is wide and widening on virtually all socioeconomic indicators of levels of living one could think of (cf. González Casanova, 1968).

Mexican peasants have responded to the existing differentials by shifting in considerable numbers from the high density, low income areas to those more attractive economically. This migration was directed primarily towards the Federal District and the States of Mexico, Nuevo León and Baja California.[4] The migrants continued to pour in all through the 1950's and the 1960's as a result of the sheer misery in the rural areas aggravated by a steady population growth.[5] For a considerable part of the migrant population, the migration did not produce an immediate economic advancement in terms of a raise in real income and levels of living. Most migrants simply transferred their poverty from the countryside to the city. Thus the agrarian crisis, which to an important extent was provoked by a policy in which economic growth was identified onesidedly with industrialization, on its turn created the subproletariat which constitutes industry's large reservoir of cheap unskilled labor.

[3] In 1965, 0.5 percent of the total number of agricultural enterprises produced 32 percent of the National Agricultural Product, the upper 2.9. percent generated even 76.3 percent of the N.A.P. The lower 50 percent produced only 4 percent of the N.A.P. (Wionczek, 1971: 31; Aguilar, 1970a: 51).
[4] They received 70.6, 10.5 and 9.5 percent, respectively, of the migration balance of those 13 civil divisions which had more migrants arrive than depart during 1960-1970 (Bridges, 1973: 278).
[5] The magnitude of this process is further illustrated by the fact that between 1950 and 1960, the rural population grew at an annual rate of 1.5 percent, while natural increases and migration together produced an annual growth rate of 4.8 percent in the urban areas (Singer, 1969: 152).

As in the case of agriculture, also within the industrial and commercial sector great disparities exist. The most obvious differences show between the more "traditional" sectors, containing most of the low productivity, labor-intensive industries and artisan shops, at the same time low-wage strongholds, and the big "modern" capital-intensive enterprises, in the commercial sector parallelled by the differences between the street vendors and the big commercial houses. These differences, as the intersectoral and regional disparities, have been worsened by the continued enlargement of scale in the Mexican economy.

2.3. Enlargement of Scale in the Economy

This tendency stands for an increasing concentration (growth in absolute size) of capital, leading to centralization (growth in relative size) of capital. The economic "boom" of the 1960's led to a considerable increase in total investment and in economic productivity. Yet the general capital labor ratios have remained low and the gap separating Mexico from the industrialized nations has not been closed. A great proportion of the capital invested in the various sectors of the economy is in the hands of a small minority of Mexican and foreign interests. This situation is very pronounced in the manufacturing industry where at the height of the "boom" (1966), 1.5 percent of the total number of enterprises accounted for 77.2 percent of the total sum of invested capital. Among this total number of 136,000 units, no more than 400 enterprises dominated the scene, one third of them companies directly or indirectly controlled by foreign interests. In commerce, 4.4 percent and in services, 2.9. percent of the total number of units represented 84.4 percent and 77.2 percent respectively, of the total sum of invested capital in those sectors (Aguilar, 1970a: 51, 59). We mentioned earlier the tendency towards concentration in agriculture. Here a limited number of families (probably no more than 500) dominate the sector by owning the best lands, having access to irrigation, credit and technology.[6]

The sectors of industry, commerce and services together counted 630,195 units (1965). Among them, the top 8,000 (1.2 percent) represented 70.9 percent of the total sum of invested capital in the three sectors (Aguilar, 1970a: 52). Within the category of large to very large companies also a considerable concentration has taken place. Among the 500 largest companies in the Mexican economy, 37 represented 45.1 percent of the total sum of capital invested in all of them (1968). Singer (1969: 157) analyzes this same trend and indicates that around 18 percent of the G.N.P. was produced by the 400 largest companies.

The concentration and centralization of capital has been accompanied by the increasingly monopolistic organization of the economy (Singer, 1969: 158). This applies especially to the commercial sector, although also in

[6] Aguilar (1970a: 54) mentions 160 of the most important families by name.

manufacturing already almost two-thirds of the industries had a monopolistic market structure (1965). Aguilar (1970a: 75 ff) shows that these processes of enlargement of scale in the economy have resulted in the emergence of a small economic elite of approximately 1,000 families, directly or indirectly controlling the economic sector by owning the nation's capital or by serving as intermediaries for foreign investment. Within this rather small sized economic elite, controlling the nation's lands, mines, factories, commercial enterprises, banks (the "Big Nine"), insurance companies, mass communication media, etc. approximately 100 families operate on a national level. Among them no more than 25 are the real business tycoons of Mexico. The group of magnates operating primarily on the state and regional levels counts approximately 300 families. The other 600 families have investment of lesser importance in and around Mexico City or on the state and local levels.

The great concentration of the riches of the nation in a few hands has taken place in the last three decades (cf. Carmona, 1970b: 86 ff). Some capitalists have roots in the period of postrevolutionary reconstruction during the Calles government (1925-1928) or were owned by *Porfiristas* who accomodated to changing conditions, but most of them date from the period of economic expansion during the Second World War. The combination of low wages, high profits and low taxes made rapid accumulation possible, a process speeded up even further by the dynamics of development itself, the growing possibility for speculative gains, especially in real estate (urbanization), the impact of foreign investment and the effects of inflation (especially in the 1940's and the first half of the 1950's), this all further facilitated by a political and legal framework that permitted an unhindered course of these processes.

2.4. *Economic Growth in Dependence*

The process of economic growth has received a great impulse through the activities of foreign companies. Their interests have taken on a considerable magnitude and they have assumed key positions in various sectors of the economy. Among the direct foreign investments, 80 percent consist of U.S. capital (De Rossi, 1971: 70). They have been directed mainly towards the sectors of industry (74.2 percent) and commerce (14.8 percent). This represents a considerable change from foreign investment policies in the past which concentrated on mining, the energy sector and on communication and transport. In 1970, the direct U.S. investment made in that year, equalled 6 percent of the Mexican G.N.P. (Durand Ponte, 1972: 274). Foreign private investment has been channeled more and more through the structure of multinational corporations

This has brought Mexico the by now familiar pattern of the presence of corporations with a volume of sales often approximating a mediumsized nation's G.N.P., with complex administrative and accounting procedures that escape from local control, with an influx of capital, technology and administrative know-how that usurpes local resources. From the end of the 1950's on,

27

TABLE 4:   FOREIGN INVESTMENT IN MEXICO 1941-1969 (MILLIONS OF DOLLARS AT CURRENT PRICES)

administrations	foreign investments			
	direct (a)	indirect (b)	total	annual average
Avila Camacho (1941-1946)	131	56	187	31
Alemán (1947-1952)	251	207	458	76
Ruíz Cortines (1953-1958)	486	432	918	153
López Mateos (1959-1964)	511	2,414	2,925	488
Díaz Ordaz (1965-1969)	606	3,268	3,874	775

Source: Carmona, 1970b: 71

(a)   does not include reinvestments, only new investments that were officially published.
(b)   long term credits to state organizations and enterprises dependent on them; short term credits (for less than one year) are not included.

TABLE 5:   SECTORAL DISTRIBUTION OF TOTAL PRIVATE FOREIGN INVESTMENT IN MEXICO 1911-1968 (PERCENTAGES)

economic sectors	private foreign investments				
	1911	1940	1950	1960	1968
agriculture	7.0	1.9	0.7	1.8	0.7
mining	28.0	23.9	19.8	15.6	6.0
oil	4.0	0.3	2.1	2.0	1.8
manufacturing	4.0	7.0	26.0	55.8	74.2
electric energy	8.0	31.5	24.2	1.4	–
commerce	10.0	3.5	12.4	18.1	14.8
communications and transport	39.0	31.6	13.3	2.8	–
other services	–	0.3	1.5	2.5	2.5
total	100.0	100.0	100.0	100.0	100.0

Source: Wionczek, 1971: 205

the presence of U.S. corporations in Mexico has expanded through the creation of subsidiaries directly or through the acquisition of existing local companies. The situation has arisen where from the 187 biggest U.S. multinational corporations, responsible for more than 70 percent of total direct U.S.

[7] According to an investigation of Harvard Graduate School of Business Administration (Vaupel and Curhan, 1969).

28

investment abroad, 172 are represented in Mexico through a total of 412 local subsidiaries (1967).[7] With this number of local subsidiaries, Mexico occupies the first place in Latin America and the fifth in the world after Canada, Great Britain, France and Germany. Among all subsidiaries, 56 percent has 100 percent U.S. capital, 19 percent had a majority U.S. investment and another 19 percent had a minority U.S. investment. The degree of control over 6 percent of the subsidiaries was unknown.

The industrial sector has been favored by U.S. capital. Within this sector the investment concentrated on the manufacturing of chemicals, pharmaceuticals-cosmetics, processed foods-drinks and household equipment-electronics. Together these accounted for 71 percent (31.4, 20.6, 10.8 and 8.2 percent respectively) of all U.S. investments in manufacturing in the period 1946-1967 (Vaupel and Curhan, 1969). Most of the U.S. controlled industries (82 percent) are located in the area around Mexico City (De Rossi, 1971: 71). Their production has been directed mainly towards the internal market. All companies, except two automobile assembly plants did not export more than 3 percent of their total sales. The general picture of foreign investment and control in Mexico indicates substantial interests in the capital goods and basic intermediate goods industries, crucial areas of the economy characterized by high levels of technology and a "dynamic" growth potential (Barkin, 1975: 72). Most of the foreign import-substituting investments have, paradoxically enough, resulted in a sharp increase in the dependence of the economy on

TABLE 6: FOREIGN FINANCING OF TOTAL MEXICAN PUBLIC INVESTMENT PER SECTOR, 1965-1970 (PERCENTAGES)

sector	foreign share of public investment
agriculture	20.4
industry	36.6
transport and communications	25.6
basic development	30.7
social welfare	11.4
administration and defense	13.1
total	25.9

Source: Durand Ponte, 1972: 232

[8] This policy determined that:
(a) The basic sectors of the national economy, as the oil and petrochemical industry, electric energy, the railways, telegraph and telephone should be completely state owned.
(b) Investment in the finance and credit sector, radio and T.V. networks, forestry resources and gas distribution are to be 100 percent Mexican owned.
(c) Several other types of industrial activity, explicitly defined by law and closely related to the basic industries or having a strategic significance with regard to the future industrial developments of the country, should have a majority participation of Mexican capital (See Wionczek, 1971: 188 for a listing of these industries). All other areas offer unlimited opportunities for foreign investment.

foreign suppliers although the structure of the imports changed from an emphasis on consumption goods to raw stuffs, half-products, spare parts and machinery for the newly established industries (Wionczek, 1971: 153).

The reaction towards the growing foreign influence in the economy under the earlier mentioned Mexicanization policy,[8] initially defined by Cárdenas in the 1930's, has not always been very effective. Enforcement is left up to the executive who often has not been able to resist the relentless pressure of foreign investors. The recent changes in the way foreign interests realize control, e.g. through technology transfer rather than direct investment, forms an additional complicating factor (Vaitsos, 1973). Finally, the immense foreign debt Mexico has incurred, and that has made it one of the most indebted nations in the world, has prohibited strong action against the foreign interests in the economy. A considerable part of the investments made by the public sector has also been provided by foreign sources. From the total foreign debt accumulated by the Mexican government in the period 1942-1965, around 55 percent represented credits given bij private foreign institutions, 45 percent came from U.S. government affiliated institutions (EXIM Bank, A.I.D., etc.) and international organizations like the World Bank and the Inter American Development Bank (Carmona, 1970b: 73). The situation has arisen now where the yearly payments on interest and redemption of previous public foreign debts (long term and short term) equal 90 percent of the total sum of credits and loans (through indirect investment) which Mexico annually receives and which averaged a total of 1,146.7 million dollars a year at the end of the 1960's (Wionczek, 1971: 197). Carmona (1970b: 74 ff) estimates the total Mexican debt for 1970 at around 7,700 million dollars, 3,000 million of which represents direct foreign investment (80 percent by U.S. companies), 3,200 million long term indirect investment and 1,500 million short term private and public foreign debts. This estimate is not very different from one made by Wionczek (1970). These debts together with the heavy U.S. presence in the economy, the dependence on the U.S. market in imports as well as in exports (both over 70 percent), the volume of border transactions, and the tourist trade, form conditions that pose limits to government decision making in the economic and political sphere and severely affect the possibility to initiate any process of economic and/or sociopolitical change that would not leave these foreign interests untouched.

2.5. Conclusion

Let us briefly summarize the basic tendencies of the Mexican development strategy.
(a)   The growth of the Mexican economy over the last three decades has been promoted through a strategy of industrialization. Agriculture was deliberately sacrificed after having financed the industrial take off out of its surplus. This economic growth has been very unbalanced and it has sharpenend the inter - and intrasectoral inequalities and the regional differences in Mexican society.

Moreover, industrialization through import substitution has ultimately led to an increasing dependence on foreign imports with the goal of economic independence still further away.

(b)   The agricultural sector experienced structural change as a result of the emergence of the great capitalist agricultural corporations, producing export crops, which took the best lands while exploiting the surrounding peasants as wage laboreres. The rest of the agricultural sector, the small property owners and subsistence farmers, were neglected and subsequently pauperized, also as a result of the strong population pressure in the rural areas. Large segments of the impoverished peasantry have migrated to the cities in search of betterment of their situation. In most cases, however, the rural proletariat has become the urban proletariat, filling the reservoir of cheap unskilled labor for the urban based industries.

(c)   The accumulation of capital has been based increasingly on the depression of popular consumption. The extreme inequalities in income distribution added to an at times inflationary situation and a low tax structure, have permitted high profit rates. These profits, at least those made on national investments, have been reinvested insufficiently in long term productive enterprises. The poverty of the popular strata has hampered the expansion of the domestic market. The middle strata, grown with the expansion and the diversification of the economic sector and the growth of the government bureaucracy, yet excercises an insufficient demand. Further industrial growth, especially of those industries dependent on mass consumption, would depend on changes in the income distribution which on their term would require some drastic changes in the power relations within the political structure.

(d)   The Mexican economy has become dependent more and more on direct and indirect foreign, e.g. U.S., investments. Foreign economic interests have become a powerful pressure group. They do not dominate the situation in any direct way but pose sharp limits to external and internal economic policies. The import and export trade has been largely directed towards the U.S.A. The importance of U.S. tourism and border transactions has further increased the dependence of the Mexican economy, with obvious political consequences.

(e)   From measures of a structural reform nature in the 1930's a change has been made to measures for economic and social growth which do not basically affect vested interests, e.g. the national and foreign entrepreneurs. In fact, the popular sectors in the cities as well as in the countryside have borne the brunt of a process in which the growth of certain productive forces and services was presented as a policy that was to end underdevelopment.[9]

Within this general picture of unbridled dependent capitalist development, Monterrey takes a deviant position. Its entrepreneurial activity has been

[9] In this context Wionczek (1971) rightfully asks in the title of his book the relevant question "growth or development?"

mostly directed towards the establisment of a development following national capitalist patterns.

3. SOCIAL CLASSES

3.1 *Introduction*

The class situation of Mexican society represents a totality of structures and substructures interrelated through intricate patterns of interdependence and conflict and reflecting the highly complex production structure, as outcome of the economic and social changes that have taken place since the Revolution. Among those writing on social class in Mexico there is little consensus with regard to the composition of the class structure. To a certain extent this goes back to problems in the use of class models and levels of analysis, partly however, it also reflects the complex structuring of the object of analysis itself.

In this study the urban working class will concern us most. Classes, however, obviously form part of a class structure. Within this structure each class' specific identity is also modelled by the nature of the relationships that are established among all of them. We will focus on the classes that stand for the broad historical categories that have been a part of the evolution and development of Mexican society, in particular in its postrevolutionary phase. To prevent confusion the term "classes" will be reserved for these categories, while their internal differentiation will be discussed in terms of "class segments".

A very general outline of these classes will be given as to their internal composition, the interrelationships between the various class segments, their economic and social bases, interests and group sentiments. The tendencies towards effective political action with these classes of class segments, or the degree of latency in them as potential factors in the political struggle, will be explored and further elaborated in a discussion of the class relations.

3.2 *The Class Situation*

3.2.1. *The bourgeoisie*

One of the remarkable results of the dynamics of class in Mexico in the postrevolutionary period has been the emergence of a bourgeoisie through two interrelated processes: private economic activity and the expansion of the public sector (Labastida, 1972: 135). These processes have resulted in the formation of (a) an economically dominant segment that includes, in order of importance, big business men (real estate, insurance, etc.), bankers, industrialists, merchants and the new *latifundistas*, e.g., the big agricultural entrepreneurs (cf. Stavenhagen, 1971: 53 ff); (b) a politically dominant segment which subsumes the highest echelon government officials, including the managers of public enterprises, leaders of the functional interest groups within the official political structure, and national politicians (Scott, 1959: 83; cf. Brandenburg, 1964: 158-159).

The core of the economically dominant segments consists of 1,000 families who share the possesion of great fortunes.[10] The distribution of income in general is highly skewed towards the entrepreneurial elite whose profits in recent decades have increasingly expanded, especially in cases of rising productivity and stagnating wage levels. This situation by and large also prevailed during the heydays of full capitalism in the Western industrial societies, with this great difference that in particular the industrial bourgeoisie played a dynamic role in the rapid transformation of the socioeconomic structure, through accumulation of the economic surplus and continuous reinvestment, thus promoting futher development. In Mexico, except for Monterrey, the small economic elite behaved differently. The combination of inflation, with the exception of the 1960's, exceedingly favorable profits and the growing inequalities in the distribution of income, which prevailed from 1939 on, have proven to be a wasteful way of inducing savings (Singer, 1969: 181). Puente Leyva (1969: 47) estimates the private savings in Mexico in the 1960's at around 9 percent of the G.N.P. while the total profits, dividends, etc. amount to no less than 27 percent of the G.N.P. The difference between these two percentages roughly indicates the part of the G.N.P. dedicated to consumptive purposes by the profit receiving business elite. This means that a considerable part of the G.N.P. was spent in a way unrelated to the nation's productive capacity. Investment in general was not forthcoming unless it could be recovered in three or four years, a situation that has prevailed from the 1940's on. The relatively small contribution to capital formation made by the bourgeoisie has further strengthened the role of investments initiated by the government or provided for by foreign sources, a phenomenon that has made it virtually impossible for them to regain the initiative later on. Their cooperation with a national autonomous solution to the problem of underdevelopment has been minimal.[11] Many Mexican entrepreneurs function as intermediaries for foreign interests in the Mexican economy, managing local subsidiaries of foreign corporations or tying their business to foreign interests in the financial, technological or commercial field. The group of Monterrey entrepreneurs, as will be explained later, deviate from this pattern and there the beginning has emerged of a dynamic national industrial bourgeoisie

Both segments of the bourgeoisie have shown a growing degree of internal cohesion. The economically dominant segment has organized in sectoral organizations that increasingly have taken unified stands on issues relating to their basic interests.In this process,the segments of the bourgeoisie located in the state of Mexico and the Federal District and in Nuevo León carry the

---

[10] The minimum size of the individual fortunes was estimated by Aguilar (1970a: 76) at 30 million pesos.
[11] In terns of A. Gunder Frank they should be characterized as a "lumpen bourgeoisie" (Gunder Frank, 1970).

heavier "weight", the first mentioned one based on its proximity to central political power, the latter because of its pure economic strength (cf. De Rossi, 1971: 47 ff). Next to this growing internal integration of each of the two segments, a trend can be discerned towards a rapprochement between them on the basis of an increasing compatibility of actual and perceived interests. This latter process has presented itself on two levels:

(a) A basic agreement or understanding has crystallized between the two segments with regard to national policy orientations and the division of labor between the private and the public sector. The agreement on the main lines of national economic and financial policies has been the result of succesful lobbying by the entrepreneurial sector. The continuing subordination of the interests of the agricultural sector to those of the urban industrial sector, may have counted as a more basic element, underlying their rapprochement (Labastida, 1972: 103). The government has provided elaborate protectionist legislation to industrial interests and has supplied the infrastructure industry needed. Finally, the activities of the State firms and enterprises of "mixed" capital have served even more to interweave the two categories' interests (González Casanova, 1967: 63 ff).

(b) The economically and the politically dominant segments have come to share a mode of life, they participate in the same social activities, live in the same residential areas, send their children to the same schools and last but not least they intermarry.[12] In this process, the politically dominant segments have come to acquire certain plutocratic features (Labastida, 1972: 134). With the economic elite, they have begun to share the highly privileged position, which the Mexican bourgeoisie has traditionally claimed and ingeniously defended.

Those prominents who left public service have become rentiers, owners of real estate or *latifundia*, bur many more became industrialists, managing national of foreign enterprises.[13]

The rapprochement in the economic and social spheres is, however, not likely to result in a complete homogenization of the bourgeoisie and an eradication of all internal differences. The integrative tendencies coexist with an effort in the political sphere to maintain some formal distinctions that intend to prevent direct dictation of government policies by the entre-preneurial sector. These distinctions are to an important extent the result of ideological prescription. At the same time, they permit the maneuvering through which the politically dominant segment has to accommodate the pressures and counter pressures which it receives from the various functional interest groups, it is supposed to represent. The verbal attacks by the official-political elite on "the rich and the wealthy" relate to this process and should be interpreted as populist word play, meant to maintain legitimacy as

---

[12] This applies in particular to the Mexico City region. The society pages of the daily *Novedades* present ample information on the integrating tendencies in these spheres of life.

[13] Cf. Labastida, 1972: 134; Aguilar (1970a: 47 ff) mentions a number of former presidents and other prominent politicians who form part of this trend.

34

representatives of popular interests.[14] They do not necessarily indicate a conflict of interests with the entrepreneurial sector.[15]

The economically as well as the politically dominant segments have not developed into strictly closed or exclusive units. The channels for social mobility into the bourgeoisie have not been blocked. The top government positions have long been recruited from the middle strata (Labastida, 1972: 136 ff).

Certain plutocratic tendencies are indeed present, but the establishment of a real plutocracy is still far away. The situation of the entrepreneurial sector, wrongly defined by Aguilar (1970a: 75) as an "oligarchy", is not very different. Tendencies towards oligarchization do exist, but they coexist with a considerable amount of flexibility and possibilities for mobility from below. Aguilar's own list of 1,000 families contains quite a number of recent entries (Aguilar, 1970a: 67 ff).

In mode of life, cultural orientation and group consciousness, the old landed aristocracy has constituted the reference group for a considerable part of the present bourgeoisie and the upper segment of the middle class. (Scott, 1959: 84). The cultural outlook and self-definition of the bourgeoisie is no different from those found in the traditional Latin American ruling classes, who have tended to view themselves as a divine elite and have cultivated, parallel to the sharp economic differences, an immense social and cultural distance towards the popular strata.[16]

3.2.2. The middle class

The emergence of the present middle class should be explained against the background of the macroprocesses of economic and social change that have taken place since the Revolution.[17] In Mexico it has been a rather recent phenomenon, in its expansion strongly related to the parallel processes of urbanization and economic development (cf. Whetten, 1968: 63 ff). The

---

[14] The tendency has become especially developed under the administration of President Echeverría, who at times even succeeded to arouse the private sector's hostility (in particular a segment of the Monterrey industrial elite), without being able, or willing, to curb or control it, making himself vulnerable to charges of demagoguery See f.e. *Latin America, a Weekly Political and Economic Report*, vol. VIII, 12, March 22, 1974.

[15] The model of a mediator government that the Mexican government tries to implement through its official party integrating sectors of the various classes, pretends the creation of a national consensus and reconcilation of conflicting interests

[16] See Mannheim (1956) for a revealing essay on the essentials of this "aristocratic culture".

[17] This is not meant to suggest that in previous historical periods this societal segment was totally absent. Palerm Vich (1968: 88) shows a "middle class" to be present in colonial and postcolonial prerevolutionary society. He recognizes at the same time, however, that the background, composition and orientation of the present middle class reveals little roots in these periods.

[18] In the period 1930-1969, 30.0 percent of the absolute growth in employment has been contributed by the government sector itself. Compare f.e. manufacturing 18.2 percent, construction 5.7 percent, transport 4.2 percent (Labastida, 1972: 145).

growth and diversification of the industrial sector changed the composition of the working class. The number of employees in low and medium level management positions and the segment of medium level technicians increased. The industrial growth further stimulated the organization of numerous small supply and repair shops, managed independently without additional personnel. The increasing importance of this category of the self-employed has presented itself even more strongly in the urban commercial sector where the increase in the number of trades people, restaurant keepers, hoteliers, mechanics, etc. has expanded the number of middle-class position in particular under the influence of the tourist trade.

The government bureaucracy, however, has rendered the greatest contribution to the expansion of the middle class. Many institutions that form part of the Mexican state machinery have developed parallel to and in association with "the middle class." The State became the supreme dispenser of occupational opportunities as a result of its interventions in the economy and the mushrooming of government activities in other areas.[18] The social and economic possibilities of the middle class have become more and more a function of State policies. Except for the telegraph and telephone operators and school teachers, those segments dependent on state activity for their employment have tended to form a support base for the government (Aguilar, 1970b: 329 ff). At the same time, they form the recruitment area for party officials and labor leaders (Scott, 1959: 83). The socioeconomic position of the state employed is a rather privileged one. The government has granted them special benefits as low cost housing, medicare and yearly bonuses which obviously shores up their tendency to support the status quo represented by their *patrones* higher up.

The middle class in Mexico is largely an urban phenomenon. The various post-Revolutionary land reforms did create a category between, on the one hand, the small group of new *latifundistas*, owners and managers of the agroindustrial enterprises, and the masses of pauperized farm laborers and subsistence farmers. Its relative size, however, is small: 7.8 percent of all farm operators own between 5 and 25 hectares, and 6 percent own between 25 and 200 hectares. In total these categories represent 6.3 percent of the economically active population in agriculture in 1960 (Stavenhagen, 1971: 48).

The urban middle class has a rather heterogeneous structure.[19] It comprises a wide range of positions representing great internal differences in occupations, income and status. Common elements are a predominantly urban background, a more than elementary degree of education (in some of the segments, bur not in all) and a position in the organization of the economic process which does justify neither their classification as part of the bourgeoisie, nor as part of the proletariat. This element, however, does not cement

---

[19] This is a phenomenon found throughout Latin America and posing considerable theoretical and methodological difficulties to analysts trying to define the class with some degree of precision. See Dahrendorf (1968: 51 ff) for the conceptual problems involved.

36

the middle class to a class in its own right. The internal cohesion is rather weak. Structural heterogeneity will result in differences in interests on concrete policy issues, further complicated by a considerable variance in class identification, reference group orientation and the definition of antagonist classes within society as a whole (Scott, 1959: 61 ff; Stavenhagen, 1971).

Various authors (Scott, 1959: 78; Ratinoff, 1967: 70 ff; Aguilar, 1970b: 328) have pointed at the mobility consciousness prevailing among those occupying urban middle-class positions. This may relate to the fact that most of them arrived through processes of mobility from below, creating aspirations of a further climb and a corresponding fear of proletarization. Especially in the middle and upper middle-class segments, a main effort is still dedicated to an accentuation of the social distance towards below while minimizing the distance towards the bourgeoisie.[20] For many, the bourgeoisie is the reference group whose mode of life is imitated, often at great cost.[21] The national income distribution shows that major portions of the middle class actually do live very modestly. The share of the lower middle strata has stagnated, while among the higher strata it has slightly increased (cf. Singer, 1969: 130 ff).

The aspirations with regard to upward social mobility refer to a movement on an individual basis. The realization of these aspirations depend primarily on particularistic and personalistic qualifications that on the medium levels still function as primary criteria of recruitment and selection. The fact that also here the labor supply exceeds the number of positions available, has emphasized this tendency even more, instead of an institutionalization of competition for the available jobs on the basis of less "subjective" qualifications. The exchange of favors, family connections, "protective" relationships, the distribution of sinecures through the official party and similar forms of particularistic relations have remained the mechanism through which members of the middle class secure occupational opportunities.

3.2.3. The proletariat

The process of class formation of the proletariat has been strongly conditioned by the processes of urbanization and industrialization, discussed in the previous paragraphs. In combination with the continuing agrarian crisis, aggravated by an increasing demographic pressure, these processes led to an expulsion of labor from the agricultural sector, finally resulting in massive migrations from the countryside to the cities, where the weakly developed economic apparatus appeared incapable to absorb the migrants in any substantial numbers. The industrial growth has been heavily concentrated in the regions around Mexico City and Monterrey. Together these industrial areas accounted for 65 per cent of the gross production in the Mexican manufac-

[20] See Gillin (1966) for this preoccupation among the Latin American middle class with hierarchy.
[21] This is a phenomenon found throughout Latin America, already noted in Crevenna's (1950-1952) early studies.

37

turing industry in 1965 (Censo Industrial 1965). Industrialization here has proceeded at an impressive pace but the trend has been towards a concentration of production in capital-intensive units, adding to the problem of under — and unemployment, now estimated to affect around 40 percent of the total Mexican labor force (Domínguez, 1974: 3). Despite small improvements in levels of living, most of the urban migrant population changed its rural poverty for an urban poverty.

Within the proletariat in a wide sense, a major division line should be drawn between the urban and rural segments. In individual situations obviously "overlaps" and transitory stages will exist,[22] but their general location in the economic process, their interests and organization are sufficiently distinct to warrant their definition as separate segments. This study is concerned with the urban segment of the proletariat.[23] Within this category a distinction should be made between the regularly employed, the urban proletariat in a more narrow sense, and the subproletariat.

The definition of the subproletariat as a separate "subclass", does not imply a complete absence of integrating elements between the two segments. However, the differences between them in structural position and corresponding interests, appear to be greater than the internal divisions between the various subsegments of the regularly employed proletariat. The relationship between the two is not free from paradoxical elements. The urban proletariat in a more narrow sense, has originated from the subproletarian under- and unemployed masses. They have formed its recruitment base. At the same time, however, the continuing presence of this labor reservoir has undermined the former's negotiating position, obstructed its struggle for the improvement of the working conditions, helped to maintain inferior wage levels and hampered the efforts to change the prevailing pattern of income distribution.

In the course of the process of urban-industrial growth the urban proletariat has developed a more and more differentiated internal structure. It is employed in sectors of the urban economy (industrial, commercial, services) that know considerable differences between and within themselves. It contains a large number of occupational groups and further shows a considerable degree of internal stratification on skill, income and status.

[22] The rural proletariat fills the ranks of the urban subproletariat, which in turn forms the recruiting ground for the proletariat. Migrant studies indicate the persistence of intensive contact with the rural area of origin after migration (an example in Lewis, 1965). The relationship between rural and urban proletariat may also be a more direct one, e.g. in those cases where the worker has a dual status. González Navarro (1969: 223 ff) notes that in the Valle de Mexico, from 70 to 80 percent of the *ejiditarios* work in the factories in the Mexico City area. Here they can earn three to four times as much as in the fields. They lease their land, hand it over to sharecroppers or work it under some other kind of arrangement, but in any case they do not cut completely their relationship to the land.

[23] See Stavenhagen (1971: 49 ff) for an exposition on the rural segment of the proletariat, its internal structure and its evolution.

Obviously the characteristics of the setting in which production has been organized forms a basic differentiating factor. This applies in particular to the segment employed by industry. The variations on the underlying pattern of organization of the productive forces account for a rather heterogeneous industrial environment. The various types of technological structure and the related phenomena of division of labor, social organization and economic structure, have created settings ranging from labor-intensive industries utilizing rather simple technologies to modern capital-intensive highly mechanized or automated enterprises. Despite the tendencies towards concentration and centralization, a considerable part of the industrial labor force is still employed by artisan shops[24] and small industrial settings. The predominance of a wide variety of small, dispersed firms, where paternalism and personal or family ties characterize the relations between the employer and a small number of workers, poses serious obstacles to an organization and integration of the workers on the basis of a common location in the organization of the economic process (cf. Petras, 1969: 209 ff).

The industrial proletariat has diversified its occupational structure and it has left the stage where it formed a homogeneous group of equally unskilled people.[25] At first, a new category emerged among the industrial workers, the semiskilled, differing from the unskilled less in technical qualfications than in some extrafunctional skills that are required through training and experience, and that relate to the capacity to accept responsibility, to adapt to changing conditions, to perform a job intelligently. In more recent times the categories of skilled laborers have appeared as a result of the growing mechanization and automation in certain industrial sectors. These have received technical education and on the upper levels they shade off into the white collar strata. As far as wages, prestige, responsibility and authority within the working situation is concerned, they constitute a privileged category. The distance in income, social status and other stratification related variables between the worker "aristcracy" and the bottom segments is considerable, a phenomenon more generally present in Latin America (Petras, 1969: 210). Obviously then, these differences in skill, mentioned above, are accompanied by other attributes and determinants of social status, that in the end serve to differentiate the industrial proletariat even further.

The presence of this internal segmentation of the working class does not necessarily rule out class conflict on the basis of structurally generated, more basic differences in interests, but it seems reasonable to assume some changes of the short-term issues and above all of the patterns of conflict in the concrete political struggle.

---

[24] Ibarra (1970: 30) indicates that more than half of the Mexican industrial labor force is employed in the "traditional low productivity sector," which should contain most of these small artisan shops counting less than five workers.

[25] See Dahrendorf (1968: 48) on the problem of the so-called "decomposition of labor".

3.2.4. *The subproletariat*

The members of the subproletariat share a number of characteristics that refer to (a) their location in the economic process, (b) their job stability, and (c) their socioeconomic situation and perspectives.

(a) Most of the members of this "subclass" engage in more or less unproductive activity in the services and circulation sectors. Here they are involved in a daily struggle for subsistence through a variety of marginal jobs, like ambulatory vendors, car watchers, shoe shiners, newspaper and lottery vendors, domestics, occasional day laborers and the like. These occupations are located in those sectors of the urban economy where low levels of productivity and technology prevail (cf. Petras, 1969: 212).

(b) The jobstability of the large mass of semiemployed and irregularly employed individuals is extremely low and may not extend beyond the day, not to mention the "selfemployed" in this subsistence sector. This lack of steady imployment has a number of correlates, as: an income below the legally established minimum, no labor contract, no access to social security and related services like medicare, disability payments, compensations in case of involuntary dismissal, retirement pay, low-income housing, profit sharing, etc. (cf. Muñoz García *et al.*, 1972: 328 ff).

(c) The paradoxical element in the situation of the subproletariat is that their marginal jobs not only yield incomes inferior to those of the regularly employed; in addition they are barred access to those institutions that were designed to protect the economically weak. Many among them are recent migrants to the city. They come from economically backward rural areas where little opportunity for education is offered and where the economic structure does not contain possibilities for employment outside the agricultural sector. The proportion of migrants with marginal jobs tends to become smaller in the course of their residence in the city, but this trend is too weak to eliminate the substantial differences between natives and migrants in terms of the likelihood to occupy marginal jobs (Muñoz García *et al.*, 1972: 332). The inability of the industry to provide jobs has caused a fierce competition for those opportunities of regular employment opening up. Formal criteria of education, training and experience have become more and more important in determining entrance to the occupational structure. With regard to these criteria, the migrants are securely handicapped.

The desperate economic situation of this part of the urban population, showing in extreme low levels of living, child labor, badly balanced diets, etc., has of course its social psychological correlates. Oscar Lewis (1964) has offered extensive descriptions of the situation of daily deprivation the subproletariat is suffering. In discussing their responses, he points to the critical attitude towards the dominant classes, the distrust of the government and hatred of the police and other institutions of control. On the basis of these characteristics he views them as a potential base for social movements against the existing social order (Lewis, 1964: xxviii). However, the reality of Mexican political life is that as yet, this potential has not been translated into action. They are not unionized and accumulate little experience in class action. Their political behavior, with few exceptions, has been dependent of official politics and largely status quo oriented.

The explanation of this phenomenon has to be sought for primarily in the specific economic positions they occupy and in the types of problems they have to concern themselves with. On these points, the subproletariat differs considerably from the steadily employed urban proletariat. The urban workers' immediate concern is with wages and improvement in working conditions. The subproletariat is focused on subsistence, finding a job, housing, securing minimal services of water and electricity (cf. Petras, 1969: 214). The highly dispersed nature of their economic activities tends to atomize and isolate instead of to unite them. Many of their occupations generate individualistic attitudes and commercial values (the penny capitalism of the street vendors), others (for example domestics) are subject to relations of personal dependence and paternalism. The subproletariat in general will function as an industrial reserve army, although only part of it could be directly employed and their presence directly destabilizes primarily the position of the unskilled (cf. Quijano, 1971: 33 ff).[26]

3.3. Conclusion: The Class Structure

The Mexican class structure and its main features are rather recent phenomena. During the Revolution, the disintegration speeded up of the archaic class structure, that had already begun during the *Porfiriato*. The economic and social changes of the postrevolutionary period further contributed to the crystallization of a class structure that conformed more to capitalist patterns. The result has been a class structure, representing extreme economic and social inequalities which even on the Latin American scene are parallelled in few cases. This structure is well set and preserved by an elaborate system of class control, yet it is not totally inflexible. The continued internal differentiation of the classes and the emergence of new classes or class segments, such as the administrative segment of the bourgeoisie, the middle class, the segment of the skilled among the proletariat, has meant an upward mobility for those who occupied the newly created positions in the economy and the government apparatus. The incapacity of the urban economy to absorb the labor supply, which made the jobless subproletariat expand at an ever growing rate, should not make us forget that steady employment as well as some upward occupational mobility must have been the personal experience of a considerable

---

[26] This reservoir is of a considerable magnitude. Muñoz García *et al.*,(1972: 336) estimates the size of the marginal segment at 23.7 percent of the economically active population in the age group 21-60 in the area of the Federal District.

number of people.[27] Apart from its significance for the attitudes and outlook of the persons concerned, this obviously will have a demonstration effect for those people occupying stagnant positions or for those who are desperately trying to enter the job market, a phenomenon artfully exploited by official politics.

4. THE POLITICAL PROCESS

The way in which the classes and class segments express themselves in the political arena, or the class relations, reveal the issue orientation and the specific patterns of the structurally generated conflict in Mexican society. The single most important characteristic of the political process is again the leading role of the State which has provided the greater part of the legal political and ideological framework which has served the process of socioeconomic development in the last four decades.

4.1. *The Official Party*

The official government party, Partido Revolucionario Institucional, P.R.I., was founded in 1929 (under a different name) and expanded in the following years as a political instrument integrating the various different revolutionary groups within the common framework, transcending the purely personalist character of the politics and modernizing the polity on a national basis. From the very beginning on, the party had a heterogeneous membership and also the ideological orientations were rather diverse. In those beginning years it developed following populist patterns (cf. Di Tella, 1965). A specific ideological commitment was not required and it became an umbrella for positions covering the entire political spectrum. Since then, the party has remained ideologically vague. It claims the principles of the Revolution, as set forth in the 1917 Constitution and various other documents, as its guiding theme.

The party structure reflects the effort to integrate people across class lines within one organizational framework, while preserving the possibility for interest respresentation. Representatives of each of the three basic sectors on which the party is built, the peasant, labor and the popular sector, run the party apparatus and participate in the harmonization of competing claims made by the functional interest associations within each sector. They articulate the demands of the sector as a whole and lobby for satisfaction of these demands with the executive. The struggle within and between the sectors has

---

[27] These numbers are hard to specify exactly. As an indication we may count Labastida's estimate (1972: 139) that around 30 percent of the population has been able to maintain or augment their real incomes over the last three decades. These represent the entrepreneurial sector, segments of the middle sector and the technical experts and skilled workers in the modern industries.

42

remained rather limited despite these activities. The proliferation of interests that has accompanied the growing differentiation of the class structure has not resulted in an equally differentiated power structure. In each of the sectors, power has been held by one large association or combination of interest groups. The leaders of these power blocks are closely tied to the inner circle of the party. This makes the arbitration possible of conflicting demands within the party "oligarchy" where at the same time the decisions are taken on the integration of these demands with the long term objectives concerning national economic, political and social development (Anderson and Cockcroft, 1972: 228 ff).

Since its formation, the party has never lost an election on the presidential, gobernatorial or senatorial level. The two opposition parties P.P.S. (*Partido Popular Socialista*) operating on the Marxist left, and P.A.N. (*Partido de Acción Nacional*) representing the politically conservative segments,[28] perform no more than ceremonial roles in the electoral process. These are dissident groups, constituting small pressure groups, and partipating in the political process, less motivated by any expectation of success, in terms of a. sizable vote,[29] than by anticipation of cooptation by the majority party which customarily produces favors and rewards in return for support for the party and loyalty to the regime. The cooptation pattern has operated rather intensively with regard to the dissident groups on the political left among them the P.P.S. and various other political movements that originated during the last two decades.[30] The party has been concerned to a much lesser degree with overt cooptation of right-wing dissidents, not only because they represent a much smaller threat to the political and socioeconomic status quo, but also because of the potential problems of legitimation to a party that claims to be the only heir to the ideals of the Mexican Revolution (Cockcroft, 1972: 234). The conservative opposition party, P.A.N., has been tolerated by the regime and presents countercandidates in presidential elections. According to Brandenburg, P.A.N. as well as the other opposition parties are supported financially by the government, despite the image of legitimate independent political organizations that they are carefully cultivating. The ultimate objective of such a procedure would be to provide some political institutions, next to the official party, through which a greater variety of ideological argument and policy discussion can be channeled, obviously under ultimate government control (Brandenburg, 1964: 144-165). Those parties or movements aspiring to an independent power position of any substance without an alliance with the official party and refusing official cooptation, have been mercilessly

---

[28] Representing big business men, the small town clerically oriented middle class, bourgeois and middle class professionals, religious peasant groups in some part of the country (cf. Anderson and Cockcroft, 1972: 235)

[29] In presidential elections the "opposition" never succeded in polling more than 25 percent of the vote (1952).

[30] Examples are: the M.L.N., led by Cárdenas, which ultimately supported the P.R.I. in 1964, further the C.C.I., an opposition peasant movement, which also joined government ranks.

suppressed.[31] This way the inner circle of the ruling party has managed to keep dissident groups in check. The participation of the populace has been limited mainly to election time when they are mobilized (and manipulated) by the party functionaries following the traditional patterns of dependent political development.

Within the party, the elite tends to perpetuate itself in power through a tight control over nominations and elections. This control extends to the office of the presidency. Incumbent presidents have a decisive say in the nomination of their successors, who over the years have been drawn invariably from the midst of the top party leadership.

The P.R.I., as we have seen, is meant to fulfill an important function as mediator of disputes and as promotor of consensus and in doing so actually functions as an important apparatus of class control. Its structure of sector organizations opens the possibility of a political expression of class member-ship, but potential class conflict is being neutralized by watering down any militant demand through the subjection to arbitration by a ruling group that has developed its own interests and harbors its own long term plans with regard to the future development of the nation. This dependence on the decisions in the party top is rigidly enforced. Any independent promotion of class interests is likely to receive a repressive response.

4.2. The Political Expression of Class Membership

The Mexican class structure does not find its direct and unequivocal con-tinuation in the political structure. Class membership has been translated into political action through complex processes of interest articulation and ex-pression, the main features of which will be outlined in the following para-graphs.

4.2.1. The entrepreneurial sector

Parallel with the broadening of their economic base in the last few decades, the Mexican entrepreneurs have greatly expanded their influence on the government policies affecting the sector, through an increasing number of interest organizations. These pressure groups have developed into powerful and effective instruments of interest representation for the various segments of the bourgeoisie.

The most important organization are: the *Confederación de Cámaras Nacionales de Comercio* (CONCANACO) with 254 chambers, the *Confeder-ación Nacional de Cámaras Industriales* (CONCAMIN) with 51 chambers, the

---

[31] For recent instances of this repression, see: the handling of the railroad workers strike in 1959, the repression of the F.E.P. and other leftist groups in the mid 1960's, the massacre at Tlatelolco in 1968; for examples of the repressive violence in the countryside, see: the discussion around the assassination of the peasant leader Rubén Jaramello in 1962 (Careága, 1971: 91), further *Latin America, a Weekly Political and Economic Report*, vol IX, 1, January 3, 1975.

Confederación Patronal de la Republica Mexicana with 21 *Centros Patronales,* further the *Asociación de Banqueros de Mexico* and the *Asociación Mexicana de Instituciones de Seguros.* These are by law "consulting agents of the government with regard to the needs of the national industry and commerce" (González Casanova, 1967: 66) and in practice function as a congress of employers with a decisive influence in the legislative and administrative affairs that affect these sectors. These are well-organized, well-financed institutions that recommend legislation and propose policies, either at their own initiative or as a critical commentary of government proposed legislation, and discuss with the government possible modifications of economic and financial policies. This way the entrepreneurial sector participates directly and on the highest level, in the process of political decision-making without formal representation in the government or in the official party (Padgett, 1966: 130). In this process they have a considerable bargaining power, further strengthened by their capacity to frustrate unwelcome government policies by freezing new investment and intensifying the flight of capital to foreign bank accounts.[32] In case a problem presents itself which affects the entire sector, the presidents of the employer's organizations, with exception of the *Asociación Mexicana de Instituciones de Seguros,* meet, together with their staff experts, in order to work out a collective standpoint. In all other cases the chamber of the specific sector affected, meets to define its own solution, at all times very aware, however, of the backing of the others in any situation where action should be necessary (González Casanova, 1967: 65).

The growing cohesion of the entrepreneurial sector has decreased individual lobbying and replaced it with a collective approach, the Monterrey entrepreneurs as most important single pressure group recently being the most outspoken representatives. The former distinctions between the entrepreneurial organizations have lessened in importance. Up until the mid-1950's the CONCANACO used to represent the "traditional" interests and in fact favored foreign investment and free trade. The policies of the CON-CAMIN, on the other hand, have become influenced in the last few decades more and more by its section CANACINTRA (*Cámara Nacional de la Industria de Transformación*) representing the entrepreneurs who had been involved in the "boom" in import-substituting industrialization during the Second World War. They opted for Mexican capital, al least initially, cultivated good relations with Mexican banks and credit institutions and developed a close working relationship with the government, the source of credit,[33] tariff protections, tax exemptions and export subsidies (cf. Mosk, 1950: 21-52; Vernon, 1963: 133 ff). At the same time they took a less instinctively antagonistic approach towards organized labor. Apparently this group of entrepreneurs has understood that an effective conflict regulation in the industrial

---

[32] These treats were carried out as a warning to the new president in 1970 (cf. Cosío Villegas, 1972: 73) and repeated in the last months of the Echeverría-administration.
[33] Almost one-third (30.1 percent) of the total national investment was made by the public sector in 1966 (Ibarra, 1970: 116)

sector would require the organization of all interest groups involved. As long as conflicting forces are diffused and lack unity and organization, regulation is virtually impossible (cf. Dahrendorf, 1968: 226). This strategy included a conciliation with the C.T.M. in 1945 and a subsequent involvement of labor in their industrialization plans with as obvious objective to neutralize the labor unions and to reduce their effectiveness as an instrument for the promotion of labor interests.

4.2.2. The middle sector

Middle-class pressure groups have sought interest representation through the popular sector of the official party. To this purpose, in 1943, the *Confederación Nacional de Organizaciones Populares* (C.N.O.P.) was founded. It was given a federation structure very similar to the one the labor confederations had. The relationship between the C.N.O.P. and the government, however, has not been formally regulated by a special code as in the case of the peasant and labor sector. The extreme diversity of the sector, reflecting the structural heterogeneity of the middle class itself, may have been a complicating factor here. It comprises nine subsectors: (a) government employees and teachers, (b) members of cooperatives, (c) small farm owners, (d) small industrialists and business men, (e) professionals and intellectuals, (f) artisans, (g) youth groups, (h) women's organizations, (i) various other small groupings.

Each of the subsectors has been further subdivided into different interest groups, a situation which brings Scott (1959: 169) to remark, that the most amazing achievement of the sector lies with its ability to avoid disintegration rather than with its marked political succes. This obviously overstates the case. Actually the degree of "success" they have had, relative to the other sectors, in realizing a number of material and social aspirations for strategic segments of the popular sector has managed to keep not only the direct beneficiaries together but has also united the others hoping for a share of the pie.

The government employees form the backbone of the C.N.O.P. organization. Within the sector they occupy most of the elective offices. They have been granted benefits far beyond those enjoyed by other Mexicans in comparable positions. In exchange they have exhibited a great loyalty towards the regime in general, and towards those politicians who mediated their demands in particular. In addition, the leading C.N.O.P. representatives have taken a political stand approaching the one of the entrepreneurial sector on many issues. They have opposed changes in the taxation system, backed the agroindustrial entrepreneurs against the landless rural proletariat and the *ejiditarios* and supported the emphasis in government spending on urban improvement and investments in the industrial sector (Padgett, 1966: 127).

The various subsectors of the confederation represent as many followings, tied to leaders who "produce" for them on the basis of their understandings with top government officials. Interest representation follows the clientelist patterns, part of the traditional system of *caudillos* and *cacicques* that left a

46

cultural heritage of personalism and an emphasis on relations based on kinship, *compadrazgo* or friendship and which has assumed new and powerful functions as an instrument of class control in Mexico's changing sociopolitical structure.

4.2.3. *The labor sector*

The role of organized labor in Mexico has been very unlike the traditional pattern under western industrial capitalism which included an active and autonomous particpation in the struggle for the emancipation of the working class. Its role has been a very dependent one. The 1917 Constitution affirmed the right of the workers to form unions and recognized the right to strike. This legal recognition, however, did not change organized labor from a passive to a dynamic factor in societal change. From the beginning on, the labor movement has not been able to escape the prevailing pattern of cooptation by official politics. Those unions opting for an opposition line, have been mercilessly suppressed, following the pattern of action against rebellious workers and peasants that long since has been a part of Mexican history. These three elements of government initiative, cooptation and suppression alternatingly have characterized the course of the Mexican labor movement.

The history of the labor movement goes far back, bur first during the period of economic expansion under the *Porfiriato* the labor organizations developed some roots (cf. Buve, 1972). Initially, these organizations took the form of mutual aid societies and cooperatives, counting mainly artisans and independent workers among the membership. These developed into a weak syndicalist movement resulting in the formation of the *Círculo de Obreros de México* in 1870 and the *Congreso Obrero Permanente* in 1876. Both were superseded by the labor movement that emerged from the 1910 Revolution and that left the cooperativist and mutual aid elements behind, concentrating instead on wages and working conditions (Iglesias, 1970: 29 ff). This new labor activism emerged from the strike movement of the first decade of this century, culminating in the strikes among the miners of Cananea (Sonora) in 1906 and among the textile workers of Rio Blanco-Orizaba, Nogales, Santa Rosa and Atlixco in 1907, "acts of heroism" that still are remembered as such on the banners carried in present day May Day manifestations. These strikes were all brutally suppressed by the army (Salazar and Escobedo, 1923: 23 ff). In this same period the anarcho-syndicalist movement emerged with as its most illustrous representatives, the Flores Magón brothers who played a leading role during the beginning phase of the large labor organization *Casa del Obrero Mundial,* founded in 1912 (Iglesias, 1970: 33 ff; also Flores Magón, 1970).

With the expansion of its membership in subsequent years the *Casa* gradually entered on a more reformist course. In 1915 it was coopted by Obregón, chief lieutenant of Carranza, in his struggle against Zapata and Villa. It delivered six worker battalions in exchange for support for the union movement and government recognition of the right to strike. After the military successes of the *batallones rojos* and the strike movement of 1916, however, the government feared to lose the initiative. The promises to the workers were not honored and the *Casa* became the object of fierce suppression (De la Cerda Silva, 1961: 121 ff). The fact that ultimately the worker claims were incorporated in the 1917 Constitution as part of a total package of reformist measures was less the result of effective labor pressure than the outcome of the government effort to define a legal framework that would canalize the worker demands and facilitate their ultimate control (cf. Iglesias, 1970: 50 ff).

The first great Mexican labor confederation of the postrevolutionary period was founded in 1918. The *Confederación Regional de Oberos Mexicanos* (C.R.O.M.) gained heavily in membership until 1928, while operating with strong presidential patronage. Next to the C.R.O.M. emerged the *Confederación General de Trabajo* (C.G.T.) which initially represented a small radical opposition to the reformist stand of the C.R.O.M. and to its close association with the government (López Aparicio, 1958). After 1928 the two labor confederations rapidly disintegrated. Splinter groups proliferated as different leaders and followings left the C.R.O.M. and the C.G.T. In addition many other new groups were formed (Padgett, 1966: 92). President Cárdenas tried to end these divisions within the labor movement by actively supporting the formation of a new organization, the *Confederación de Trabajadores de Mexico* (C.T.M.) which he intended to use as a vehicle for the mobilization of support for his national labor policy. The C.T.M. claimed to represent a radical line, based on a Marxist analysis of Mexico's social and economic problems, which did not prevent, however, an active collaboration, with the government and with industry especially from the late 1930's on[34]. Cárdenas and his successors strongly pushed the C.T.M. as an all encompassing confederation acting as spokesman for the entire labor sector. Their ideal, however, failed to realize. Next to the C.T.M., the C.R.O.M. and the C.G.T., many autonomous state level labor organizations have persisted, although certainly in the late 1930's and 1940's, these unions did not offer very serious competition. All continued to operate as part of the labor sector of the official party. In 1945 the C.T.M. signed an "industrial labor pact" with the employers organization CANACINTRA, in an effort to reconcile labor and management interests. This compromising attitude of the C.T.M. leadership led to further splits in labor unity. Discontented leaders left the confederation followed by their clientele.[35]

---

[34] In this period it changed its motto from *por una sociedad sin clases,* towards a classless society, to *por la independencia económica de Mexico,* towards the economic independence of Mexico.
[35] Among them was Vincente Lombardo Toledano who attempted to create a new confederation, the *Unión General de Obreros y Campesinos Mexicanos* (U.G.O.C.M.), which initially was refused official recognition through the Ministry of Labor but later was coopted.Luis Gómez and Valentin Campo founded the C.U.T., Diaz Muñoz organized the A.O.C.M. These latter efforts were all unsuccesful in the long run.

48

In the early 1950's the *Confederación Regional de Obreros y Campesinos* (C.R.O.C.) emerged and expanded under strong government patronage, although it never got into a position from where it could seriously challenge the dominance of the C.T.M.[36] Anxious to achieve labor unity while maintaining its supremacy, the C.T.M. banded together with the C.R.O.M., the C.G.T. and the unions of railroad workers, workers in the mining and metallurgy sector, the petroleum workers, the telephone workers, the workers in the motion picture industry and several smaller independent unions. Together they formed in the late 1950's the *Bloque de Unidad Obrera* (B.U.O.) The "opposition" to the C.T.M. united in the *Central Nacional de Trabajadores* (C.N.T.). Affiliated were: C.R.O.C., C.R.T. (*Confederación Revolucionaria de Trabajadores*), the electrical workers union, a federation of textile workers, the federation of sugar cane workers and several independent unions (De la Cerda Silva, 1961: 150 ff). The composition of the C.N.T. Leadership suggested that also in the formation of this "opposition" to the B.U.O., the government was in firm control.

Both *centrales*, B.U.O. and C.N.T., form the labor sector of the P.R.I. The mere fact of affiliation with one or the other block does not necessarily mean that the confederations or individual unions all adhere to a specific "line". Between the C.T.M. and the C.G.T. at times, a considerable animosity has appeared, manifesting in their quarrelling veteran leaders Velázquez and Rivas. The railroad workers, electrical workers and petroleum workers at various times have taken deviant positions (cf. Scott, 1959: 167).

The pluralistic picture on labor side and the failure to change the multiconfederation structure into a single confederation, has several reasons. First of all, it has a legal basis. The federal labor code recognizes the freedom of the worker to affiliate with one or the other union or to remain unorganized.[37] Moreover, individual unions are free to decide whether or not they want to associate with a given federation or confederation (Trueba Urbina and Trueba Barrera) 1970: 148 ff). The government, however, has ultimate control through the provision that all unions should register with the reconciliation and arbitration board in the area where they operate and further with the Ministry of Labor if their activities fall under federal jurisdiction. These boards, on the local as well as on the federal level, have an equal number of labor and management representatives and they are presided over by a government official. They have the authority to refuse registration to a new union organization when they judge its objectives, statutes or proceedings to be in violation of the labor code.

In political practice, the labor laws offer ample opportunity for the government to intervene and to manipulate the unions. The efforts to unify

---

[36] Scott (1959: 164) suggests that President Ruíz Cortines used the C.R.O.C. to mobilize support for some of his reformist measures, opposing a rightist faction in the P.R.I. that had entered in alliance with the C.T.M.

[37] A freedom undermined by the closed shop policies of most local unions (Basurto, 1972: 53).

the labor movement as a single instrument under a single directorate which would unconditionally serve the political needs of the men in government, however, have not been entirely successful. Concessions had to be made to the highly personalistic features of union politics which, more than differences in ideological perspective, has accounted for the proliferation of the labor unions. In addition an entire segment of the union movement, the so called *sindicatos blancos,* has remained under control of employers who have resisted the incorporation into official federations and continue to promote paternalistic attitudes towards their workers. The government has continued to lean heavily on one confederation as the C.T.M., or the C.R.O.C. in the beginning of the 1950's. Those unions refusing affiliation with government supported confederations and not belonging to the *sindicatos blancos,* were object of cooptation efforts, including the incorporation of their leadership into the patronage system of the official party. Leaders who refused were removed, imprisoned or assassinated. Their movements were crushed and disbanded or had to continue under a leadership imposed by the government (cf. Iglesias, 1970: 131). Spectacular postwar examples include: the petroleum workers movement of 1946, the railroad workers movement of 1948, the miners movement of Nueva Rosita in 1950, the telephone workers, railroad workers and electrical workers movement of 1958-1959 and finally several smaller student worker movements in the 1960's (Cockcroft, 1972: 254; Iglesias, 1970: 133). These concern at the same time economically strategic sectors in which the degree of organization of the workers was relatively high.[38]

In bargaining situations with labor it has invariably been a government tactic to concede small economic improvements to politically and economically strategic sectors (urban labor), while at the same time strongly resisting any serious effort to implement those changes that could have power consequences on a national level.

The Mexican labor history exemplifies the dependency of organized labor, facing government initiative and strong intervention by the executive. In relation to this phenomenon González Casanova (1967: 27, 233) has noted that in Mexican political practice even labor strikes frequently will represent dependent action.[39]

---

[38] Union membership among the total work force in the electricity sector runs as high as 88.8 percent, in the extractive sector it is 59.2 percent and in the transport and communication sector 57.0 percent (1964). The degree of unionization of the entire Mexican economically active population was only 10.5 percent, which primarily should be attributed to the extremely low degree of union membership among the peasants and among those employed in commerce and in the services sector.

[39] He shows that since 1920 the fluctuations in strike frequency and numbers of participating workers coincide with presidential successions. Regrettably he does not provide the information on the number of man days lost that would be needed to complete the argumentation. He indicates that during the administration of presidents sympathetic towards labor, the numbers of strikes and participating workers increased sharply. Quite the opposite occurred under presidents indifferent towards labor interests and leaning towards the entrepreneurial sector.

He maintains that, given the fact that the strategy and tactics of the labor movement gravitate towards executive policies, strikes have not only been promoted by the expectation of support and protection by these policies (in the case of a president known for his prolabor sentiments), but inclusively at times have been directed and manipulated by the Executive as part of his overall tactics in playing one pressure group off against the other. Exceptions are: (a) the strike movement of 1933, which was a spontaneous reaction against the conservative policies of the *Maximato* (post-Calles period), (b) the strikes of 1943-1944, which represented a show of force against the administration of Camacho who tried to soften the prolabor policies of his predecessor, (c) the strikes of 1958-1959, in which a sector of the labor movement consisting of railroad workers, electrical workers and telephone workers, tried to change the internal structure of their unions and to implement a more militant and independent course of action (González Casanova, 1967: 28 ff; Iglesias, 1970, 136 ff; for the movement of railroad workers, see: Gill, 1971). These are the only examples of genuinely autonomous labor action on a large scale in postrevolutionary labor history, and they do provide an indication of the magnitude of labor as a latent power factor on the Mexican political scene. This, despite the fact that they terminated in the usual way through cooptation and or suppression.

Government control over organized labor has been accompanied by the emergence and maintenance of oligarchical structures within the labor unions themselves. The leadership of the major confederations has been dominated by "old" union bosses and some of them, like the C.T.M.'s Fidel Velázquez, have been in power already for more than thirty years. These bosses or *lideres charros* have well succeeded to maintain power through the use of force and suppression of rivals and dissidents as well as through their ability to "deliver" to their following as a result of their firm integration in the government clientelist machine. The oligarchical pattern which we find at the confederation level repeats itself at the lower levels. Here the influence of the higher levels weighs heavily and will lead to the imposition of the leaders in affiliated unions.

The corruption in these unions has become endemic and one of the more spectacular examples of a wider system of corrupt practices that has become institutionalized in virtually every sphere of social, economic and political life in Mexico (Cf. Carrión, 1969: 114 ff). This phenomenon forms part of the patrimonial bureaucratic and particularistic heritage in which the separation between private and public affairs was not strictly drawn and loyalties on a particularistic basis overshadowed a universalist loyalty to the State (Wertheim, 1961: 36 ff). In recent times it has even received new strength through the expansion of state activity and through the increasing appeal of U.S. lifestyles that entail consumption patterns very few can afford without some extra earnings. Corruption cases are more frequently publicized than used to be the case. These indications of changes in normative conscience, however, may not necessarily, indicate changes in political practice. The

51

almost weekly revelations in journals like *Siempre, Sucesos* and *Por Qué?* (closed by the government in September, 1974) and the regular self-scrutiny of the presidental election campaigns may even temporarily promote further corruption. In the case of the union movement, however, the frequent outbursts of discontent over corrupt practices, defying the usual hazards of *pistoleros* and hired thugs indicate that here these changes have more substance, even if, as is the case in Mexico, they are not permitted to canalize into a direction that would give it a more permanent power dimension in the political system. In this context we should point at the issues involved in the spontaneous strike movements of the last few decades (notably in 1958-1959 and in 1968), the emergence of more activist orientations among segments of workers in the public sector (railroad workers, electrical workers, telephone workers), in some industries in the private sector (textile workers, miners) and among the workers in the agroindustrial enterprises in the North of the country.

Besides those segments of the population that have been integrated into the government or entrepreneur controlled and manipulated organizations, great masses of the population do not belong to any of the popular organizations at all. Almost one-fourth (23.4 percent) of the workers in the industrial, commercial and services sector have not been unionized. In the agricultural sector the unorganized comprise 93.6 percent of the segment of rural workers (1963). This situation has existed without great modifications from 1939 on (González Casanova, 1967: 145 ff). The urban and rural subproletariat are, however, even more marginal to the official political structure. Opposition parties do not seem to have a grip on them, looking at the voting patterns in presidential and senatorial elections (González Casanova, 1967: 149 ff). The only way they can make themselves heard is throught the paternalistic mechanisms of traditional Mexican politics. Official politicians, or those aspiring to that status, will try to create a "constituency" that will give them support in their political career in exchange for some concrete "rewards" (often in the area of public services), achieved through their intervention in the government bureaucracy. Their role as an intermediary is a clearly limited one. The politician will not try to organize or politicize the marginal sectors at the grass roots level or continue agitation after his political position has been secured. Actions like these are not covered by the rules of the game and they are invitations to suppression (cf. Cockcroft, 1972; Anderson and Cockcroft, 1972).

4.3. Some Concluding Remarks

Mexican politics shows sharp contradictions between the normative model and the descriptive model of its political system.[40] The normative model, as

---

[40] In individual cases, as one often can observe, this leads to an almost schizophrenic situation, where two different frames of reference are alternately used according to the requirements of the moment.

part of the official Mexican political ideology, obviously serves the maintenance of the legitimacy of the system threatened by political practice. In this model the pluralistic picture of Mexican politics clashes with the practice of one party rule, where the opposition is either coopted or suppressed. The definition of the official party as consisting of three sectors independent of each other, each having a considerable degree of grass roots participation, conflicts with the practice of a pyramidical structure and oligarchic control. The interest groups united in the sectors are highly dependent on government initiative which sets the pace of action at the basic levels, eliminating any possible uncontrolled mobilization effort. State power has become strongly centralized, which can be clearly noted in the extreme dependence in political, military and financial spheres, showing at the state and local levels.

The idiosyncrasies of Mexican politics often show a remarkable historical continuity in style, despite the vast changes in the postrevolutionary political system. In this respect the present descriptive model of the political system, with its emphasis on the various dimensions of hierarchy and distance, its all pervading personalism, its suppressive tendencies, bears some resemblance to more ancient authority patterns and in particular to those of the Porfirio Díaz administration.

It would be too simplistic to assume a simple persistence of traditional elements. In many cases they have been reformulated and assumed different functions with regard to the exigences of socioeconomic development. It should also be realized that the formula of the one official party structure and the integration of the various social classes within the framework of "national" development through the formation of "intermediary" organizations by the State, has been used in many Third World nations,[41] although of course the Mexican formula has a historically and culturally specific scent to it. The system promotes a consensus, which will express itself less in a consciously militant constituency, than in the consciousness that, given the existing power structure, economic improvements, if ever, can only be obtained through the "intermediary" organizations. The elaborate system of controls to which these organizations have been subjected, in addition to the periodic outbursts of labor unrest, indicate that this consensus may stand for an enforced attitude that is rooted in resignation rather than in an original indifference and political apathy, as several students of the Mexican situations claim (cf. Flores Olea, 1972: 492; González Casanova, 1968: 178).

From a functional point of view, the political system has served well. This may explain the relative stability of the power structure as a whole despite the polarizing tendencies of the economic growth process. It has shown to be an effective instrument for the exercise of control and the neutralization of class conflict, at least in its most open and violent form. It is hard to think of how economic growth could have been realized through inflationary measures,

---

[41] Cf. Zolberg (1967) for the West African case, further Di Tella (1965) for the Latin American experience.

Figure 6: Basic tendencies of the Mexican development process

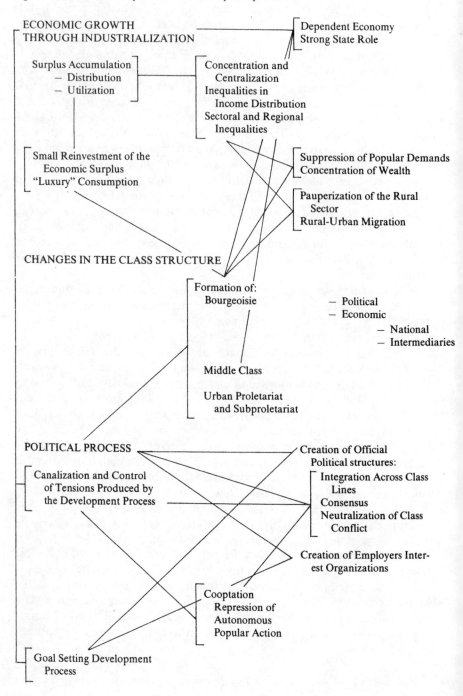

depressing the real wages of substantial sectors of the working population, with sharp inequalities in income distribution and with enormous differences in life chances between the upper and the lower strata, without incorporating labor in structures under absolute political control. More recently, however, the political process and the economic and social processes appear to have been less perfectly coordinated (cf. Flores Olea, 1972: 499). New strata have emerged, others have been profoundly changed. Claims have been generated that only partially can be met within the existing power structure (cf. R. Smith, 1968: 5). A culture of rising expectations has led to an increase in popular discontent and a shift away from populist policies (Cockcroft, 1972: 258). The emergence of small groups within the educated elite, refusing cooptation (cf. Medina and Aguilar, 1971: 35 ff), led to strong suppressive action that has increased the tension between the normative and the descriptive models of political reality and further threatened the legitimacy of the system.[42]

The government desperately has tried to preserve the present pattern of development through ad-hoc reforms in the spheres of taxation, public investment and social welfare without attacking its basic contradictions, a policy which ultimately may threaten the overall rate of economic growth itself.

---

[42] See the happenings around the student worker movement of 1968, the student movement in Monterrey, leading to the urban guerrilla actions of 1971, and the rural guerrilla in Guerrero in 1972-1974.

CHAPTER IV
MONTERREY

1. INTRODUCTION

The industrial city of Monterrey[1] has played a leading role in the Mexican process of economic growth from the beginning of this century on. It has done so largely through a self-generated process of development of the classical industrial-capitalist type. Within the realm of Latin American theories of dependency this does make Monterrey into an important deviant case. These theories[2] locate the basic factors responsible for Latin American underdevelopment at the level of the world economy where the processes of international exploitation and their power consequences limit the autonomous capacity for growth and development of the dependent nations, making them expand only as a reflection of the growth of the dominant economies. Frank (1972: 10 ff) emphasizes, in his early version of dependency theory, the ultimate fultility of a national capitalist development which would leave the general structure of dependency relationships tying the economy to the world capitalist system, untouched. Historically such developments have taken place in regions that were geographically and economically isolated from the metropole and in situations where wars or depressions in the metropole temporarily interrupted the ties with the world economy. After (re)incorporation into the world economic system, their autonomous processes of industrial development were deranged and channelled into a direction which only (re) affirmed external dependency. Frank mentions several examples, among them Sao Paulo (Brazil) and Medellín (Colombia), both dynamic industrial growthpoles with, contrary to his thesis, still a very substantial participation of national capitalists (cf. Hagen, 1962; Singer, 1974). The same applies and even

---

[1] In this study "Monterrey" stands for "Metropolitan Monterrey," which next to the city of Monterrey includes the suburbs of San Nicolás, Santa Catarina, Guadalupe, and Garza García. The analysis on this level is indebted to the studies of Mauro (1964) and De León (1968). Especially the last mentioned book, written by a local leader of the P.C.M., offers unique information on Monterrey labor history and on the idiosyncracies of the local industrial bourgeoisie. Despite some flaws, the book is the first comprehensive study on the subject but was boycotted by the local press, because of the radical commitment of its author. Cf. *Oigamé*, May 16, 1970, containing a letter by De León informing on this subject. *Oigamé* was an independent Monterrey weekly published in the period 1969-1971 and containing all the particulars of the Monterrey small history of the time.
[2] for a critical discussion of these theories, see O'Brien (1973)

more so to the case of Monterrey. The question arises now what factors, next to the one already mentioned by Frank, made these areas into deviant cases within a general context of dependent economic development. We will answer this question for the case of Monterrey, elaborate the basic characteristics of the industrialization process and its correlates in the sociopolitical sphere. At the same time this will specify the context within which the processes dealt with in the study of the industrial workers, will be analyzed.

2. THE ECONOMIC STRUCTURE

2.1. The Process of Industrial Development in Monterrey

The history of industrial development in Monterrey seems to substantiate Frank's thesis on the importance of a relative degree of isolation from world economic influences in the case of self-generated processes of industrial growth. The region was weakly integrated into the colonial system because of a peripheral location and economic insignificance. Gold and silvermining were non-existent; the area was not very attractive for the establishment of a *latifundia* system. This means that two major factors were absent that in other areas of Latin America were instrumental in the development of underdevelopment. In this rather sparsely populated outpost of the colonial empire regionalist sentiments developed already at an early stage.

The independence of Texas and its later annexation by the U.S.A., however, changed the geographical isolation of the area. Monterrey ended up close to the U.S. border and as an almost natural sally port for North Mexican trade through Texas further to the North (Marasciulo, 1952). During the American Civil War this function of the city became well developed, also under influence of the liberal trade policies of a local *cacicque*. The blockage of the Southern ports led to a desviation of trade, in particular involving cotton, through Monterrey where branches of several Southern commercial houses (a.o. Calderon and Company) were founded (De León, 1968: 9). After the Civil War several hundreds of Southern businessmen emigrated to Mexico. Several of them settled in Nuevo León, where they began entrepreneurial activity in mining and commerce.

In 1865 the first textile mill, La Fama, was established in Santa Catarina, a village located shortly West of Monterrey. In 1872 a second mill was founded in El Cercado, Nuevo León,[3] two years later followed by a third one in La Leona, located close to Santa Catarina. This textile industry formed the starting point for further industrial developement and was typically the outcome of commercial capitalism, based on trade and the accumulation of trade profits. Industrial production was still in the hands of merchants and es-

---

[3] The capital for both mills had been provided by the families Rivero and Zambrano (later also involved in the foundation of the Monterrey metallurgical industry).

pecially the textile industry, which was labor intensive and needed a relatively small initial investment, suited their needs (Mauro, 1960: 38).

In the 1880's economic development speeded up under the influence of dynamic governor Bernardo Reyes.[4] Gradually capital accumulated from trade, mining and the incipient industry. The implementation of tariff bariers by the U.S.A. together with the gradual disintegration of the monopoly of trade in Northern Mexico after the construction of the railways, cut this process short and forced a change in the investment patterns. The new industrialists abandoned their trade activities and sought exclusive dedication to industrial production. Commercial capitalism was progressively replaced by industrial capitalism (Mauro, 1960: 39).

In the period from 1891-1900, 101 new companies were founded in the State of Nuevo León. Many of these were small industries, developed as a function of the growth of the city, and produced consumption goods for the regional market. Among these new industrial establishments, however, figured also two companies that introduced big industry to Monterrey and would condition to an important extent the course of the process of economic developement in the area.

In 1891 the brewery Cuauthemoc was founded with capital mainly provided by associates of the previously mentioned commercial house of Calderon and Company. Among them was an entrepreneur of German descent, José Maria Schneider, who together with the Mexicans: Isaac Garza, Francisco Sada and José Muguerza,[5] formed the factory management. Starting in 1899 the company began to expand vertically, founding factories for the production of glass, paper, cardboard, crowncork.[6] Later it diversified its interests towards the metallurgical sector (1942: Hojalata y Lámina S.A.) and the chemical sector (1945: Celulosa y Derivados S.A.).

The group Cuauthemoc presently counts some thirty industrial enterprises divided into two subgroups: *Cervecería* and *Vidriera*. It also comprises a number of banks and credit-finance associations. A complete picture of the group is presented in Table 7.

The other leading enterprise in the process of industrial development in Monterrey has been Fundidora de Fierro y Acero de Monterrey, founded in 1900 by a small group of entrepreneurs which counted some foreign immigrant participation. The administrative board included: Vicente Ferrara (Italian), León Signoret (French), Eugene Kelley (American), Antonio Basagoiti (Spanish). Mexican members were: Isaac Garza (entrepreneur behind the Cuauthemoc group), Ernesto Madero (brother of Francisco I. Madero) and Adolfo Zambrano (representing the textile industry in the State of Nuevo

---

[4] Reyes governed the state from 1885-1909. He expressed strong regionalist sentiments, brought political stability and encouraged strongly new industrial ventures (Saldaña, 1965: 20).
[5] Grandfathers of a dynasty that still pulls the strings in Monterrey.
[6] These last three companies, together with a factory producing metal wares, were grouped in 1929 in FA-MO-SA (Fabricas Monterrey S.A.).

58

TABLE 7:   Composition of the Cuauthemoc Conglomerate*

extractive industry	manufacturing industry	financial sector	commerce and other
Industria del Alcalí	Cerveceria Cuauthemoc	Cia. General de Aceptaciones	Proveedora Del Hogar
Materias Primas de Monterrey	6 establishments	Financiera del Norte	Super-Mercados**
	Malta de Monterrey	Crédito de Monterrey	Servicios Aéreos
	2 establishments	Crédito Provincial Hipotecario	Regiomontanos
	Empaques de Cartón Titán	Banco Capitalizador de Monterrey	
	2 establishments	Banco de Nuevo León	
	Fábrica de Papel	Banco Azteca**	
	Fábricas Monterrey	Almacenadora del Norte	
	Hojalata y Lámina	Almacenes y Silos	
	HYLSA de Puebla	Compañia de Seguros Monterrey	
	Fierro Esponja		
	Aceros de México		
	Aceros Alfa Monterrey		
	Tálleres Universales		
	Técnica Industrial		
	Grafo Regia		
	Vidriera Monterrey		
	Vidrio Plano		
	Keramos		
	Cristalería		
	Vidriera México		
	Cristales Mexicanos		
	Vidrio Plano de México		
	Vidriera de Guadalajara		
	Vidriera Los Reyes		
	Grupo Químico CYDSA		
	7 establishments		
	Fabricación de Maquinas		

* companies mentioned have the status of Sociedad Anónima
** probably minority participation, all others majority participation

Source: De León, 1968: 60-61
Sociedad Cuauthemoc y Famosa, informe 1973.

León). The presence of immigrants in the entrepreneurial sector during the beginning phase of industrialization, a phenomenon well known throughout Latin America (cf. Lipset, 1967), in this case, however, does not indicate a wider presence of foreign interests.

At the time Fundidora was founded already a small metallurgical industry was operating in the city. Three smelters had started operations in the years 1889-1891. Railroads were constructed in order to supply the mineral and the coal from mines, located at less than 250 kilometers from the city. At the time these were considered among the richest in Mexico. During Fundidora's first years, the bad functioning of the railroads caused various production problems. In 1906 the company reorganized and came under the direction of Adolfo Prieto, who would become one of the great Monterrey entrepreneurs. From 1911 on, the revolutionary developments in Mexico made themselves felt in Monterrey with increasing intensity. The railroads were cut repeatedly by the warring factions and eventually the city was involved in the actual struggle itself. Two times Monterrey changed hands between the forces of Pancho Villa and Venustiano Carranza. In 1914 and in 1915 actual fights between the two parties took place on the premises of the company Fundidora itself.

From 1916 on, production slowly recuperated and it continued to rise gradually, with as only interruptions the years of 1924 (labor problems) and 1932 (world crisis). World War II and the necessity to substitute imports caused considerable industrial expansion all over Mexico and the metallurgical sector formed no exception. The upward trend was continued after the war with slight fluctuations in 1946, 1952 and 1957, reflecting company insecurity at the time of the election of the new president. This is a phenomenon which can be observed on a general scale in those industries that are dependent on federal contracts (Mauro, 1960: 62) and that, as we will see later on in the case of Fundidora has led to a heavier involvement with official politics (cultiminating in a government interest of 42 percent in the steelplant later on in the 1970's).

From 1927 on, the company has founded affiliates and it has diversified its interests by investing in other sectors. As in the case of the Cuauthemoc group, a strong vertical as well as horizontal expansion of its industrial activities can be observed together with a strong integration of the industrial with the financial and credit sector. The Fundidora conglomerate is slightly smaller in size (as measured by number of companies and total investment) than the Cuauthemoc group.

The banks were originally owned by business interests. They, however, passed soon into the hands of industry. Next to these banks the entrepreneurs organized *Compañias Financieras*, finance and credit organizations that are active throughout Mexico in attracting capital from private investors (Mauro, 1960: 64). These have played an ever increasing role in providing the capital for continued economic growth. Unlike the case of traditional capitalist development, in Monterrey the financial institutions were organized and owned by industry instead of the other way around.

Besides the two conglomerates, that have set the pace of industrial development in Monterrey, a great number of other industrial enterprises have been established and among them some new conglomerates have emerged. This latter development, however, is of a more recent date and its economic and political significance is a more modest one. In this context the Santos group can be mentioned with interests in the foodstuffs industry, the real estate business and the bank and credit sector together with the Ramirez group which comprises the greater part of the automobile industry and also

60

TABLE 8:   Composition of the Fundidora Conclomerate*

extractive industry	manufacturing industry	financial sector	commerce and other
Cerro de Mercado	Fábrica de	Banco Popu-	Internacion-
Minera el Mamey	Ladrillos In-	lar de Edif.	al de
Minera del Norte	dustriales y	y Ahorros	Aceros
Hullera Mexicana	Refracterios	Central Fi-	Gas Indus-
Carbón y Cok	Harbison Walk-	nanciera	trial de
Cia. Minera	er Flir	Banco Gener-	Monterrey**
Norex	Harbison Walk-	al de Mon-	Constructora
Fluorita de	er Flir de	terrey	y Fraccion-
México	México	Financiera	adora
Fluorita de	Ferroaleaciones	General de	Constructora
Coahuila	México	Monterrey**	Popular
Cia. Minera	National Scrap		Inversiones
Central	Recovery		Urbanas
Magcobar de	Sistemas y Ser-		Monterrey
México	vicios Técnicos		Edificacio-
	Suministros		nes Monter-
	Carros de Ferro-		rey
	carril de Duran-		Fomento Fab-
	go		ril
	Cia. Metalúrgica		Sociedad
	Mexico		General de
	Tubería Nacional		Inmuebles
	Fabricaciones de		
	Alambre		
	Estructuras de		
	Acero		
	Hierro y Acero de		
	México		
	Perfiles y Estruc-		
	turas de Durango		
	Tubacero**		
	Ce-rrey**		
	Cementos del Norte**		
	Productos Alimen-		
	ticios**		
	Motores Diesel de		
	Durango**		

* all companies mentioned have the status of *Sociedad Anónima*
** minority participation, all others majority participation

Source: Compañia Fundidora de Fierro y Acero de Monterrey S.A., Informe Anual 1969.

has interests in financial institutions.[7] In these cases again a close association between industrial and financial interests can be observed.

The Cuauthemoc and Fundidora groups and the new smaller conglomerates maintain connections through shared interests in the bank and credit sector and the interchange of management personnel. This latter phenomenon

[7] Both the Santos and Ramirez families are mentioned in the list compiled by Aguilar (1970a).

61

seems to occur on a much wider scale in the Monterrey industrial sector. De León mentions several cases in which members of Monterrey entrepreneurial familes combine their position in either one of the leading companies with a membership on the administrative boards of a number of other industries and financial institutions (De León, 1968: 66 ff). The extent to which this phenomenon reflects interlocking financial and business interests is not revealed. It can be safely assumed, however, that in Monterrey, where business often has remained a family affair, these connections will have a significance that goes beyond a mere exchange of personnel.

2.2. The Process of Economic Growth in Wider Perspective

Although the process of urban growth in the Monterrey area had already advanced before (the area counted already a population over 50,000 in the 1880's), it received its strongest impulses through the industrial expansion since the turn of the century. Especially after 1940 the growth of the city has been rather spectacular. The migration factor explains close to half of the growth during the last three decades. The other half is the result of natural growth and of the expansion of the Monterrey agglomeration, which brought

TABLE 9:   The growth of the population in the Monterrey agglomeration 1900-1970

year	population	difference	percentage growth
1900	62,000	–	–
1910	79,000	16,000	26
1921	88,000	10,000	13
1930	134,000	44,000	50
1940	186,000	54,000	40
1950	356,000	170,000	91
1960	680,000	324.000	91
1970	1,200,000	520,000	76

Source: 1900-1970 Dirección General de Estadística
Censo General de Población, Estado de Nuevo León; Balán, 1967: 46

new populations within its limits (Balán, 1968: 45). The migrant population of Nuevo León counted 424,032 on a total population of 1,694,689 in 1970 (Censo 1970). The Monterrey area houses over 70 percent of the state population. Most of the economic activity of the region is concentrated here. This explains why the migration movement has almost exclusively been directed towards Monterrey and surroundings. The majority of the migrants come from the neighbouring states of Coahuila and San Luís Potosí.[8]

The tremendous growth in population has been accompanied by considerable changes in the economic structure of the region. The primary sector

[8] The census does not state the in-state migration towards the Monterrey agglomeration.

TABLE 10: The distribution of employment of the total economically active population over the three sectors of economic activity, Nuevo León, 1930-1970

sector	1930*	1950	1970
primary	60	42	18
secondary	12	22	37**
tertiary	28	36	45
	100.0	100.0	100.0

* excluding domestic labor
** includes construction and energy, excludes extractive industry
Source: Mauro, 1964: 66
         Censo 1970

(agriculture and mining) had already lost its importance at the end of the last century, but maintained some relevance in other parts of Nuevo León. The tertiary sector, representing the various services such as trade, banks, transport and communication, etc., has continued to expand although at a lesser rate than the secondary sector (industrial production). Within the Mexican context, Nuevo León had already in 1930 a rather advanced economy. Since then, the increase in importance of the secondary sector at the cost of the primary sector has been rather spectacular. The general pattern is typical of the take-off phase of the industrial revolution.

These shifts in relative importance of the three economic sectors with regard to employment, have not substantially altered the percentage of the total population which is gainfully employed. The absolute number of positions has risen from 83,469 in 1900 to 491,829 in 1970 (Mauro, 1964: 41 and Censo 1970), but the proportion of the total population employed has remained pretty stable. It decreased from 25.4 percent (1900) to 22.1 percent (1910), when during the beginning stage of industrialization some employment in the artisan sector was destroyed, but stabilized on 31.7 percent (1921), 30.3 percent (1940), climbed to 32.3 percent (1950) and 33.6 percent (1960), but fell again to 29.0 percent in 1970.[9] The official rate of unemployment does not appear to be exceptionally high (Censo 1970: 3.8 percent).[10]

During the period of industrial expansion from 1930 to 1970, the population directly employed by the manufacturing industry increased from 14,557 to 145,705 (Censo 1970). In recent decades the growth in industrial production has been substantial, culminating in an average annual rate of close to 11

[9] Mauro, 1964: 87; the C.I.E. projects a percentage of 35.1 for 1980 (Hacia una Planeación, 1970: 60). The numbers of the gainfully employed for 1900, 1910, 1921 and 1940 should be considered estimates due to deficient statistics. In the last few decades the younger age brackets and consequently also the size of the school-age population have increased with obvious effects on the size of the economically active population.
[10] Actually of course the phenomena of unemployment and also subemployment affect a much greater part of the population. Dominguez (1974) estimates that more than 40 percent of the total Mexican labor force is affected by these phenomena. In Monterrey this percentage will be less, but certainly will exceed the official unemployment rate.

63

TABLE 11: Value added by manufacturing, employment and productivity per worker employed by the Nuevo León manufacturing industry, 1955-1965

industry	value added (in mill pesos of 1955)		employment				productivity (in pesos of 1955)	
	1955	1965	1955	%	1965	%	1955	1965
food	137.7	338.9	8,683	12.7	14,070	12.0	15,858.6	23,269.4
drinks	55.3	144.6	2,871	4.2	3,683	3.2	19,261.6	43,958.7
tobacco	33.7	388.5	1,573	2.3	2,101	1.8	21,424.0	184,911.9
textiles	71.5	88.8	5,743	8.4	3,498	3.0	12,449.9	25,385.9
shoes and apparel	43.2	127.9	6,427	9.4	9,336	7.8	6,721.6	13,699.7
wood and cork	6.7	13.9	1,025	1.5	1,547	1.3	6,536.6	8,985.1
furniture	16.2	17.9	2,325	3.4	1,460	1.3	6,967.7	12,123.3
paper	40.5	140.4	2,325	3.4	3,631	3.1	17,419.4	38,556.9
printing	10.8	59.2	1,367	2.0	2,900	2.5	7,900.5	18,207.0
leather	9.5	21.5	1,026	0.5	721	0.6	9,259.3	29,819.7
rubber	1.4	12.9	137	0.2	708	0.6	10,219.0	18,220.3
chemicals	55.3	550.9	2,803	4.1	7,972	6.8	19,728.9	66,959.4
stone, clay, glass	159.3	485.9	10,461	15.3	18,674	16.0	15,228.0	22,603.6
basic metallurgy	527.8	850.1	6,837	10.0	11,769	10.1	77,197.6	72,232.1
fabricated metals	85.0	301.4	6,837	10.0	12,636	10.8	12,432.4	29,004.4
machinery	36.4	129.9	2,871	4.2	5,907	5.0	12,678.5	21,990.9
electrical	36.4	391.6	2,530	3.7	8,690	7.4	14,387.4	42,600.7
automobiles and other transport equipment	18.9	167.1	1,846	2.7	6,820	5.8	10,238.4	24,501.5
miscellaneous manufacturing	4.1	13.8	684	1.0	993	0.9	5,994.2	13,897.3
totals	1,349.7	4,244.3	68,371	100.0	117,116	100.0	----	----

Source: Hacia una Planeación, 1970: 79, 80, 82

64

percent in the 1960's. Part of this growth, however, was the result of the establishment of capital-intensive industries and did not automatically translate into a proportional increase in the use of the production factor "labor" (cf. Table 11). The employment effects have been more important in other areas of the economy stimulated by the industrialization process, while in addition the low-productivity sector has greatly expanded (Puente Leyva, 1969: 57).

The number of industrial enterprises in Nuevo Leon increased from 4 in 1891 to 101 in 1900, to 1,310 in 1940 and 5,839 in 1970. The average annual increase between 1900 and 1940 was 30, since 1940 151 industrial establishments.[11] Among these enterprises 92.0 percent are located in the Monterrey area. They employ 93.9 percent of the total industrial labor force in the state and represent 97.2 percent of the total industrial investment in Nuevo León (1970).[12]

Small enterprises still predominate in numbers. Among the total number of 5,372 enterprises in Monterrey, 71.2 percent (3,825) had a declared capital investment of 30.000 pesos or less. They represent small repair shops and artisan workshops, employ a few workers (5 or less) and have little in common with the large-scale industrial enterprises that have set the pace of industrial development in the region. A 22.7 percent (1,220) represented enterprises with a capital investment between 30,001 and 1,000,000 pesos; 5.8 percent (312) had a capital investment between 1,000,001 and 50,000,000 pesos. Only 0.3 percent declared investments superior to 50,000,001 pesos (Directorio Industrial: 1970). This latter category counted 15 enterprises, 10 of which form part of the Cuauthemoc and Fundidora conglomerates. Investment has been concentrated in few industries. In 1965, 14 percent (675) of the total number of enterprises in that year (4,820) accounted for 98.7 percent of the total capital invested in the industrial sector in Nuevo León. Among these 675 enterprises, 8 companies alone represented 22.7 percent of these total investments made (Censo Industrial 1965; De León, 1968: 81). This trend toward a concentration of capital has been very persistent and may be even more pronounced than the industrial census and the COFIDE statistics do convey. The fiscal legislation in Nuevo León, which allows a tax break for new enterprises, has led in several instances to the legal division and subdivision of existing companies which in fact continued to function as one unit. A similar trend of concentration has emerged in the financial sector as a close correlate obviously of the developments in the industrial sector.

Among the banks and the credit associations that have Monterrey origins, the scene has been dominated by two banks (Banco Mercantil de Monterrey and Banco Regional del Norte) and two credit institutions (Financiera del Norte and Compañíá General de Aceptaciones). The latter two form part of

---

[11] De León, 1968: 43 and Directorio Industrial, 1970: xxi. These data of course only approximate the average yearly number of new industrial establishments as we lack data on the number of enterprises that disappeared each year. The Directorio Industrial mentions 116 such enterprises in the period 1967-1968. They virtually all concern small industrial establishments.

[12] *Boletín COFIDE*, 4, no. 25, July 30, 1970.

the Cuauthemoc group and concentrated 50 percent and over 75 percent respectively of the total assets of all these institutions in the state of Nuevo Léon in 1967 (De León, 1968: 48, 53).

The tendency towards concentration in commerce has been equally manifest, although less than in industry. Next to the commercial branches of the big conglomerates and the presence of the great houses as Casa Chapa, Salinas y Roche, Casa Holck and the appearance of Sears Roebuck, Woolworth and others, the sector counts thousands of small marginal establishments with investments not exceeding a few thousand pesos. The intermediate level of commerce located between the great enterprises and these small shops, has been badly developed. This phenomenon may find an explanation in the Monterrey income distribution and the weak position of the middle strata, with the substantial contraband across the Texas border as a reinforcing factor.[13]

The process of economic growth in the Monterrey area during the last few decades seems not to have lost its largely autonomous character. Although the foreign influence is hard to quantify precisely and in all its aspects, the general impression confirms to the thesis, arduously defended by the local bourgeoisie and also by government representatives,[14] that the economy of the area is eminently "Mexican" and that its expansion rests in the continuing reinvestment of profits by a dynamic group of Mexican entrepreneurs.

The dependence on foreign produced and patented technology in Monterrey conforms to general Third World patterns. The economy still lacks in capacity to produce its own capital goods. Technical research is still underdeveloped, although some advances are made. The big conglomerates have begun to organize their own research units. As a first result Hojalata y Lámina SA (Cuauthemoc group) developed in the 1960's a new process in steel production, which was patented, applied in its new Monterrey plant and later even exported to Austria and Germany. In many other instances, however, virtually the entire infrastructure of newly established plants has to be imported. The extent to which this represents "genuine" technology, freely bought on the world market, or "special" technology only to be acquired under special arrangements with the company holding the patents, differs from case to case. The transfer of this "special" technology may lead to direct foreign participation in local companies, but the general information on this phenomenon is rather fragmentary.

The Fundidora and Cuauthemoc conglomerates have some foreign participation,[15] but it has remained rather small. Further participation in the leading Monterrey companies is minor. Some foreign companies, like Anderson & Clayton, Kraft, General Electric, Union Carbide, Caterpillar,

---

[13] Cf. "El Contrabando, Gran Freno al Desarrollo del Comercio," in *El Porvenir*, April 13, 1971.
[14] Cf. the speech of the Secretary of Industry and Commerce, as cited by *El Porvenir*, August 20, 1967.
[15] Through their affiliates Harbison Walker Flir S.A., Ce-rrey S.A. and Hojalata y Lámina S.A., Vidriera S.A. and CYDSA, respectively.

John Deere, etc., have established branches, in a few cases with members of the local bourgeoisie acting as intermediaries. The majority of industries in the Monterrey area, however, appears to be genuinely domestic and the role of foreign capital, under whatever kind of arrangement, seems relatively minor. De Rossi in a study of 42 leading Monterrey industries, found 91 percent owned by Mexicans, 7 percent represented joint ventures and only 2 percent was entirely foreign owned. Most of these industries, 88 percent, has been founded with domestic capital without any outside help.[16]

On the subject of credit provision by foreign interests, few quantitative data are available. The Cuauthemoc group maintains links with U.S. banking interests (Morgan Guarantee Trust and Chase Manhattan), through its local and national banks. The same applies to four other local banks and one credit association (De León, 1968: 92 ff). De Rossi also mentions the phenomenon of direct loans by U.S. institutions sometimes even without government mediation to Fundidora and to Compañía General de Aceptaciones, a financial institution of the Cuauthemoc group (De Rossi, 1971: 54). The specifics of these external relationships and the degree to which they supplement the activities of the Monterrey financial interests on the basis of nationally generated capital however cannot be ascertained.

TABLE 12: Degree of concentration of family income in metropolitan Monterrey, 1965

population*	income*		
	before taxes	after taxes	corrected for welfare services**
5	0.80	0.87	1.18
10	2.28	2.54	3.05
15	3.96	4.14	4.93
20	5.75	6.09	6.91
30	9.66	9.72	10.81
40	13.98	14.81	15.97
50	19.00	20.61	21.89
60	25.50	26.77	29.26
70	33.12	34.62	37.38
80	44.16	45.34	47.59
85	50.80	51.32	54.79
90	57.52	61.76	62.90
95	68.77	74.07	75.31
100	100.00	100.00	100.00

* accumulated percentages
** educational services, school breakfasts, kindergartens, medicare and other services in the field of social assistance.
Source: Puente Leyva, 1969: 14, 17.

[16] De Rossi's sample of companies in Mexico City and the Federal District indicates 74 percent as founded entirely by Mexican capital, De Rossi, 1971: 56.

2.3. The Distribution of Income[17]

The high degree of concentration in ownership and control of the means of production finds its correlate in a highly skewed distribution of family incomes. The upper 5 percent of the population account for 32.33 percent of the total family income (before taxes), the lower 5 percent for .80 percent. Tijerina Garza (1965: 74) shows that, in 1960, 68 percent of the Monterrey population belonged to families receiving an income below the level of minimum welfare,[18] taking into account the typical size of the Monterrey family, and the age and occupational structure of the population. By 1965 the situation had not improved very much. Still 67 percent of the total population found themselves in this condition of poverty (Puente Leyva, 1969: 21). The socioeconomic and political structure of Monterrey has shown considerable resistance against changes in this pattern of distribution of the economic surplus. The migration toward the city obviously has fed the low income strata and has helped to maintain their sizable importance within the population as a whole.[19] The stratum of the very poorest expanded from 1.4 percent in 1960 to 7.6 percent in 1965. The reduction in size of the lower middle strata on the income scale, their relative downward mobility (income wise) and apparent absorption by the upper lower strata has been a less self-evident phenomenon. These last mentioned strata expanded in size also through an upward movement of the "middle poor". The latter diminished in size from 21.6 percent in 1960 to 15.0 percent in 1965.[20] Puenta Leyva's analysis of the distribution of family income during the first half of the 1960's suggests the presence of a strong trend towards an expansion of the low income strata due to the influx of poor rural migrants, unskilled and willing to accept any job that guarantees subsistence, and to the impoverishment of important segments of the middle sector.

The distribution of family income has turned more unequal during the period of rapid industrial growth, showing the apparent paradox of a booming economy next to a relative impoverishment of the entire low family income brackets subsuming more than half of the population.

The main redistributive mechanisms operating in Monterrey do not

---

[17] This paragraph is indebted to the excellent study of Puente Leyva (1969)

[18] This level was normatively established on the basis of an absolute minimum intake of calories translated into expenses for food, in addition to minimum expenses for housing, clothing, education, medicare and "miscellaneous".

[19] The migration toward Monterrey involves to an important extent the selection of people who are badly prepared for any position that does not locate them at the very bottom of the occupational scale, see Balán, 1967: 181 ff.

[20] Tijerina Garza, 1965: 70, 74 and a C.I.E. investigation in 1965, cited by Puente Leyva, 1969: 21. Both investigations used a family income scale, divided in three lower strata, two middle strata and one upper stratum. The 1965 investigation shows the "poor middle class" more than halved from 33.2 percent in 1960 to 15.9 percent in 1965 and a corresponding increase of the "poor in transition" from 11.4 percent in 1960 to 28.6 percent in 1965.

counter this trend. At least they function in a way which does not consistently favor the lower income strata.

The educational services, in terms of their total costs, benefit these strata less than proportional. While they represent more than 51 percent of the population, they do not benefit for more than 7 percent (in percentage of the total student body) from the educational services superior to secondary school and for around 37 percent from secondary education. Only in the case of primary education the situation is the reverse: 61.4 percent of the student body originates from these lower strata.[21]

The services of the social welfare sector which are defined to meet the needs of the lower income strata comprise those in the medical field and the so-called *servicios de asistencia*, including school breakfasts and kindergartens. The government provides a breakfast in the primary schools of the most humble *colonías*. The kindergartens mostly benefit the working mothers of low income families. The medical services, organized through the I.M.S.S. are most intensively used by the upper and middle strata of the lower class, as the type of occupation which the very poorest frequently have does not qualify them for incorporation in the social security system (Puenta Leyva, 1969: 29).

In terms of the percentage of total cost for education, medicare and social services, the poor half of the population receives 32.5, 62.6 and 64.9 percent respectively. Especially the lack of adequate access to continued education of a professional nature, blocks the upward social mobility of the poor.[22] Their education generally remains limited to primary school which only gives access to low paying manual jobs. In the middle and upper strata, education is intensively used to maintain social status (as measured by level of occupation). Education as Balán found, is also in Monterrey closely correlated with occupation (Balán, 1967: 189 ff) and already only for that reason should be characterized as an instrument of social mobility. However, the highly unequal distribution of educational opportunities will tend to reduce the proportion of the upwardly mobile who actually have used education as such an instrument (Soares, 1965: 529 ff). The fact that the access to higher professional and university training has remained limited to a rather small segment of society comprising the higher middle strata and up, that is to say to those who already inherited a privileged social position, underlines the role of education as a means to remain in those positions, to improve if possible and to avoid downward mobility at all cost (cf. Balán, 1965: 324-337).

---

[21] The fact that the upper middle and upper strata generally send their children to private schools may have contributed to this phenomenon.
[22] It is common knowledge that in Mexico secondary education does not prepare its students for any specific job and handicaps them severely by sending them out on the job market with expectations of salary and prestige that cannot possibly be realized.

3.1. Introduction

In this paragaph the various classes will be defined that figure on the Monterrey socioeconomic and political scene. In this description, the proletariat and its interaction with the other classes, subclasses or class segments within the overall class structure is our primary concern. The analysis of the political process will reveal the essentials of this interaction between the classes and indicate the degree of correlation between economic and political power. Within this context also some attention will be given to the way the Monterrey economic interests have sought political expression on the national level.

The occupational stratification of the economically active population in Monterrey gives us some indication as to the composition of the class structure and it furnishes an order of magnitude as to each of the classes and subclasses.

TABLE 13: The composition of the class structure in Metropolitan Monterrey (1965)*

classes		sectors	
subproletariat	18.5		
		commerce	4.6
		services	13.9
urban proletariat	44.3		
		commerce	7.6
		transport	6.3
		extractive and manufactur-	
		ing industry	17.0
		construction	6.3
		artisans	7.1
rural proletariat	0.6		
		agriculture	0.6
middle sector	24.4		
		employees (industry-	
		services-commerce)	15.6
		professions (industry-	
		services-commerce)	8.8
bourgeoisie	6.2		
		industry	3.4
		commerce	2.4
		agriculture	0.4
other	6.0**		
		other	6.0
	100.0		100.0

* in percentages of the total economically active population
** occupation not identified, not declared or not classifiable. The greater part of this category most probably should be added to the marginal subproletarian occupations.

Source: defined on the basis of the occupational stratification offered by De León, 1968: 115, 279 and Ocupación y Salarios, 1965: 15.

The size of the proletarian and subproletarian segments is striking. Together they subsume 62.8 percent of the economically active population. The category of "artisans" is largely a "disguised" worker category, having a seemingly independent status. In reality, however, they are often tied to bigger companies. The segments of the bourgeoisie mentioned in the table also include the owners and/or managers of the small industrial and commercial enterprises.

3.2. The Monterrey Class Structure

3.2.1. The bourgeoisie

In Monterrey, as we have seen, the process of industrialization has been dominated by a small number of entrepreneurial families whose interests have become heavily interwined. De León Garza estimates this number of families at around fifty (De León, 1968: 67).[23] Aguilar mentions two Monterrey entrepreneurs (Garza Sada, Garza) in his list of the twenty-five magnates of Mexico. Two more (Jaime Garza, Prieto) figure under the hundred most important Mexican families (Aguilar, 1970a: 67-70). The next group which comprises a number of 300 families and represents the economically dominant groups on the state level, counts nine Monterrey families (Benavides, Clariond, Garza Sepúlveda, Aurelio González, Llaguno, Lobo, C. and J. Maldonado, Gregorio Ramírez, Santos). The various other branches of the Garza-Garza Sada-Sada clan (group Cuauthemoc) should be added to this number, although the families in this case are heavily intertwined and could be considered one group.

An important part of this Monterrey bourgeoisie consists of "traditional" families, that is to say, families that have been active in Monterrey economic life since the end of the last century. This applies in particular to the families associated with the Cuauthemoc and Fundidora concerns. Others have amassed their fortune in more recent times, notably since the expansion of the import-substituting industry during the Second World War. Among them quite a few have done so as managers for the "traditional" families.

In the course of the process of economic development the entrepreneurial families have greatly diversified their interests, expanding their corporations vertically and horizontally towards the extractive industry (mining), manufacturing, banking, trade (the commercialization of their products) and the construction and urban development sectors. Among the leading Monterrey entrepreneurs these interests are often interrelated and further concentrated by kinship and intermarriage (De León, 1968: 65-73). The entrepreneurial sector has become a rather close knit group with community characteristics and signs of strong group solidarity. This is not to say that at times internal

[23] "Family" here means "extended family."

71

divisions and competition do not exist.[24] They have been known, however, to make common front whenever they felt their interests threatened.[25] As *Regiomontanos* they claim to be markedly different from other Mexicans. They confess a strong regional pride, which centers around values like industriousness and dynamic entrepreneurship in addition to a certain feeling of independence towards the central government in Mexico City.[26] This feeling of independence, backed up by a high degree of financial autonomy and the existing group solidarity, has not led the entrepreneurs to neglect the relationship with the government. It has given them, however, special bargaining power in their dealings with government officials (cf. De Rossi, 1971: 54).[27] At the same time, they have not restricted their investment activity to the home region. In recent years the Monterrey entrepreneurs have expanded their operations to other parts of the republic and they have even acquired interests abroad.[28] The size of the *Regiomontano* bourgeoisie is increasing slowly, not only by the sheer expansion of the number of enterprises, but also by a growing tendency among the shareholders of the big companies to leave management responsibilities to professional executives. These executives subsequently may even be integrated in the entrepreneurial group through the acquisition of company shares from the shareholding family (cf. De Rossi, 1971: 57)

Despite its proximity to the U.S.A. the cultural dependence with regard to this country is not overwhelming. Frequent contact are maintained through education in the United States and business trips, but the actual impact appears to remain limited to the technical and administrative sphere and in

[24] The animosity between the Fundidora and Cuathemoc groups, however, has never assumed major proportions. They have continued to exchange managers who take positions on the administrative boards of each other's companies. An example is the Fundidora top man, Manuel Barragán, who participates on the board of Cia. General de Aceptaciones, the most important financial institution of the Cuathemoc group.

[25] See: the happenings during the Cárdenas regime in the 1930's, the conflicts with the government in the mid-1940's, in the beginning of the 1960's, and during the first half of the 1970's. These issues will be discussed later on.

[26] Their lifestyle appears to be different from entrepreneurs in other parts of the republic. They have preferred to reinvest their profits instead of transferring them to European bank accounts. In addition, their luxurious consumption has remained limited. "You won't find here the black Cadillacs with chauffeur and the palace-like mansions," as a representative of one employer's organization told me in April, 1971. The almost puritan ethic of the sternly Catholic segment of the bourgeoisie (cf. also section 3.4.3.) reminds of Max Weber's analyses of the role of religious ideas during the rise of capitalism.

[27] The weak position of the public sector in the Monterrey economy has contributed to the power of the entrepreneurs. Public intervention has remained limited to the economic infrastructure (railways, electricity, water drainage, etc.) and the government has been rather reluctant to invest in other sectors, with the exception of the 42 percent interest in the Fundidora steel plant acquired in the 1970's.

[28] The Cuathemoc group has established subsidiaries (beer, malt, carton, glass) in Mexico D.F. Nogales, Guadalajara, Culiacán and Tecate. In addition, HYLSA has founded a metallurgical industry in Puebla. CYDSA has established plants in Guadalajara and in Coatzacoalcos (Veracruz). Vidriera S.A. has a plant in Guatemala; the Cuathemoc brewery has one in Honduras.

general to the style of management.[29] In this aspect the Monterrey bourgeoisie would certainly deviate from the rest of the area population where the U.S. cultural influence is rather widespread (cf. (Solís Garza, 1971: 86). In general one could say that in Monterrey probably most advances have been made towards the creation of a national bourgeoisie.

3.2.2. *The middle class*

The expansion of the middle class, as we have seen, is to a great extent a function of the macroprocesses of urbanization and industrialization, together with the growth of the public administrative apparatus. This process has presented itself in Monterrey on a more limited scale than in the capital primarily because of the relatively modest presence of the public sector in Nuevo León. In fact, middle class professions count less than one fourth of the economically active population (1965). The class structure is rather polarized, the middle class being squeezed in between the small bourgeoisie and a numerous proletariat. Its internal structure and dynamics and its position in the general combination of social and political forces, are here more important, however, than its present relative size.

Heterogeneity in composition is one of the middle class' most outstanding features. Medium-level executive personnel, professional administrative personnel and medium-level technical personnel here are each other's company. The upper and lower class boundaries are often difficult to define and especially the one with the proletariat cannot be sharply drawn. This phenomenon has its correlate in a lack of homogeneity in interests, the extremes being formed by the lower level employees whose real family income has shown a tendency to decrease and who live in constant danger of proletarization and the higher level professionals aspiring to the membership of the bourgeoisie.[30]

In the manufacturing industry, 21.1 percent of the population employed shares middle class occupations; the executive professions count 4.8 percent and the working class occupations 74.1 percent.[31] A relatively greater amount of individuals with middle class occupations are employed in sectors other than the manufacturing industry, notably in the tertiary sector. We lack data on the expansion of middle class jobs in industry in earlier time periods which makes a comparison difficult with the growth of manual labor. In the Western industrial nations, the development of advanced technology and automation

---

[29] This is a general observation that is somewhat difficult to specify and to substantiate further. It goes back to a rather pervasive impression I got from personal interviews. My impressions find some support in De Rossi, 1971: 55.

[30] The entrepreneurial sector has made an effort to secure the supply of professionals, stimulating the foundation of the Instituto Tecnológico de Monterrey, Mexico's M.I.T., and supplying financial aid on a regular basis to the Universidad de Nuevo León.

[31] Hacia una Planeación, 1970: 87. The percentage of executive professions is rather elevated because of the considerable number of rather small enterprises (cf. also table 14).

has led to a growing proportion of workers in white collar positions where they presently outnumber the manual workers (cf. Van Doorn, 1963; Miller and Form, 1964: 60 ff). The present scarcity of highly skilled workers has prevented repetition of this trend in Monterrey yet. Again, only 21.1 percent of the total population employed in industries has white collar jobs. The prevailing low levels of education, together with the lack of adequate educational facilities and the absence of financial incentives in the generally depressed wage situation, still stand in the way of a rapid expansion of the category of highly qualified technical workers who in Western industry form such an important segment of the industrial white collar population (Haciá una Planeación, 1970; Garcia, 1971).

3.2.3. The proletariat

Using the earlier presented stratification of occupations as a very general indicator, the proletariat can be estimated to include around 44 percent of the economically active population (1965). It consist of segments employed in different economic sectors and, next to the artisans, comprises dependent workers in commerce, in the extractive and the manufacturing industries, in transport and in the construction industry. These segments number 16.0, 17.1, 38.5, 14.2 and 14.2 percent respectively, of what can be called the urban proletariat (cf. Table 13). The agricultural proletariat is very weakly represented in the Monterrey area.

The segment of the proletariat employed by the manufacturing industry has increased strongly in size over the last few decades (cf. section 2.2.). It presently counts almost 108,000 workers in the state of Nuevo León (1970).[32] This expansion has taken place next to the growing concentration of industrial production in big enterprises, the working environment which, according to Marx, would play such a vital role in the development of class consciousness. Yet it appears that a considerable proportion of the industrial proletariat still is being employed by small and medium-sized enterprises. Balán's study (Balán, 1967)[33] indicated 11 percent of the industrial working population as self-employed without the help of personnel (this will include most of the artisans);[34] 19 percent was employed in enterprises counting from 2 to 5 men personnel, 14 percent counted 6 to 20, and 23 percent 21 to 200 men personnel. About a third (33 percent) was employed in enterprises counting 201 men

---

[32] On the basis of the percentage proportioned by the C.I.E. (Hacia una Planeación 1970) of 74.1 percent for working class occupations on the total number of occupations in the industrial sector, we arrive at a number of 107, 967 (74.1 percent of 145,705) persons, using the 1970 Census data.
[33] The percentages form an approximation of real size, because nonproletarian strata were also included in Balán's study, although in minor numbers.
[34] The proportion of people working independently is greater in the higher age brackets, e.g. over 41. The probability to work on one's own increases with age.

74

personnel or more.[35] Yet the number of industrial workers employed by large firms is not very impressive. Using Balán's percentage as an estimate, the size of this category of workers can be put at 35,629 men (33 percent of 107,967) using the 1970 census data. This number should be considered a minimum estimate, given the limitations of Balán's study.[36] The total economically active population in the state counted 491,829 (Censo 1970). It follows that in fact only 7.4 percent of this population represented workers, employed by industrial enterprises counting over 200 men personnel.

The total population employed by the manufacturing industry in Monterrey still contains a high proportion of unskilled labor. They counted 37.4 percent as against 33.7 percent for skilled labor and 2.7 percent for apprentices in 1969 (Hacía una Planeación, 1970: 18). Within the industrial proletariat in a more narrow sense, these categories represent 50.4, 49.2 and 0.5 percent respectively.[37] The entire skill distribution of the Monterrey industrial sector is presented in table 14. When entering the labormarket the workers generally lack any kind of formal qualifications. Most industries, except for the artisan shops and other simple-technology settings, have instituted training programs in order to satisfy the demand for skilled labor in those sections which require an elevated level of technification (Hacía una Planeación, 1970: 23).

The tremendous growth in the supply of labor has tended to depress the general wage level of the worker population, affecting in particular the wages of those without special skills. The income differentials between the various segments of the working class have increased, but not in a spectacular way. The differential between the skilled and the unskilled,[38] which seems sizable, is less due to an absolute high wage level for the skilled than to an absolute low wage level for the unskilled. The legally established minimum wages for the region (1000 pesos a month in 1971) is hard to enforce. Some companies, moreover, employ new workers as *eventuales,* which means they cannot unionize and can be fired on short notice, making it even easier to employ labor against inferior wages. However, even the legally established minimum wages will not save a family from pauperization. The "level of minimum

---

[35] The percentage of workers employed by big enterprises may in fact be greater, given the practice of big companies to subdivide into smaller units, each getting independent legal status. These units subsequently can apply for a tax break as "new" industries. Some additional advantages for the entrepreneurs are involved. The new labor code obliges those companies employing more than 100 workers to provide housing for these workers. Bigger companies may duck this rule through subdivision. They further have the opportunity to break the unity of organized labor in their companies, forcing the union to organize separately for each of the subdivisions. Divide and rule!

[36] See note 33; further, the data refer to the state industrial population, although it should be added that the few industries that have been established outside the Monterrey area, are mostly small sized.

[37] Note: 37.4 percent of the industrial labor force, 145,705 in 1970, equals 50.4 percent of the industrial proletariat, 107,967 in 1970, a.s.o.

[38] Puente Leyva (1969: 56) mentions a differential of 57 percent: compare Goodman (1972) who mentions a differential of 24 percent for Buenos Aires (1966), cf. also Chaplin (1969: 178) and Petras (1970: 16).

75

welfare", established by the earlier cited C.I.E. investigation (par. 2.3.) is located far above the minimum wage level. Following this standard, 67 percent of the Monterrey families should be considered as living below the poverty line (1965) The relative increases in income in the first half of the 1960's were concentrated among the categories of directors and top executives (50 percent), professionals (28 percent), skilled workers (8 percent and artisans and operators (1.5 percent). All other categories appear to have experienced relative decreases in income (Ocupación y Salarios, 1965: 41). Among them, the medium-level technical personnel, the so-called *técnicos medios*, and the highly specialized categories of skilled workers receive salaries which, although not "high" in any absolute sense, are located on a level considerably above the minimum wages. In this respect they form a "worker aristocracy," often used by the management as intermediaries in its dealings with the other workers. These *obreros de confianza,* or "trusted workers," enjoy a privileged position. They are not allowed to unionize and mostly fulfill the functions of foremen, supervisor, etc. Through *empadronamiento* they formally leave the ranks of the workers and are transferred to the monthly payroll.

Despite the generally depressed wage levels, the industrial worker population as a whole forms a privileged category in comparison with the other proletarian segments of the economically active population. Their privileged status obviously stands out in a situation of an expanding disguised unemployment due to the mushrooming marginal occupations. Industrial workers at least have a steady job which gives them a fixed salary, however inferior it may be. They enjoy regular wage increases at the time of the revision of the collective contracts. These raises may be small but in Monterrey they virtually always have been superior to the national average.[39] The system of profit sharing, that was instituted in 1964,[40] has meant a small extra income for a considerable number of workers; this despite its sabotage by several companies. In addition, most of the larger industrial enterprises, in particular those belonging to the Cuauthemoc and Fundidora conglomerates, have instituted programs of social assistance in the areas of education, housing, recreation, alimentation and the financing of consumer durables. These programs aim at the integration of the workers within the companies and form part of their mechanisms of conflict management and control. They will be discussed more extensively later on.

The dependent workers in commercial enterprises, the construction workers and the transport workers, are worse off compared to the industrial workers, to say nothing about the subproletariat. Our earlier exposition on the Monterrey income distribution has shown that the main redistributive mechanisms as education, medicare and other social welfare services, do not

---

[39] These raises are related to raises in the cost of living. They are not a function of the increases in labor productivity that in virtually all industries exceed by far the salary increases. Cf. De León, 1968: 131 ff, and Hacia una Planeación, 1970: 82.
[40] The measure formed already a part of the Constitution of 1917 but had never been implemented.

TABLE 14: Occupational structure of selected industries, Monterrey area, 1967

production participation of each type of worker per branch of industry (percentages)

industry	top-level executives	medium-level executives	profes-sionals	admini-strative personnel	medium-level tech-nicians	skilled workers	semi-skilled workers	unskilled workers	total
food	1.1	1.2	0.5	7.0	6.8	13.0	0.2	70.2	100.0
drinks	2.0	4.9	7.5	40.0	2.0	3.6	–	40.0	100.0
textiles	1.0	1.3	1.0	19.0	2.2	59.9	1.0	14.6	100.0
shoes and apparel	0.8	1.0	0.6	5.6	2.8	53.6	8.7	26.5	100.0
wood and cork	4.4	2.2	–	6.6	2.2	29.5	–	55.1	100.0
furniture	1.4	3.1	1.1	9.4	1.4	22.4	–	61.2	100.0
paper	2.2	1.1	2.2	25.1	7.6	4.0	3.4	54.4	100.0
printing	3.3	7.7	1.4	14.4	8.8	25.0	13.3	26.4	100.0
rubber	3.3	3.7	1.5	20.4	4.4	35.0	3.3	28.2	100.0
chemicals	1.5	1.4	4.6	17.5	13.0	33.2	2.9	25.9	100.0
stone, clay, glass	1.0	1.5	1.1	10.6	3.9	25.7	0.5	55.7	100.0
basic metallurgy	0.2	1.0	3.6	5.3	2.1	52.6	0.5	34.7	100.0
fabricated metals	1.5	3.3	2.0	15.6	10.0	33.1	4.2	30.3	100.0
machinery	3.0	5.0	1.9	34.5	7.5	42.2	–	5.9	100.0
electrical	1.0	2.9	4.3	10.9	11.5	19.4	–	50.0	100.0
automobiles and other transport eq.	3.8	4.2	1.6	29.4	7.0	15.1	5.7	33.2	100.0
miscellaneous manufacturing	1.7	0.8	0.5	8.6	4.7	11.3	–	72.4	100.0

Source: Hacia una Planeación, 1970: 19

77

favor the lowest income strata, which include the subproletarian categories of workers, in any special way. Education favors primarily the middle strata and upwards, while one needs to be regularly employed in order to profit from most of the other services in the welfare package.

The shortage of adequate housing facilities in the Monterrey area hits most of the working class hard. Here, again, the very poorest suffer most. The housing situation, as a correlate of the existing income distribution, forms a good indicator of the levels of living in these low income brackets. Those workers employed for more than a year in companies counting a labor force of 101 or more can claim housing from their employers by law (*Ley Federal del Trabajo, articulo* 136). In Monterrey, big industry traditionally has supplied housing to various categories of workers in the *colonias* surrounding the factories. Most of the Monterrey workers, however, are employed by smaller enterprises. Some of these may count more than a hundred workers, but the law may be difficult to enforce. In the case of others no claim for housing can be made at all.

In a study of the problem, Puente Leyva (1967: 55) concludes that almost half of the population in the Monterrey area has to live in dwellings that are totally inadequate as far as construction, services and health conditions are concerned. At the same time the possibility to obtain financing for new housing is extremely limited for those lower strata that would need it most.

The inadequate living conditions are very much concentrated in the proletarian *colonias*. De León (1968: 152 ff) reports on the housing situation in eight *colonias* that have existed already for quite some time and traditionally have a working class population.[41] Among a total of 28,400 houses, 5.8 percent were improvised houses of various types of material, 70.1 percent were shacks and dilapidated slum dwellings lacking all elementary services, 18.1 percent were workman's houses, often old but fit for habitation. Only 5 percent represented dwellings in good conditions, often recently constructed. In these *colonias*, the services like water, drainage, electricity and gas are generally lacking and most of the streets go without pavement.

In a study realized in 1966 among those having an income below the legal minimum (27 percent of the economically active population), it appeared that 56.3 percent of this population rented their houses. Among the others 36.5 percent owned the house, 1.8. percent was still paying the installments, 2.7 percent had a house given to them by their employers, 2.7 percent inhabited a house under other conditions. Most of these houses were slum dwellings of inferior construction on rented sites. Around 85 percent had roofs made of wood or corrugated iron, 54 percent had an entirely wooden construction. Only 59.5 percent possessed running water either in the house itself or from a public tap. The area average is 80 percent.[42]

---

[41] The *colonías* are: Independiente, Hidalgo, Estrella, Niño Artillero, Garza Nieto, Juárez, Pedro Lozano, Progreso.

[42] *Boletín Bimestral C.I.E.*, no. 22, August 1966.

A 1970 COFIDE report[43] suggests that in the second half of the 1960's at least some improvements had been made in housing construction. It informed that in that same year 60.4 percent of the houses in the Monterrey area had brick walls (26.6 percent in 1960), 11.5 percent were made of *adobe* (56.3 percent in 1960), 20.9 percent were made of wood (6.2 percent in 1960) and 7.2 percent were made of mud and cardboard (10.9 percent in 1960).

Still, inadequate living conditions continue to affect a considerable part of the working class. However they most seriously influence the living conditions of the subproletarian segments of the population.

3.2.4. *The subproletariat*

The masses forming the subproletariat comprise almost a quarter of the total population of the area and their living quarters constitute a *cinturón de miseria* surrounding the city. Almost a third of this population receives an income far below the legally established minimum. The others barely make this minimum or receive an income slightly below this level (Puente Leyva, 1969: 21). They generally earn their living through a variety of odd jobs in the services and circulation sectors, that represent often no more than a form of disguised unemployment and in themselves do not offer any posibility of improvement (Balán, 1967: 183). In fact they form part of a labor reservoir which by its mere presence depresses the wage level of the unskilled and semiskilled workers in particular and has a debilitating effect on the pressure group functions of organized labor. Their levels of living are low, even by Monterrey standards.

The lower third of this subproletarian population had an average family income that in 1965 did not exceed 600 pesos a month, or 75 percent of the legal minimum wages at the time. Tijerina Garza (1965: 71-73) mentions a few additional indicators of their levels of living. In the area of nutrition large deficiencies did exist: 10 percent of this group had only two meals a day, 43 percent suffered more severe nutritive deficiencies, 40 percent of the children in school age went to class without breakfast. With regard to health: 73 percent suffered from some kind of illness and lacked good health, 15 percent had lung disease (mostly tuberculosis), 8 percent suffered from anemia. Tijerina Garza further reports that a third of the houses, in which the individuals belonging to this subproletarian segment live, are in the worst possible conditions. These dwellings counted an average of two rooms with an average occupancy of 3.5 persons per room.

The upper two-thirds of the subproletarian population comprises families recieving an income that either equals or approximates the legal minimum. Although they still consume less than 2,000 calories per person daily,[44] their's is not a situation of acute hunger and misery.

---

[43] Cited in *El Porvenir*, April 5, 1971.
[44] The recommended daily intake of calories is 2500. Cf. Puente Leyva, 1969: 106.

The paradox of the situation of these poor strata is again that only a minority, 26 percent of the total number of families, is reached by the income redistributing mechanisms of the social security organization, I.M.S.S., which proportions medicare and administers other welfare revulations.

3.3. Entrepreneurs and Political Action

The activities of the Monterrey industrial bourgeoisie in the political arena have been organized against the background of a continuous tension between the strivings of the industrialists towards regional autonomy and the central government asserting its supreme authority.

In discussing the background of this phenomenon the heritage of the 19th century *caudillo* era should be remembered, that left disintegrating tendencies seeking to cristallize around some feelings of regional unity all over Mexico. These tendencies, vigorously fought by Porfirio Díaz, nevertheless persisted and the very ideosyncratic economic and social structure of the state of Nuevo León generated a strong economic base for their expression. All through this century the central government has opposed the efforts of the industrialists to monopolize also political power within the state of Nuevo León, besides economic power and social prestige. Their constant struggle to gain control over a wide range of political positions ranging from the state governor, officials of state government, members of the judiciary, members of the labor arbitration boards, officials of the Monterrey municipal government, has met varying degrees of success through the years. Apart from direct control over the leading officies on the state and municipal level, however, the industrial sector has employed other subtle and not so subtle pressure mechanisms to influence public policies.[45]

The conscious drive toward regional independence emerged for the first time rather strongly during the beginning phase of the Díaz regime itself. At that time, the Monterrey entrepreneurs operated close to the regional center of political decision making. Their relationship with state governor, Bernardo Reyes, was one of mutual support. The latter assumed the role of benefactor of the incipient industry and designed the legal administrative framework that permitted an uphindered industrial expansion. The industrialists, on their turn, helped to support Reyes' political ambitions on the regional and national level by fortifying the economic base for the power of the state. This close "marriage de convenance" was broken up through the removal of Reyes by Díaz in 1909. At that time his power had become a real threat to the central authorities (Saldaña, 1965: 20 ff).

The interdependence of economic and political power has never again been so complete as in the Reyes period. Since then, the central governement has stepped in repeatedly to prevent the emergence of a competing power center

---

[45] Cf. "Los Niveles del Poder" in: *Oigamé*, May 23, 1970.

that would dispute the government initiative in policies affecting the industrial sector.

The activities in the political sphere have been structured somewhat differently between the Fundidora and the Cuauthemoc conglomerates. Those interests connected with the Fundidora group traditionally have enjoyed a greater access to the level of national politics and their activities form part of the effort to influence decision making processes on that level, also reflecting their greater dependence on federal contracts. The interests tied up with the Cuauthemoc concern have lacked this facility and primarily have been regionally oriented. They had a weak relationship with the Mexican state apparatus and at times operated in clear opposition to official politics.

The differences in orientations emerged already during revolutionary times. The Madero family[46] had financial interests in Fundidora. The company consequently leaned towards the constitutionalist side. The entrepreneurs of the Cuauthemoc group, however, supported Huerta, the leader of the counter revolutionary movement that ultimately resulted in the imprisonment and assassination of Franciso I. Madero. In 1914, Monterrey was occupied definitively by the constitutionalist armies.[47] The mines, that had been closed as a result of war action, were reopenend in order to reestablish Fundidora's prewar production levels. The Cuauthemoc brewery, however, was seized by the revolutionaries *para beneficio de la Revolución*, as a reprisal for the political stand its owners had taken. These left the city for the U.S.A., where they had to wait a few years before the brewery was returned to them in 1916. Despite their accommodation with the changed postrevolutionary situation, they have never overcome their sense of alienation from the "new politics" since that period. Repeatedly the central government and the entrepreneurs have clashed on the issue of regional political control, the initiative each time residing with the interests related to the Cuauthemoc group.

The tension between the two parties reached a high during the government of President Cárdenas (1934-1940). The Cuauthemoc interests opposed his election to the presidency which led to Cárdenas' refusal to visit the city during his political campaign. They maintained the opposition to his reformist and prolabor policies at full force for the entire period of his administration and initially they even supported covertly the *Acción Cívica Nacionalista*, a movement of fascist leanings, later disbanded by order of President Cárdenas (Ashby, 1967: 91; De León, 1968: 79). In this period they lacked complete political control over the state government.

In 1936, the conflict between Cárdenas and the Monterrey entrepreneurial sector broke out into the open. This development was motivated by a labor management dispute that had originated in the Vidriera glass factory, be-

---

[46] Fransico I. Madero was the leader of the revolt against Porfirio Díaz in 1910.
[47] These armies were led by general Pablo González, who appointed General Antonio Villareal as temporary governor of the state of Nuevo León. Villareal had been a collaborator of Ricardo Flores Magón, anarchosyndicalist and precursor of the Mexican Revolution.

longing to the Cuauthemoc group. Cárdenas decided to intervene personally and travelled to Monterrey. After a visit of several days, during which he met with representatives of labor and management, Cárdenas presented a plan for the settlement of the strike. At the same time he took advantage of the opportunity and defined openly and systematically his position and strategy with regard to the development of the industrial sector, the position of labor and the evolution of labor management relations (Ashby, 1967: 34). To the entrepreneurs he issued a stern warning to the effect that any attempt to shut down the factories or to alter the production process in any other way in order to frustrate the emancipation of the workers, would be met by government intervention. In the area of labor politics, Cárdenas' statement of position led to the creation of the special relationship between government and organized labor as embodied in the C.T.M. The Monterrey industrial interests, however, were in no mood to cooperate with official organized labor. All through 1938 they joined efforts in a campaign intended to stop union organizing and to destroy the C.T.M. as a viable union movement in the state. The *Acción Cívica Nacionalista* reappeared and attacked striking workers. This situation led to another intervention by Cárdenas. An attempt was made at a general strike which had some success in vital sectors of the Monterrey economy (public services) and eventually brought the workers some concessions (Ashby, 1967: 92).

From the early 1940's on, the Monterrey entrepreneurial sector has attempted repeatedly to influence the issue of regional autonomy through the organization of political power on the municipal, state and national levels. To this purpose the Cuauthemoc group supported the conservative opposition party, P.A.N., that had been founded in 1939.[48] The Fundidora group gave support to the *Partido Liberal*, while seeing to it, however, that the good working relationship with the central government was not disturbed (De León, 1968: 80). The political struggle was most manifest on the state level, where initially the attempts to gain power did not meet a great deal of success. During the administration of Governor Arturo B. De la Garza (1943-1949) who represented the rural middle sector and organized urban and rural labor, especially the Cuauthemoc group engaged in sharp opposition. The issue of the acquisition of the Monterrey water and drainage works by the public sector in 1944, was used to launch a frontal attack on the De la Garza administration. Relations became even more strained after the central government intervened temporarily in one of the Cuauthemoc enterprises, Cristalería S.A.

The succession of De la Garza marked a victory of the entrepreneurial sector. They launched a vicious attack on the successor to be, reformist Livas Villareal, and pressured President Miguel Alemán to impose a governor who

---

[48] During the presidential elections of 1940, P.A.N. backed Almazán, the military zone commander of Nuevo León, against the official candidate and later president, Avila Camacho.

would be more favorable to the entrepreneur's interests.[49] With Morones Prieto (1949-1952), the Fundidora group thus acquired a strong influence in the government of the state, an influence that was shortly interrupted by the interim reformist government of José Vivanco (1952-1955), but further continued with Rangel Frías (1955-1961), at present still a member of the administrative board of Fundidora (De Leon, 1968: 82 ff; Mauro, 1964: 79 ff). This latter group had left the *Partido Liberal* episode behind and had accommodated itself to the official party, P.R.I. Thus, their political pressures could be channeled more effectively. Consequently they gained access to political power positions safeguarding at the same time their federal contracts. The Cuauthemoc group, however, continued to support the opposition party, P.A.N., which has frustrated their attempts at direct control over the formal political positions on the state level.

Under the government of President López Mateos (1958-1964), Livas Villareal was nominated to succeed Frías as state governor, again very much against the will of the industrial bourgeoisie. In particular the Cuauthemoc interests took an uncompromising attitude. The introduction of standard primary school textbooks in the entire republic by the federal authorities was taken up by the industrialists as an issue exemplifying the "intolerable interference" by the central government with the powers of the state. Their resistance created a crisis in the country (De Rossi, 1971: 51). Again a political movement, *La Cruzada Regional Anti-Comunista* was tacitly supported as part of the political action against the central government's decision, mainly because they lacked the possibility to exert pressure on official politics from within.

In 1967 Eduardo Elizondo was elected governor of Nuevo León. He belonged to the industrial financial bourgeoisie and had changed his affiliation from P.A.N. to P.R.I. in order to make the election possible.[50] His arrival to power gave the local bourgeoisie direct access to the highest state office and to a series of lower offices over which he had appointive power. The continued weakness of the public sector in the state economy accounted for the absence of sufficient counterweight against the industrialists' efforts to control the vital political decision-making positions in Nuevo León. The tendency towards regional autonomy assumed again full force, obviously followed by a reaction of the central government. In the beginning of 1971, the Monterrey industrialists communicated to President Echeverría their misgivings about his new economic policies.[51] Several months later the government reacted, reaffirm-

[49] Livas Villareal was to return as governor in 1961 during the presidency of López Mateos; for this interesting issue, see: "Los Niveles del Poder," in *Oigamé*, May 23, 1970.
[50] Elizondo was a son of a Monterrey banker and a son-in-law of Nuevo León's "eminence grise" in P.R.I. politics Manuel L. Barragán, member of the administrative board of Fundidora, co-owner of the Coca-Cola factory and big landowner in the state. Elizondo was a protegee of Díaz Ordaz which was the origin of his later difficulties with President Echeverría. Cf. Alisky, 1971: 15 and De León, 1968: 84 ff.
[51] See: *Latin America, a weekly political and economic report*, vol. V, no. 7, February 12, 1971 and no. 19, May 7, 1971.

ing its authority and forcing the governor's resignation over an issue of local university policies. He was replaced by the reliable P.R.I. senator, Luís Farias.[52] Here, the central government interfered again to prevent the emergence of a semi-independent power block in the North.

Despite some internal cleavages that have appeared at times, the industrial community always has represented a close knit unit well aware of its interests and ready to defend these by all means. The *Centro Patronal* of Nuevo León, the "employers union," has a greater membership than any of the other *Centros* in the country, including Mexico City (De Rossi, 1971: 54). The state of Nuevo León also appears to be the only one capable of organizing a *Cámara de Industria de Transformación* that is truly of a regional type. Together with the regional offices of the *Cámara Nacional de Comercio*, the *Centro Bancario* and next to representatives of state and municipal government, they account for a strong participation in COFIDE, the committee for industrialization and economic development of the state of Nuevo León.[53] Through COFIDE, the Monterrey entrepreneurs have a controlling influence over a number of basic aspects that concern the future economic development of the state.

The *Centro Patronal* as a "union organization" is known for its somewhat more traditional and conservative attitude, containing remnants of a strong antiunion orientation that has been directed in particular towards the official unions, the *sindicatos rojos*. The *Cámara de la Industria de Tranformación*, which provides an organization in which all the entrepreneurs involved in the manufacturing industry participate, is less motivated by instinctive antiunionism and has taken a more "modern" approach.

The entrepreneurs' *personal* and *direct* role in organized politics has always been minimal, which obviously does not exclude intervention of a more covert nature. Intermediaries: individual politicians, parties or movements have been used as primary vehicles for political action while the entrepreneurs themselves have remained in the background. Political participation in interest organizations and other organizations with a pressure group character however is high. The *Centro Patronal* and the sectorial organizations, together with the other *Cámaras* in the country have a definite impact on the elaboration of new laws affecting industry. They further take part in discussions of wider problems influencing economic development such as communications, education, etc. (De Rossi, 1971: 187) and play a leading role in matters affecting national policies on industrial development and international trade. Though these organizations and also through private channels of influence the entrepreneurs of course practice at the same time the "personal" approach

---

[52] Ibid., no. 24, June 11, 1971.

[53] COFIDE has been assigned the tasks of promoting new industrial investments and further to create the infrastructural conditions, such as terrains, water, energy, etc., that make the establishment of these industries possible, with a particular emphasis for those regions in the state outside Monterrey, conform the new decentralization policy. It counsels potential investors on problems relating to taxes, credits, labor affairs, etc. See: *Boletín COFIDE*, 4. no. 19, January 15, 1970.

84

in the promotion of their interests. This approach is particularly facilitated by their place at the social and economic top. which makes communication with leading government officials easier, based on felt equality.[54] The entrepreneurs of the larger enterprises pay a visit to Mexico City at least once a week and they often keep an office in order to facilitate the contact with the government departments. The Fundidora group even has its general headquarters and its general manager situated in Mexico City, 600 miles away from the factories in Monterrey.

3.4. *Labor, Two Forms of Dependence*

The political expression of class membership in the case of the Monterrey proletariat reflects two forms of dependence: (a) with regard to the official political apparatus, and (b) with regard to the *patrón*, the employer. The dependence with respect to the official political structure resembles on the local level the situation that we have described for the national level and for the particulars we refer to Chapter III, section 4.3.3. The second mentioned form of dependence e.g., vis-a-vis the *patrón*, requires a more extensive expostion here. Before we proceed to this issue, some data on the organization of the labor movement, its ideology and some elements from Monterrey labor history, will be presented.

3.4.1. *The labor sector: organization and perspectives*
Basically, organized labor can be divided into two blocks. The division lines coincide with the two forms of dependence mentioned above. On the one side operate the federations of C.T.M., C.R.O.C., C.G.T. and a number of other unions (railroad workers, mining and metallurgy workers, telephone workers, etc.) or so-called *sindicatos rojos*, oriented towards the official political structure. On the other side we find the federations of F.N.S.I., *Federación Nacional de Sindicatos Independientes,* and F.S.A., *Federación de Sindicatos Autónomos,* or the so-called *sindicatos blancos*, oriented towards to the *patrón*.

It is difficult to get their exact numerical importance. The federations themselves have the tendency to inflate the numbers of affiliated workers. According to their own statements they had in 1971:[55]

F.N.S.I.:	65,000
F.S.A.:	22,000
C.R.O.C.:	25.000
C.T.M.:	25.000
C.G.T.:	5,000
other:	10,000
total	152,000

---

[54] This lobbying activity may involve a considerable amount of armtwisting as the often angry relationship with the Echeverría administration shows, the industrialists repeatedly threatening to freeze investment and to organize a capital flight.

[55] These data represent the state membership of the respective federations.

The *Centro Patronal*, which tends to deflate union membership, estimated, for the same period, the total number of unionized workers in the Monterrey area at around 100,000. F.N.S.I. and F.S.A. would represent 45,000 and 15,000 workers respectively. C.T.M. and C.R.O.C. each 15,000 and the rest around 10,000 workers. The real magnitude of union membership should be located between these maximum and minimum statements.[56]

On the basis of our earlier estimate of the proletarian occupations among the economically active population (44.3 percent) and utilizing the 1970 census, the proletariat should comprise 217,880 persons among the employed. This represents around 83 percent of the total number of persons employed in commerce, the extractive and manufacturing industry, transport and the construction industry. Taking into consideration that the union membership contains a certain percentage of employees, teachers, etc. and other categories of "middle class" professions and estimating the total union membership between 120,000 and 130,000 workers, it follows that about 40 percent of the Nuevo León working class is not organized in any union. These are workers in small industries who are not organized because of personal ties with the company and/or repressive action by the *patrón* fearing union interference with exploitative practices. In addition most companies employ a part of their labor force as *eventuales*, workers who formally are in a trial period. As such, they are contracted only provisionally and for limited periods of time. This formula is used, however, to keep them on montly contracts for rather long periods during which they are not allowed to unionize and the company can limit its obligations under the federal labor code. Finally, the gap in union affiliation is further explained by the high percentage of unorganized workers in the construction sector.[57]

The labor movement, it can be concluded, is rather divided organizationally. The *sindicatos blancos* and the *sindicatos rojos* obviously show differences in political perspective and, consequently, in strategy and tactics. These differences, however, have also conditioned the structure and functioning of the respective union organizations. The *sindicatos rojos*, moreover, are deeply divided internally as a result of the power politics of the union leadership.

The F.N.S.I. and the F.S.A. were founded in the wake of President Cárdenas' intervention in the labor management conflicts of 1936. Their organization was inspired by the Monterrey entrepreneurial sector, among them in particular the Cuauthemoc group. The objective was to block the advances of the recently founded C.T.M., an instrument of government policies for which they did not conceal their fervent dislike. The F.N.S.I. initially affiliated with the opposition party P.A.N. It abandoned this party in 1954 after having

---

[56] The difference between state membership and area membership cannot possibly account for the differences.

[57] The segment of the construction workers as a whole can be estimated for 1970 at close to 31.000 workers (14.2 percent of 217.880).

86

confronted the difficulties of solving the multitude of problems tied up with the daily representation of the interests of the membership, without the advantage of government patronage (Scott, 1959: 183). Since then, they have affiliated with the P.R.I. labor sector, however, as part of the anti-B.U.O. block. The F.S.A. unions have remained "autonomous", that is, they have not joined the "official" party in one way or another. They reject any political involvement and profess strict "neutrality". The influence of the *patrón* in union affairs is most manifest. F.S.A. unites a small number of unions in a few big industries (glass, chemicals, iron and steel, machinery) belonging to the Cuauthemoc conglomerate, in the electrotechnical industry and in the transport sector. The federation structure is very weak.

The absence of the *líder*, the traditional Mexican union boss, marks a clear difference between the *sindicatos rojos* and the F.N.S.I. and F.S.A. The heads of both federations are called "general coordinators" and their task indeed appears to be primarily one of coordination and administration. Their leadership bears little resemblance to the *lideres charros* of the *sindicatos rojos*. The functioning of the F.N.S.I. and F.S.A. unions further reflects the specific definition of the tasks of these organizations that limit the defense of worker interests strictly to the legal framework provided by the new federal labor code.[58] Anything exceeding this narrow legalistic administrative approach has been excluded. The infiltration of official politics in the unions and the corresponding coexistence of trade unionist and political issues is virtually absent. In addition, the fact that they are not an instrument of government policy has reduced the political infighting characterizing the *sindicatos rojos*. There is less overt manipulation of the rank and file by the leadership of the affiliated unions. The instances of abuse and corruption by those in positions of power are less frequent.[59]

The C.T.M. has the longest history of the official labor movement in Nuevo León. It started to organize workers in 1936. The C.R.O.C. followed in 1952. Together they organized most of the *sindicatos rojos* in the state. The C.G.T. has remained small. The federations show intra- and interorganizational divisions due to the workings of *personalismo*, together with the tendency of the leadership to accumulate power, to combine positions within the union organization and the official political structure and to use the former as a political base for gaining personal political power in official politics. The rivalries between these *lideres charros* frustrate the development of any collective solidarity and mutual support in the case of a labor conflict affecting

---

[58] In individual cases, the limits imposed by the *patrón* may carry a much heavier weight in defining union action, cf. *Oigamé*, August 8, 1970 and August 15, 1970.
[59] The general coordinator of the F.N.S.I. suggested (interview May 1971) a change of name from *sindicatos blancos* to *sindicatos limpios* ("clean unions") as appropriate.

workers affiliated with either one of the three federations.[60] Inter- and intrafederational animosities and schisms have been further encouraged by the subdivision of the larger companies, forcing the unions to divide thus creating the possibility for the entrepreneurs to play one union off against the other. The general situation is one of a fragmented and deeply divided labor movement canalizing a fair amount of its energies towards intramovement struggle and the competition for political followings. This last mentioned phenomenon has emerged most clearly in the case of the Monterrey subproletariat whose tremendous growth alerted local politicians to their potential significance as a political base.

In 1964 the government of Livas Villareal encouraged the organization of the poor settlers on the fringes of the city, the so-called *colonos*, with the objective to get control of the invasions of unused terrain in the city.[61] In subsequent elections, these organizations proved to have a considerable mobilization potential. *Colono* unions also affiliated with the C.T.M. and the C.R.O.C. to gain access to official patronage.[62] In 1970, the *líder* of the C.G.T. began to organize the *colonos* in an overall structure, the *Central de Defensa del Pueblo*, with the obvious intention to create a political following.[63] His activities had the clear blessings of the state governor, who already for some time had tried to play the C.G.T. off against its bigger competitors, C.R.O.C. and C.T.M. (De León, 1968: 253).

This affiliation with a specific labor federation, which acts as an intermediary for the distribution of official patronage from above and the mobilization of support for official politics from below, often has less than voluntary aspects in a situation where blackmail and straight repressive tactics

---

[60] In recent years the interorganizational rivalries emerged with regular frequency while the *rojo* federation leaders fulfilled their political duties as *diputados* in the state congress of Nuevo León, of which the C.R.O.C. leader was president (*Oigamé*, May 30, 1970). Within the unions the complaints of abuse of power were widespread among the rank and file. A frequently heard allegation was, that the leaders made a deal with the employers, settling labor conflicts while receiving a percentage of the final settlement in exchange. The charges of corruption, mismanagement and nepotism in the supply of jobs led in 1971 to a temporary split in the C.T.M. when 92 affiliated unions, representing around 10.000 workers, refused to accept the *líder* any longer (*El Porvenir*, February 13, 1971). He was shown to own a ranch in the Southern part of the state where he forced workers who were dependent on him for the solution of their employment problems to work without pay (*Oigamé*, November 31, 197. These abuses eventually led to his assasination by disgruntled workers (*El Porvenir*, May 30, 1970). The *líder* of the C.R.O.C. was a leading state politician and one of the prominent landowners of Guadalupe, a Monterrey suburb which had experienced a strong expansion of popular settlements (*Oigamé*, June 27, 1970) His son had been named executive director of COFIDE, the state industrialization and economic development board, in which the employers' interests are so strongly represented: a beautiful example of cooptation!
[61] *Oigamé*, November 31, 1970.
[62] Cf. *El Porvenir*, May 23, 1971.
[63] *Oigamé*, October 17, October 31 and November 14, 1970.

by the authorities against those local leaders not willing to abdicate in favor of "official" mediators, are common phenomena.[64]

The differences in political perspective, strategy and tactics between the *sindicatos blancos* and the *sindicatos rojos* obviously are most clearly expressed in their orientations towards labor management relations. The declaration of principles of the C.R.O.C. utilizes Marxist jargon, mentions the existence of a two-class structure in which the class relations are based on the exploitation of one class by the other and recommends class struggle as the most appropriate means to achieve the emancipation of the proletariat.[65] The perspective of the C.T.M. is rather similar.[66] The F.N.S.I., on the other hand, explicity rejects Marxism-Leninism as an alien doctrine producing "disastrous results" and affirms the adherence to liberal bourgeoisie principles, in particular "private property", as the ultimate determinants of personal liberty and dignity.[67] It defines as its primary objective, the development and maintenance of a dialogue in an atmosphere of mutual respect and understanding. On the company level, the role of these unions has been focused on the mediation of problems related to the implementation of the labor laws. Its pressure group function has long remained dormant. During the entire period 1948-1968 the F.N.S.I., the greatest labor federation of Northern Mexico, did not organize one strike or strike threat. Six strikes were organized from 1968 to 1971.[68] They concerned, however, minor unions.

The F.N.S.I. action in case of a labor conflict reveals a tactic which is rather different from the one practiced by the *sindicatos rojos*. Its moves are

---

[64] See *Oigamé*, November 14, 1970. The slumdwellers' dependence from official politics, mediated through the unions, as far as basic public services, employment, social services, etc, is concerned, makes that these official pressures cannot be ignored without impunity, as we have been able to observe repeatedly.

[65] *Estatuto de la Federación Revolucionaria de Obreros y Campesinos de Nuevo León,* Aprobados en el 3er Congreso General Ordinario celebrado el 23 de Agosto de 1964.

[66] *Estatutos,* C.T.M. Comite Nacional, Mexico D.F., Julio 10 de 1940.

[67] *Declaración de Principios, Estatutos, Promociones y Servicios.* Federación Nacional de Sindicatos Independientes, Monterrey N.L., 1965. The statute further mentions the union as a "purely professional organization" that should operate at "the margins of politics" (art. 6); it indicates that its struggle should proceed through "purely legal means" not prejudicing "the common good" (art. 8); the objectives of this struggle before all should concern wage increases, taking however into consideration "the possibilities" of the company, in order to prevent "sterile agitation" that in the first place would prejudice the workers themselves (art. 11); "private property is the motive of work and the firm base for personal dignity and independence" (art. 14); the union should "defend the right to private property of all mankind in addition to the right to transfer this property through inheritance" (art. XI); it should "struggle with great force" against "the doctrine of Marxism-Leninism, which proclaims the class struggle through violent means, denies the workers a full cultural development, private property, the right to have a family, and takes his freedom, the doctrine aims to weaken and oppress the fatherland, substituting it for an international organization facilitating the penetration of forms of imperialism and changing the modern State for a dictatorship" (art. 16 and XXII); finally, the union proclaims "the integration of capital and labor" on the basis of "harmony, cooperation and progress."

[68] This phenomenon may have been part of the general labor unrest that preceded the promulgation of the new labor code in 1970 and later accompanied the problems around its implementation.

primarily intended to establish discussion and negotiation with the *patrón* over proposals made by the union. The *rojo* unions on the other hand, present a package of claims together with an ultimatum containing a strike threat. As the *Centro Patronal* states it: "the *sindicatos blancos* deny the existence of a class struggle. They tend to avoid confrontations and in negotiations present a smile instead of a pistol, thus preserving the rest and harmony necessary for an undisturbed development of the production process."[69]

This orientation prevails even more strongly in the F.S.A. These unions explicity deny having pressure group characteristics. Their activites do not go beyond the provision of counsel and advice to the membership in problems relating to the implementation of the labor laws.[70] The continuity of production should never be endangered by collective action, because in that case common interests would be threatened: "if the *patrón* goes well, so does the worker." In these unions the influence of the *patrón* is rather marked. Negotiations for the collective contract are organized directly between him and the union representatives without the participation of labor lawyers. Their presence is common practice with the other unions, but as the F.S.A. leader maintained: "they tend to create conflicts and then earn their money on the case." The federation claims to have harmonious relations with the employers: "we are good friends, drink a beer together and negotiate in an atmosphere of mutual respect and comprehension." The F.S.A. has never had one strike in its 35 years of existence.

These differences in perspective and behavior between the *sindicatos blancos* and the *sindicatos rojos* do not necessarily mean that the *rojo* unions will take a more militant or radical stand. In both union organizations militants are out. The leadership is firmly committed to the political status quo. Their antagonism against a greater militancy in union affairs is deep. Over the years they have moved swiftly to eliminate any tendency working in this direction. A similar fate has struck the efforts to democratize the unions and related actions threatening the power position of the existing leadership.

The absence of any militancy in the affiliated unions was explained by the F.N.S.I. leaders from the effectiveness of the efforts, both by the unions and the employers, to create "good" industrial relations. The F.N.S.I. "eschews demagogy," refrains from "talking politics" and has banned "agitation, pressure or threats" from its arsenal of weapons.[71] F.S.A. voiced similar

---

[69] This defintion of the situation by the director of the *Centro Patronal* indicates that the *sindicatos blancos* in fact actively help to realize one of the most important objectives of this employer's union, which is: "to achieve the harmonization and stabilization of the *patrón*-worker relationship." Cf. *Estatutos del Centro Patronal de Nuevo León*. Monterrey, N.L., 27 de Julio de 1964.

[70] This according to the F.S.A. coordinator general (interview May 1971); this official occupies his position since 1937 and although representing a remarkable case of *continuismo*, lacks the other characteristics that in Mexico are normally part of the *liderazgo sindical*.

[71] These and other opinions of the federation's leadership were collected through extensive interviewing in Spring 1971; additional information on the role of the F.N.S.I. was gathered in February 1974.

90

opinions, pointing to its relationship of "mutual understanding" with the employers who "abide with the labor laws and make militancy unnecessary." Among the *rojo* union movement, the C.R.O.C. leadership maintained that it was necessary to suppres militant union attitudes as they would tend to harm the investment climate. Organized labor should be "cooperative," voluntary mitigating its demands, in order to attract new industries and help to alleviate the problem of unemployment.

The labor history of Monterrey provides ample illustration of the dependent positon in which the labor sector finds itself. Since the very beginnings of industrialization in Monterrey, the collective manifestations of labor activism, as strikes, boycotts or public manifestations, have not been frequent. Up until the 1930's the union movement in Monterrey was underdeveloped. The C.R.O.M. enjoyed some support in the textile sector in the 1920's, but the general scene was still dominated by mutual aid societies. The *Gran Círculo de Obreros de Monterrey* was founded in 1874. Its membership consisted of textile workers, artisans like: carpenters, tailors, shoemakers, hatmakers, printers, cabinetmakers, and dependently employed store employees.[72] The list of honorary members indicates that its leadership had close connections with the Porfirio Díaz government and with the regional economic and political powerful, up until the revolution. Its orientation and activities suggest this society as an early example of a dependent worker organization.

In the 1920's various rather short periods of labor unrest can be noted. Not until 1936, however, did Monterrey experience a large-scale strike movement. The unrest of the 1930's followed the promulgation of the federal labor code in 1931, that inspired the organization of various unions of workers and employees in the state. In addition, the law had created the *Junta Central de Conciliación y Arbitraje*, which however functioned rather irregularly and in its decisions reflected the heavy pressure given by the employers. The fact that these channels through which labor conflicts could be mediated ultimately were blocked by the *patrones*, contributed greatly to the wave of unrest of 1936 (Roel, 1954: 257). From this movement emerged organized labor as we know it today.

The 1940's did also show some strike activity. In 1942 labor protested the price raises of basic necessities. Two years later a series of strikes broke out, among others paralyzing Fundidora. These formed part of a wider spontaneous strike movement all over Mexico, resulting in the greatest annual strike frequency the country has ever known. The nature of these strikes and their motives have been clarified in section 4.3.3. Chapter III. In 1948 Fundidora was struck again, this time for pure trade-unionist demands. The strikers succeeded in forcing the company to concede a general wage increase of 18 percent as part of a new collective contract.

Since then, collective labor conflicts on any substantial scale have not occurred in the Monterrey industrial sector, although in the late 1960's a

---

[72] Cf. José Navarro. "Historia del Gran Círculo de Obreros de Monterrey." *El Porvenir*, April 22, 1971.

growing labor unrest could be observed. This included a few strikes protesting undesirable working conditions, a considerable number of complaints about exploitative practices and the arbitrary applications of labor regulations in several of the smaller Monterrey factories and several manifestations of labor pressing wage issues. In addition quite a number of actions can be observed, that concerned the labor organization itself, such as efforts to remove corrupt union leaders and/or to change the affiliation of the unions from *blanco* to *rojo*.[73] This unrest relates in many cases to the problems surrounding the decree of the long expected new labor code on May 1st, 1970 and its subsequent implementation, especially in the industrial sector.

Most of the genuine collective labor action in the 1960's, however, has taken place outside the industrial sector: among workers in subproletarian occupations, such as penny vendors and *colonos* at the urban fringe, or in sectors marginal to the industrial proletariat, as the workers of the Universidad de Nuevo León or sections of the electrical workers organizations. At the same time, these are segments of the working class functioning in a much less "controlled" working situation. The distribution of economic power in the area and the way it has influenced the power relations in other spheres obviously has contributed to a situation in which the collective manifestation of labor militance is minimal and the organization of an autonomous labor movement is blocked. The apparent lack of labor initiative does reflect this very visible distribution of power, as experienced by them, and indicates at the same time the effectiveness of the employers more covert mechanisms of coercion and control which segmentize, atomize and suppress the worker population. The term "apparent" has been used here, because this lack of initiative may have a less than voluntary nature. This is underlined by the fact that autonomous action does occur, although it is not allowed to develop beyond an initial stage. The increasing number of confrontations in the 1960's and early 1970's between union leadership and rank and file over issues related to the administration of the unions and in particular the procedures for election of union officials form a case in point.[74] Here "the lack of initiative" rather will represent a temporary resignation to a situation of powerlessness opposite to the *patrón* and the official political structure and an inability to counteract the more subtle penetration of their mechanisms of control in union organizations and any other form of collective labor action.

3.4.2. The mechanisms of control over the labor sector

The mechanisms of control over the labor sector form a structure of rewards and punishments that encourage conformity to the "rules of the game" as defined by the employers and/or the official political structure and at the

---

[73] See De León (1968: 252 ff), also *Oigamé*, August 1, August 15 and August 22, 1970.
[74] A great number of examples can be found in the column *Notas Laborales* of the local newspaper *El Porvenir* in this period.

same time discourage any violation of these rules. A subtle interplay of carrot and stick policies have been defined that have shown a considerable effectiveness, if the frequency of strikes and other collective manifestations of labor discontent are used as an indicator. For reasons of exposition, these mechanisms of control will be divided into, first, positive sanctions, the "carrot," and, second, negative sanctions, the "stick." In the daily situation of labor management relations, they are used of course intermittently and interdependently.

Positive sanctions:
In this area a number of mechanisms can be discerned, ranging from the complex of policies forming part of entrepreneurial paternalist and reformist endeavors to cooptation of labor leaders and individual workers through patronage, *empadronamiento* and similar means.

(a)   *entrepreneurial paternalism*
This orientation emerged in Monterrey labor management relations in the aftermath of the Mexican Revolution. Already in 1913, however, the great entrepreneurs began to supply food to their workers, starting with Fundidora and followed by the Cuauthemoc enterprises. The objective was to guarantee the continuity of production in a period when, due to the revolutionary war, the road communications with Monterrey were interrupted repeatedly, causing food shortages in the city. This organization of a food supply for needy workers later developed into the system of *despensas familiares*, food packages that the principal Monterrey industrial companies offer their personnel at wholesale prices (cf. Saldaña, 1965).

The deteriorating living conditions in the city led in 1918 to the formation of "councils of public and private welfare." The Cuauthemoc group organized a cooperative, the Sociedad Cuauthemoc y FA-MO-SA, that was concerned with the welfare of employees and workers and counted with the participation of both categories.[75] In this same period, that is two years after the revolutionary forces had returned the factory to the founding family, the brewery Cuauthemoc organized a welfare department that, however, soon coordinated its activities with the cooperative society. Both institutions expanded their activities from the distribution of first-necessity goods to other areas. In addition to food they began to provide clothing. Soon they launched the idea that each member should be enabled to buy his own house using savings deposited with the cooperative. This latter policy completed the coverage of three areas singled out by the entrepreneurs as having primary importance: *alimentation, clothing,* and *housing.* The Fundidora group developed a very similar policy.

[75] Presently the membership comprises all personnel, from unskilled workers to directors, in about one-fourth of the total number of enterprises that form part of the Cuauthemoc conglomerate, and concentrated in the beer-steel-machinery sector. Cf. Sociedad Cuauthemoc y FA-MO-SA, informe 1973.

At a later stage, after 1940, the system of credits and advances for the acquistion of consumer durables was added. At the same time the areas of *education* and *recreation* were defined as part of the responsibility of the companies.

The system of the *despensas-familiares* and the distribution of clothing still exist but only a part of the proletariat is involved, in particular those working in the big factories belonging to the Cuauthemoc and Fundidora conglomerates. De León (1968: 144) estimates those receiving the food packages, as not counting over 25 percent of the salaried worker population in the Monterrey area. Payment for the services is taken out of the weekly paycheck. While the *Centro Patronal* presented it as a nonprofit program, those involved viewed the system of the *despensas familiares* as just another profitable company business. Among the workers and especially those living in the *colonias pobres*, the practice was not uncommon to have a penny trade using their *despensa* articles and those of their colleagues, buying themselves inferior cheaper foods.

The activities of the companies in the area of housing have a long history. Traditionally Mexican industries have been surrounded by the living quarters of their workers, a phenomenon that we also find in other parts of Latin America. Fundidora started in 1911 with the construction of the first *colonia obrera*, the *Colonia Acero*, to house its workers next to the factory. This initiative was followed by the Cuauthemoc cooperative society in 1918 under the motto "everybody his own home." From this year on up till the mid-1960's the society financed approximately 2,300 homes, 1,300 of which are located in the *Colonia Cuauthemoc*. At that time less than half of the society's members owned their houses (De León, 1968: 168). In recent years, however, the construction program has been expanded strongly and by 1971 around 80 percent were reported to own their homes (source: *Centro Patronal*). Around 20 percent of the workers of the Vidriera sector of the Cuauthemoc group owned their homes in 1967. In this period similar percentages were reached by other companies, including Fundidora.[76] The building programs have speeded up in the last few years, especially after the promulgation of the new labor code in 1970.[77]

In most cases the purchase of a home will lay a heavy financial burden on the workers. A skilled worker may spend more than a third of his monthly

---

[76] Until 1970 Fundidora had distributed 862 homes to its workers. The company proportions a lot of 250 m2, arranges the mortgage and pays 50 percent of the interest. Cf. Informe Anual 1969, Compañia Fundidora de Fierro y Acero de Monterrey S.A.
[77] Art. 136 *Ley Federal del Trabajo*. Cf. Trueba Urbina and Trueba Barrera, 1970: 77 ff. The existing practice in the Monterrey area to subdivide existing companies into smaller units, however, may bring not only a tax break and serve the undermining of union power but also, since 1970, may help to duck the obligation for companies counting a hundred workers or more to provide housing for those workers who have been employed for a year or more.

income. Buying a home, then, would be beyond the means of most workers in case the other family members would not contribute to the family income. As a result of this situation, these workers are tied to the company through heavy financial obligations. The individual worker will be reluctant to leave the company or to protest his working conditions, out of fear that he may be thrown out of his house. He will not be able to participate in strikes as pay stoppages would make it difficult to meet his financial obligations.

In the beginning of the 1960's, the *Centro Patronal* organized the *Instituto Promotor de Habitaciones Populares* as a vehicle through which funds, provided under the Alliance for Progress, were channeled into the popular construction sector. *Unidad Modelo* was built, a model quarter of 2,500 houses offically intended for workers of "modest financial capability", working in the big enterprises, in particular those belonging to the Cuauthemoc conglomerate. At the end of the 1960's, the quarter was extended with *Loma Linda,* counting 2,000 homes and financed by the IADB.[78]

The system of credits and advances that the bigger companies have, helps to alleviate the immediate financial problems of the workers. In addition it serves to integrate the worker in the company, to keep him "satisfied" and to neutralize his political potential.[79] At the same time the employer, taking part of the wages for food expenditures, mortgage installments, payments for consumer durables, has a certain control over the pattern of spending of the workers. The business involved in house financing and consumer durables production represent an interest of these employers themselves and the profits made ultimately will flow back to them. This all is legitimized by the old paternalist preoccupation that the worker might play ducks and drakes with his money. The ultimate objective of this system appears to be the formation of a property owning labor aristocracy that will lose its identification with the proletariat.[80]

The activities of the companies in the area of education date back a long time. In 1911 Fundidora founded two primary schools for the children of its workers. Their establishment was the result of a personal interest of Adolfo

[78] Both *Unidad Modelo* and *Loma Linda* present the best in worker housing Monterrey has to offer. The houses are small, but neat and well kept. They stand apart on clean treelined streets and undoubtedly embody the aspirations of many a Monterrey worker. They show a difference of day and night with the poor, miserable, dirty slum areas down the road. Obviously only stable workers can obtain a house here. In fact skilled workers are highly overrepresented among the inhabitants.
[79] This function was explicitly mentioned as such, by one of the managers who was interviewed.
[80] De León (1968: 139) cites a report of the Sociedad Cuauthemoc y FA-MO-SA, written by Salvador Novo, proudly reflecting on the number of stoves, refrigerators, laundry machines, TV sets and automobiles the members of the society have been able to accumulate.

Prieto, the director general of the company in that period.[81] From 1911 up till 1970 a total of 73,193 students received their primary education through these schools. Fundidora has further developed a system of scholarships that, among others, includes the possibility of continued education at institutions of higher learning in Mexico and abroad (1969: 14 scholarships). Most of the scholarships, however, are spent on the training of workers or employees at medium technical or administrative levels (1969: 154 scholarships).[82]

A similar pattern prevails in the other companies that have organized the education of their workers, although here training courses up to the medium technical level have been emphasized even more. Virtually no attention is given to education on a superior level (Hacía una Planeación, 1970: 21 ff). In addition the companies purposefully refrain from asking official recognition of the studies completed, which limits the workers' mobility and ties them to their original company.

In the area of recreation, the companies have devoted most attention to the organization of sports activities: soccer, baseball, volleyball, etc.[83] Fundidora was the first one to build a sports stadium for its workers (1925) Other companies followed soon. Ample attention is also given to the organization of *fiestas* and similar phenomena of collective ritual that affirm feelings of solidarity, as part of the integration of the entire body of personnel within the company and the identification with its objectives.

Apart from their more diffuse effects on the individual workers' aspirations, his desire for individual mobility, etc., the mechanisms of "entrepreneurial paternalism," offer ample opportunities for control by management through their selective and arbitrary application. The big companies have a grip on the patterns of spending (food, clothing, consumer durables, housing) of a considerable part of their work force and have developed a profitable business for those administering these programs. They control a fair portion of the worker's free time and dominate his mobility chances insofar as these depend on education or training. The worker's indebtedness to the company or to the credit agency for which the company acts as an intermediary, further adds to their dependence, at the same time increasing the potential for control by management.

---

[81] Prieto presented "education" as the vital factor determining upward social mobility. According to a present Fundidora director, he used to say: "the sons of our workers should become the future labor aristocracy of Mexico." The tremendous shortage of skilled personnel at the time, most probably also motivated Prieto's decision to further education. Presently, the costs of these programs for the respective companies are reduced; 50 percent of the total expenses for education is tax deductible.

[82] Cf. *Informe Anual 1969*. Compañia Fundidora de Fierro y Acero de Monterrey S.A.

[83] For examples, see *El Porvenir*, March 31, 1971.

(b) *other measures of a reformist nature*
Besides the policies mentioned above, the Monterrey industrialists have developed a number of reformist measures as part of an overall strategy of "making concessions when confronted with worker demands" (Puente Leyva, 1969: 68). In many cases these "concessions" represent in fact almost insignificant improvements "conceded" after a ritual of "tough negotiations" with coopted union leaders. These measures, given their safety valve function, have been a major tool of conflict prevention and have served to preserve the "atmosphere of understanding and mutual respect" that in managerial ideology describes a situation without collective labor conflicts.[84] Among these measures figures the wage policies of the big Monterrey companies since the end of the 1940's, which has included the custom of granting increases, as part of the two yearly revisions of the collective contracts, that exceed the national average by a small margin.

A similar role has been performed, particularly in the larger companies, by the system of profit sharing decreed in 1962 and implemented in 1964 (Padgett, 1966: 170 ff; Iglesias, 1970: 165).[85]

Despite their modest scope, the profit sharing measures initially met strong management opposition and suffered from sabotage. Some companies refused to open their books to union officials in charge of the control of profit statements. Other presented calculations of profits that raised union claims of double bookkeeping practices. Profit shares given to the workers were often insignificantly small.[86] In reaction to the widespread efforts to sabotage the law, extensive labor unrest arose in the Monterrey industries in 1964, (De León, 1968: 144). Pretty soon, however, the managers understood, first, that profit sharing in no way implied a threat of worker participation in the administration of their companies and that they only had a right to request access to "the books"; second, that in its application official indulgence was shown; and last but not least that the measures in fact could have a considerable utility as another means of conflict prevention where it would affect the workers' job satisfaction in a positive way without great cost to the

---

[84] Cf. *Informe Anual 1969*, op.cit.
[85] The share to be paid to the workers, specified by law, is small. In practice it equals little more than 2 percent of the gross annual company income before taxes (Padgett, 1966: 172). In addition the law excludes certain companies and certain categories of workers. Very small companies or those in the first two years of operation, as well as existing companies changing to an entirely new line of products, are excluded. Within the companies that do participate, top management personnel are not included in the profit sharing plan. The same applies to the categories of apprentices and part-time laborers who have worked less than 60 days during the year for the company concerned. Moreover, the law specifies that given the necessity to speed up the industrialization of the country, the right of capital to a "reasonable" interest and the needed reinvestment of capital have to be reviewed before determining the workers' share (art. 118 *Ley Federal del Trabajo*).
[86] For the first year the law was applied (1964), Padgett (1966: 172) reports profit shares in bottling plants as low as 20 pesos.

employers.[87] As one manager, quoted by Padgett (1966: 175) remarked: "the whole thing has a certain psychological appeal for the wage earner."

In the same period, e.g. the beginning of the 1960's, the bigger companies had begun to organize departments of industrial relations[88] in order to coordinate and mediate their labor policies and centralize the personnel administration. Some have a longer history, such as the earlier mentioned *Departamento de Bienestar* of the Cuauthemoc brewery, founded in 1918. The most important tasks assigned to the departments concerned the increase in productivity while maintaining peace on the labor front (Michelsen Terry and Otálara Bay, 1970: 68).

Tension and conflict in industrial labor-management relations obviously may take different means of expression, including bargaining, boycotts, sabotage, absenteeism, turnover, etc. as well as strikes (Kerr, 1964: 171 ff). The studies by Hyman (1972: 53 ff) Knowles (1952: 210) and Turner (1967: 190 ff) suggest these forms of conflict, their covert or overt variety and their individual or collective expression as action alternatives. In any industrial setting in which worker discontent arises in reaction to conditions of absolute or relative deprivation, it is bound to express itself in some form. Whether it will be a strike or an increase in the rates of absenteeism or turnover will depend on the circumstances of the case, among which the distribution of power and the stage of development of the labor movement take an important place (Hyman, 1972: 54). In a situation like Monterrey, where autonomous collectively organized labor action in a conflict situation would meet strong repressive action from the "other side," workers would most likely express their discontent with work or living conditions in other ways. Labor turnover and absenteeism would be among the most significant alternative courses of action. The problem is, that these may not be "pure" indicators of industrial conflict. Especially turnover may also be influenced by business cycles and changes in administrative labor policies, while both may receive the impact of those problems of adaptation to industrial work patterns by workers with a rural background,[89] that cannot be properly classified as "industrial conflict." Yet they are among the few general indicators that are available and, despite the methodological problems involved, are useful if handled with some caution.

The data presented by Michelsen Terry and Otálara Bay (1970: 88) show that less than 20 percent of the departments of industrial relations in all

[87] These reasons were mentioned to the author by representatives of employers' organizations in Monterrey.
[88] See Michelsen Terry and Otálara Bay (1970: 69 ff) for a complete definition of the objectives and the activities of these departments. This study contains the results of an investigation on the functioning of the departments of industrial relations in the Monterrey area.
[89] This issue is not without debate. While Moore and Feldman (1960: 49) underline the importance of these adaptation problems, Bonilla (1964: 197) and Chaplin (1967: 215) indicate their impact on turnover and absenteeism to be minor. We have researched the problem in Chapter V, section 3.5.

98

companies investigated (N = 189, employing 261,841 personnel in 1969) handled strikes or strike threats at all during the period 1959-1969. The average frequency was 3.3 conflicts per company over these ten years. Among the total work force of those enterprises showing a turnover rate of 1 percent or more in 1969 (N = 160), the turnover amounted to an average of 12.4 percent. The average percentage of hours lost by absenteeism in all companies (N = 189) was 6.6. The average size company with a total work force of 1,385, would suffer a loss of 22,060 man days of 8 hours each per year or 16 work days for each member of the personnel (1969). This all means that while the frequency of collective conflicts is very small, the phenomena of absenteeism and turnover has caused losses that equalled the impact of a few weeks' strike in every company each year (Michelsen Terry and Otálara Bay, 1970: 88). It may indicate the existence of a situation of industrial conflict that has remained hidden behind the facade of peace on the labor front.

(c)   *The role of the government*
In this area of paternalist and reformist policies the government has the role of *gran patrón* with supreme discretionary powers with regard to the enforcement of the labor laws and the distribution of social welfare measures.

The Ministry of Labor administers the federal inspection and control in this area, next to its organization of the conciliation and arbitration boards that function at the municipal, state and federal levels and handle concrete instances of labor management, interlabor or intermanagement conflict. The possibility for appeal to the highest level is important as the boards in the Monterrey area have tended to favor management interests. These appeals requesting government intervention and mediation have occurred particularly in matters relating to profitsharing where the assistance is called of special committees in the Ministry of Labor and in the Ministry of the Treasury.

The I.M.S.S., the Mexican Institute of Social Security, mainly benefits organized urban labor. It virtually excludes the unorganized sections of the urban proletariat, the urban subproletariat and the rural proletariat, marking again the government's image as "supreme benefactor" of the first mentioned category.[90] The entrepreneurial sector, after initial hesitation, has cooperated fully with the social security system. The *Centro Patronal* subsequently even undertook the task to promote the program, when it became clear that it directed itself primarily to the needs of the solidly employed industrial worker population and relieved management of a number of responsibilities in this area.

Negative sanctions
The big Monterrey industrialists traditionally have favored cooptation

[90] The total number of beneficiaries in 1967 was 560,000 on a total state population of approximately 1,500,000 (De León, 1968: 207).

through paternalist and reformist measures and/or clientelist mechanisms, over openly suppressive measures. *Oberos de confianza* occupying strategic positions, like supervisors, *mayordomos* and the like, are often coopted by management to act as intermediaries in labor management relations, bypassing the unions in case the union leadership itself is less than cooperative. "Rewards" may include *empadronamiento*, a rise to the white collar ranks, the selective application of paternalist measures (housing, credits, scholarships, etc) or straight bribery. The traditional system of patronage relationships between the *patrón* and an atomized, individualized work force is only persisting in the smaller and medium-sized companies. Its presence was widespread during the beginning phase of industrialization in Monterrey. Stories still abound entrepreneurs like Prieto, Sada a.o. who used to walk the factory calling the workers by their first names, discussing their family problems and distributing small presents. This phenomenon, however, has virtually disappeared with the growing size and complexity of the companies.

Only when cooptation fails, suppressive measures are taken. "The Monterrey entrepreneurs prefer incentives over punishment."[91] This statement is not just an example of entrepreneurial ideology. For decades already the management of the Monterrey industries has attempted to obtain labor support and to reduce the possibility of collective labor conflict through the distribution of small "favors" that often forestalled federal labor legislation. The entrepreneurs, however, posses an enormous capability for repression and the few times it has been converted into action has increased their credibility as potential suppressors of those categories of workers unwilling to step in line. The fear of the power of the *patrón* and the awareness that it may be used quite arbitrarily, may limit the willingness of the workers to take overtly militant courses of action or simply to change the union to a more effective instrument defending their interests.[92] The fear of company spies may further contribute to the situation in which workers "withdraw" from the working environment on an individual basis, in the way analyzed by Michelsen Terry and Otálara Bay (1970).

Most of the more spectacular cases of suppression appear to be located in the medium and small-sized companies. In this sector the instances of exploitation are most clearly marked. The control over labor traditionally has been strict, based on the personal arbitrariness of the *patrón*. Here also the resistance of management against the implementation of the new labor laws has been greatest. This opposition was not only motivated by its possible implications for the distribution of power within the company, but also prompted by the fear that a strict adherence to the new labor code would force

---

[91] Interview *Centro Patronal* in Monterrey, March 1971.
[92] Actually this point was mentioned by several of the respondents among the worker population.

a considerable number of the more "traditional" medium and small-sized enterprises into marginality.[93]

The most directly suppressive measures the companies can take are (a) the instant dismissal of individuals or groups of workers, and (b) the lock out, which in Monterrey practice has involved up to several hundreds of workers at the same time (cf. De León, 1968: 253). In these cases a variety of legal tricks are used in order to duck the provisions of the general legal code or the federal labor code and to remove the worker(s) from the job, often without the indemnification required by law (cf. art. 50 *Ley Federal del Trabajo*). These proceedings are facilitated by the "understanding" between management and coopted or bribed union leaders and/or *obreros de confianza* and, on the local level by the orientation of the conciliation and arbitration board which has favored the employer's point of view already for a long period of time.

Most of the dismissal cases concern workers who are suspected to have activist orientations or who have been involved in action related to the implementation of labor laws, problems of union democracy or changes in union affiliation from *blanco* to *rojo*. Opinion leaders, action leaders, etc., operating outside the company approved framework, run a serious risk of harassment and ultimate dismissal. Activists will be blacklisted as "undesirable individuals" not to be employed by any of the Monterrey industries. The often blatantly repressive dimension of the Monterrey "labor climate" illustrates the ample maneuvering room which management has vis-a-vis the workers in case of labor conflicts.[94] They can practically proceed at will, confident of the fact that in the last resort the conciliation and arbitration board and the courts will be on their side. The individual workers is left powerless and does not stand a chance. The following quote puts this situation into words:[95]

... I am one of the millions of exploited workers in this country asking for justice. We all know that the humble people are not listened to, but perhaps my plea will change the hearts of the leaders who instead of making politics should be defending the worker and not deceive him. At the moment they help the capitalist because they are well treated by him. Always when the worker claims something, they will call him an agitator and the capitalists, the government and the union leaders feel very offended ... In the company where I work we did not receive profit shares this year. The leaders said there were no profits and the government accepted, because they side with the capitalists and are paid off by them. The worker is forgotten, because from him they do not gain anything. Leaders and government have rendered us to the capitalist which means the end of the worker who lacks sufficient economic means. What can we do with our low wages and the high cost of living. In the absence of a decent government we will continue to be controlled by those who determine our misfortune ... I hope that many fellow workers will awake from their situation of lethargy and that we will turn into reality the real aspirations of those who made the Revolution, and about whom the government is talking so much.

---

[93] There are strong indications, that the new labor code, together with fiscal policies, credit provicions and social security regulations, give further support to the already strong trend toward concentration in the economic sector, forcing the labor intensive, more "traditional" medium and small-sized industries into oblivion. Cf. "Trágica Agonía del Pequeño Industrial," in *Oigamé*, February 5, 1970.

[94] For some examples see: *Oigamé*, August 1, 11, 15, 22 and 29, 1970, and October 24, 1970.

[95] Letter to the editor, *Oigamé*, September 26, 1970.

3.4.3. The ideology of entrepreneurial control

The control mechanisms of a paternalist and reformist nature are being "covered" by an ideology which, especially in its formulation by representatives of the Cuauthemoc group, has achieved its greatest consistency and clarity. The orientation of this segment of the Monterrey entrepreneurial sector towards labor management relations and "social problems" in general, has been inspired by the social-Christian doctrines figuring in the various papal encyclicals that have appeared since the end of the 19th century (Rerum Novarum, Quadragesimo Anno, Mater et Magistra). The Fundidora group on the other hand, at least its more traditional representatives, have based themselves primarily on the liberal perspective as contained in the Juárez tradition, which carried an anticlerical tone. Their paternalist measures were rather founded in an attitude of *noblesse oblige*, entailing a feudalistic preoccupation of the enlightened aristocracy or would-be aristocracy with the well being of its servants. This attitude was certainly present with the members of the old Prieto dynasty. It has persisted in the statements on the special responsibilities of the entrepreneur with regard to the elimination of "the conditions that prevent the organized and responsible participation of everybody in the process of development." These responsibilities are his because "he is conscious of his social duties and traditionally has a participation in the process of solving the problems of the community. It is his honored duty to realize social justice within his company. While planning his business he has always the well being of the community in mind."[96]

The social-Christian doctrine on "the social problem" has not only inspired the ideology of the entrepreneurs of the Cuauthemoc group, but even found its way to the Declaration of Principles of the management dominated labor federation F.N.S.I. An outstanding element is the idea that private property should not be abolished, as Marx suggested. On the contrary, in order to promote social justice, it should be spread over an ever increasing number of people "serving human dignity and furthering the life chances of the individual" (Rerum Novarum and Quadragesimo Anno, 1952: 128, 116). Class struggle is rejected and the "cooperation between management and labor in an atmosphere of mutual understanding" is emphasized (Ibid, 97). The responsibility of the manager for the general well being of his workers is asserted, ultimately to be secured through the formation of property. This all should be done in an atmosphere of Christian charity. Finally, on the important subject of state intervention in the economy, the entrepreneurs share the encyclicals opinion only to approve of such action in case of obvious failure of the private sector to take care of its "responsibilities." In principle the state should be subsidary to private initiative (Ibid, 113 ff, 139 ff).

---

[96] Humberto Lobo. "Las Responsibilidades del Empresario USEM." *Boletín COFIDE*, 4, 19, January 1970.

102

From these initial variations in ideological position among the Monterrey entrepreneurs, a number of common elements have emerged in their ideas on the structure of the company and the socioeconomic context in which it functions. Among these elements, the various expressions of a "unitary ideology" (cf. Hyman, 1972: 153 ff; Bendix, 1963: 282 ff) stand out. The company itself is viewed as an organic whole functioning on the basis of a harmony of purpose existing between the parts. The basic assumption is that the interests of management and labor are not contradictory but coincide to a great extent. Given this essentially harmonious perspective of the company structure, conflict is automatically relegated to the category of irrational behavior based on either ignorance, subversion by agitators or both. Obviously, this ideology has not only served to legitimize the entrepreneurs' policies before the workers, but also before the public at large. Especially with regard to their activities in other areas, the unitary ideology has managed to give these *fuerzas vivas* a comforting definition of their own role. This phenomenon can be discerned very clearly in the statements of the Monterrey entrepreneurs themselves. It constituted an underlying element in the earlier mentioned statement on "the social resposibilities of the entrepreneur." It takes an even more prominent place in the ideas of the leading representatives of the industrialist community, Garza and Sada. Both are concerned with the industrialists' extra-industrial role.

Alejandro Garza[97] emphasizes the problem of "social justice" which, according to him, can be achieved only through an emancipation process directed at the individual. The individual is the core and motor of societal development and should be allowed to operate unbridled. This social justice, together with respect for individual integrity, private property and related elements of the "good society" will find realization within "communities" that should be established under responsibility of the private entrepreneurs. This is what Garza calls the "social function" of the company. His further explanation of the role of private corporations in the process of development reveals an interesting ideological position in which liberal bourgeois and social-Christian ideas have been fused. In this context, he underlines the role of the individual, the work for the "common good," the importance of the free enterprise system which should function unchecked, responding to the market mechanism without government interference. In the perspective of Sada, the role of the entrepreneurs assumes almost utopian dimensions. Together with the institution of the private enterprise, they stand for "the preservation and continuation of human liberty." The one-sided emphasis on productivity and product quality should be replaced by "an emphasis on the well being of all employed by the company, thus serving the collective welfare in a wider sense, e.g. outside the company."[98] According to Garza, within the industrial

---

[97] Alejandro Garza L. "El Empresario y el Desarollo." *El Porvenir*, March 10, 1971.
[98] Roberto Sada. "La Producción Fabril es un Acto Social." *Oigamé*, February 14, 1970.

103

companies "structures should be created to encourage the self-realization of man."[99]

These ideas, it should be emphasized, form part of an ideology that to a great extent is "free floating," fulfills legitimizing and justifying functions with regard to the actual needs of control and has little or no prescriptive value with regard to actual behavior.[100]

4. CONCLUSION

Monterrey appears to be a case of succesful autonomous industrialization which accounts for its specialness, not only within the Mexican but also within a Third World context.

In this case of self-generated growth a number of macro factors that in other areas stifled independent growth, were conspicuously absent. We refer here to various dimensions of its situation of comparative isolation from a world economy, which in other Third World areas formed the framework for a dependent incorporation into the capitalist system[101].

In the Monterrey situation industrialization followed classical capitalist patterns independently, as it grew out of the commercial capitalism of the second half of the 19th century. Already during the industrial take-off, the industrial and financial sectors were fused and in subsequent years the concentration of ownership and control of the means of production assumed spectacular proportions.

The pattern of accumulation, distribution and allocation of the economic surplus which supported rapid industrialization, led to the creation of a rather idiosyncratic sociopolitical system. The class structure embodied extreme socioeconomic inequalities and had become increasingly polarized between the small cohesive, dynamic industrial bourgeoisie and the sizable proletarian and subproletarian classes. Even during the period of rapid economic expansion in the 1960's these classes suffered substantial setbacks in their income situation.

The efforts by the bourgeoisie to build an industrial bastion on the basis of existing regionalist tendencies, from which the central government could be challenged with regard to the objectives and means of its development policies, led to an increasing concern with the internal political dynamics of this regional powerbase. The important potential competitor for power, labor,

---

[99] Alejandro Garza L. "El Propósito y Sentido de la Libertad." *Oigamé*, June 6, 1970.

[100] The commentary of a supervisor of welfare programs in one of the family Garza Sada's factories (interviews April 1971) is revealing: "all this talk about the social responsibility and the *visión social* of the entrepreneur is *pura basura* (hogwash). They (the entrepreneurs) are all for it, as long as it does not cost them anything and serves their interests in a narrow way, but they have neatly turned down any proposal I know of, that would have benefitted the workers in a wider sense but would have cost the *patrón* some money."

[101] See Sutcliffe (1971: 343 ff) for an exposition on the consequences of the isolation factor for industrialization policy.

Figure 7: Basic tendencies of the Monterrey development process

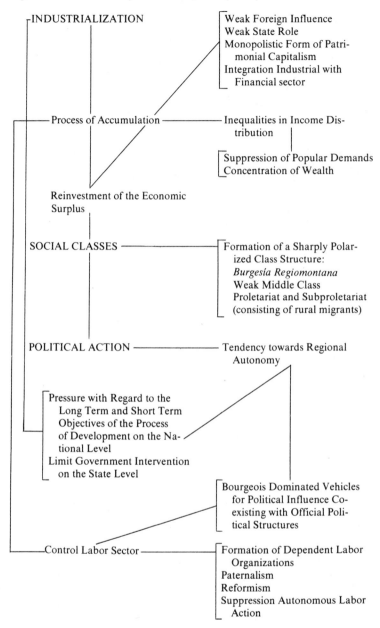

was neutralized as an autonomous political force through the creation of an elaborate system of cooptation and control. At the end of the 1960's and in the beginning of the 1970's, however, the beginnings of some labor unrest have appeared. The effectivenes of the complex of paternalist and reformist measures, legitimized by a well-developed ideology grafted on social-Christian and liberal bourgeois ideas and complemented with a series of overtly suppressive policies, may be put to a test. In this study, it is our intention to investigate, in four different industrial settings, the various worker reactions towards the dynamics of power and politics. The problem will be approached through the analysis of their work experience, working-class psychology and conditioning factors. This way we will get a closer look at those factors that, on a micro level, promote or hamper a direct translation of objectively existing inequities into a subjective feeling of discontent, influence the development of horizontal solidarities, stimulate or prevent autonomous class-based political action and that together, and on that level, condition the nature, extent and direction of the process of class formation.

CHAPTER V
THE INDUSTRIAL WORKERS

1. INTRODUCTION

Classical theory suggests the industrial proletariat to be the source of the dynamics in the class structure. But what is its real potential for change, especially in a situation as described before? The empirical study of work experience, working-class psychology and related factors should help to answer this question and give some "roots" to the more general discussion on the structural transformation of Mexican society.

The basic hypothesis involved in the study of these phenomena concerns the impact of "industrial setting". This factor refers to a number of interrelated aspects of the industrial environment: technological structure, division of labor, social organization and economic structure. Among these aspects, "technological structure" takes a primary position, conditioning the others. This relationship is not one of simple and straight determination and managerial ideas may be involved in the other aspects which may reduce the intercorrelations between all of them (Eldridge, 1968: 47). The technological structure of an industry, however, will define the general framework within which the division of labor, the social organization, and the economic structure can develop.

It will affect the division of labor where it conditions the pattern of work organization, defining the variety of tasks and corresponding skill levels that are needed to keep the production process going.

The social organization of the working environment likewise will depend to an important extent upon the underlying pattern in which the elements, man-material-tools, have crystallized. Its impact on the size and the layout of a factory is most obvious. Advances in mechanization call for a more differentiated work organization and inspire the development of an intricate and elaborate system of rules governing the working situation. These rules concern not only worker management relations, but also those between the workers themselves as they condition the frequency and the range of interaction between them (Sayles, 1958: 72).

In a capitalist economy, the technological structure of a plant influences greatly its status and development perspectives (and often its wage structure). This applies also to the Mexican situation, but in a more relative sense. Protectionist legislation may allow some archaic technologies to maintain profitable production. The ample supply of labor may interfere in the relationship between the economic status of the company and its wage structure.

"Industrial setting", as implied by the thesis outlined above, would constitute a basic factor differentiating the industrial labor force on a number of objective and subjective characteristics. In this study, it has been hypothesized as the primary explanatory variable behind variations in work experience and working-class psychology.[1] The hypothesis obviously has its roots in Marx's theses on the role of the pattern of organization of the productive forces. Its application to this study was further inspired by the work of Robert Blauner (1964). The methodological flaws of his book, that already been widely discussed (Glazer and Strauss, 1967), do not affect, in our opinion, the validity of his core hypothesis. In our study, its application has been extended from the problem of alienation to the phenomenon of class consciousness, again strongly supported by Marx himself.

The four settings offer a fair representation of the diversity and pluralism within the Monterrey industrial sector. They present distinct differences in technological structure, e.g. level of mechanization, rationalization of division of labor, bureaucratization of social organization, and in a lesser way characteristics of economic structure.

With "degree of mechanization of technology" as a basic classificatory variable, the settings can be located on a continuum ranging from manufacturing requiring relatively little mechanization and little standardization of production to manufacturing where a high degree of automation is involved. This classification comprises: (a) a craft technology with low levels of mechanization and standardization (print shops); (b) a machine-tending technology, characterized by a higher degree of mechanization and a greater degree of standardization of its work processes, the workers "minding" the machines (textile mill); (c) an assembly line technology, characterized by a highly rationalized work organization (automobile factory); and (d) continuous-process production, characterized by a high degree of automation (chemical plant).

These four settings do not necessarily represent the fixed stages of a predetermined unilinear process of industrial evolution. Historical experience does suggest the presence of a general tendency towards an increase in level of mechanization of the entire industrial structure. This tendency, however, shouls not be equated with a unilinear process of technological evolution (Blauner, 1964: 8).

The selected factories approached the technological types in their most pure

[1] Kuhn (1969: 166), on the basis of a comparative study of workers in the rubber tire and electrical equipment industries in the U.S.A. over the period 1947-1959, concludes that: "technology determines the ability of workers to press their demands and greatly affects their willingness to formulate demands." I agree with him on the importance of technological structure as an explanatory variable but have great difficulty accepting it, like Kuhn does, as a factor straightly determining the others.

108

form. That is to say, the respective technology dominated virtually the entire production process. Its variation was minimal within each plant. Thus, not only homogeneity could be achieved in the internal composition of the technological variable, but also in its effects on the other aspects of the setting.

Within the picture of general industrial development in Monterrey, the selected setting all belonged to the dynamic branches of industry in the area. This applies even to the textile industry, which declined in employment but increased its productivity quite substantially due to an extensive modernization of the industry.

2. THE FOUR INDUSTRIAL SETTINGS

2.1. *The Print Shops*

Craft industries share some technological characteristics, among which the lack of standardization of the product, the relatively low level of mechanization, and the rather high proportion of skilled personnel stand out (Blauner, 1964: 35 ff).[2] In the print shops, much of the work is still done by hand. The nature of the product clearly imposes limits on the technology that can be employed. This product may be books, newspapers, magazines or commercial printed matter, but is is constantly changing from day to day, which rules out the mechanization or automation that require a standardized product.

All the shops, except one, had experienced recent expansion and had been extensively modernized, as a consequence of the sharp increase in demand for printed matter during the economic boom. They had installed new machinery, and all but one were housed in new or rebuilt quarters. The shops had been in existence for an average period of 33 years, the youngest 15, and the oldest 60 years.

This modernization process has required a substantial capital investment per production worker. The equity capital investment now totalled 25,000,000 pesos (1971), the individual shops ranging between 1.25 and 8.5 million, on a total of 475 men employed: 130 employees and 345 workers. Yet, manual work involving traditional skills has remained very important. In fact, in only one shop, which printed a newspaper, a series of operations involving the typesetting process had been removed from the worker, and were done by machines operating with a considerable degree of automation. The fragmentation and subdivision of job tasks, typical of modern factory technology, is absent, and most jobs encompass a variety of operations. This emphasis on traditional skill has resulted in a relatively high proportion of skilled workers in the labor force. In the selected shops, 70.4 percent of the manual workers were skilled craftsmen, 17 percent were semiskilled, and 12.6 percent unskilled workers. Compare the automobile factory, which had 31 percent and the chemical plant which had 45 percent of skilled workers.

---

[2] A still highly valuable analysis of work in these settings is given by Veblen (1964: 231 ff).

The semiskilled workers form the apprentices who pass through a rather long learning period, during which the specific skills of the trade are mastered. The printing-pressmen among them are required to perfect their skills in one of the technical schools in the area, in addition to the training on the job (Hacia una Planeación, 1970: 30).

The relatively simple division of labor and the absence of fractionization of individual tasks implied by a craft technology is further illustrated by the rather simple system of job classification. Even the biggest shop that produced a considerable variety of printing products did not have more than 15 different job categories (compare: textiles, 47; automobiles 38). Most workers have an intimate knowledge of the various tasks in the trade, and often occupy different positions in the production process in the course of their careers. Especially in the small shops, a relative lack of job specialization can be noted. The printers often assist each other to get the job done and alternately set type, work on linotype operations, or run the presses.

The selected printing establishments employed an average of 59 men (43 workers and 16 employees). The smallest shop had 13 workers and 7 employees; the biggest had 89 workers and 51 employees. The variable of shop size undoubtedly has conditioned the evolution of worker management relations (cf. Lipset, 1956: 172). In the small shops, the *patrón* has ample opportunity to cultivate personal relations with his personnel and to promote their identification with the enterprise, while at the same time exercising control over their activities. In the larger shops, such direct and unmediated relations between the *patrón* and his workers are harder to realize. Yet, even in the smaller shops, the high skill level of the workers has supported their power position vis-a-vis the *patrón*, limited his power alternatives, and added a dimension to the power relations between the two parties that is lacking in other types of small-sized craft industries.

2.2. The Textile Mill

The textile industry in Mexico, as in other parts of Latin America, has been characteristic of the early stages of industrialization. The industry already existed during the colonial period. At that time, it was a craft industry, first dominated by artisans, later organized in the notorious *obrajes* (cf. Shaw, 1977). In the second half of the 19th century, the large-scale textile industry was organized. In this industry, many of the traditional skills had been made redundant by the machine system.

The selected factory had been founded in 1874 as part of the first industrialization effort in Nuevo León. It was located near three small villages that have since become part of metropolitan Monterrey. Yet, these villages have remained rather homogeneous company communities, in which the greater part of the population for generations has earned its living in this factory and in a second textile mill, founded in 1865, and located just a few miles away. Both factories have since been modernized.

This process of modernization of the old textile mill started in 1952 as part of a coordinated national effort to make the traditional textile industry more competitive and technologically up to date. The process took 12 years to complete. In this period, a complete new factory was built next to the ruins of the old one. The level of mechanization was improved. Semiautomatic spinning frames and automatic looms were installed. The work force was gradually reduced in size. Many workers were retired from the factory, although the number of looms increased from 175 in the old factory to 721 in the new one. In recent years, the company also founded a synthetics division which, however, has been organized in two separate plants, each with independent legal status.

Our research has concentrated on the mother plant, which still is producing mainly cotton textiles.

The present equity capital runs close to 20,000,000 pesos (1969). The mill employs 1,032 men: 292 employees and 740 workers (1968). Data on the total capital investment are not available. However, it can be assumed, given the size of the equity capital of the respective companies, that the size of the capital investment per production worker is lower than either in the print shops, the automobile factory, or the chemical plant. On this basis, the textile mill would have an investment of 27,000 pesos per production worker, the print shops 72,000, the automobile factory, 40,000 and the chemical plant 163,000 pesos.

Traditionally, the setting has a low skill distribution. The fact that 75 percent of the workers have been classified als "skilled" is the result of the specific system of job ranking in the industry, prescribed by the collective labor contract and does not necessarily indicate the presence of high levels of technical skills. The proportion of medium-level technicians is small: they number less than 2 percent of the total work force (printing 9, automobiles 10, and chemicals: 15 percent). The entire production process in the mill has been intensively rationalized, permitted by a high degree of standardization of the product. Most jobs are routine, largely automatic, and require speed and alertness rather than skill. This is a general characteristic of jobs in the textile industry (cf. Blauner, 1964: 59).

The job of the average textile worker is to tend a large number of spinning frames, looms, or other machinery. He is not just responsible for the operation of one machine, but has to take care of a whole series of identical spinning, weaving, knitting, or other machines. He has to adapt his activities and movements to the technical process, lest the production process be interrupted and his own production quota endangered. The high degree of rationalization is further promoted by the fact that, since the speed of the various machines is known, the maximum potential production can be determined. As a consequence, all operations within the production process have been defined as part of the collective contracts in the textile industry, together with the time it takes to fulfill each of them (up to tenths of a second), the various production quotas, and their remuneration.

The selected factory is a totally integrated cotton mill. It has a spinning, weaving, knitting, and finishing section. This means that every part of the entire production process, from raw cotton to finished products (battist, poplin, fashion fabrics, shirts, etc.), is carried out within this plant. The spinning and weaving sections have most workers. In the old factory, before modernization changed the picture, their work used to be highly skilled and especially the weavers were responsible for a variety of operations in the production of cloth. Nowadays, however, the work organization has become extremely subdivided. The system of job classification in the mill includes no less than 47 categories. The machines have reduced most jobs to a series of rather simple repetitive tasks. Presently, the most skilled and prestigious jobs are those of the mechanics who do the maintenance and repair work, and keep the machinery going.

The mill is one of the biggest of a branch of manufacturing that has declined in relative importance over the last decades. As a result of the process of reorganization of the textile industry in the 1950's and 1960's, only a few large enterprises have remained. In terms of value added, they fell in importance from the fifth place among the manufacturing industries in 1955 to twelfth place in 1965. The industry's share in the employment of the industrial working population of Nuevo León dropped from 8.4 percent in 1955 to 3.0 percent in 1965, and it is expected to decrease further to around 1.0 percent in 1980. The worker productivity, however, has risen considerably and is expected to rise another 200 percent in the period from 1965 to 1980, as a result of further mechanization and automation (Hacia una Planeación, 1970: 84).

In the selected mill, this process of modernization had been concluded. The employment situation has settled down after the many early retirements of the reorganization period that had caused a considerable unrest among the personnel.

2.3. The Automobile Factory

The automobile industry is a rather recent phenomenon in Mexico. Car-assembling was introduced on a rather small scale during World War II as part of the policy of import substitution. In this period, most of the parts still came from foreign suppliers. On the Mexican industrial scene, automobile manufacturing is a typically modern industry with a greatly diversified division of labor and a high degree of rationalization and efficiency. It has become concentrated in a small number of large firms, among which Automex (Toluca), Datsun (Cuernavaca), Volkswagen (Puebla), and the Monterrey automobile conglomerate dominate the sector.

The Mexican government has promoted the vertical integration of this industry through the protectionist measures of its import-substitution policy: 60 percent of the total value of the components of an automobile have to represent parts of Mexican manufacturers; 40 percent can be imported.

Automobile manufacturing has three stages of production: first, the manufacturing of specific components;[3] second, the subassembly into engines, transmissions, rear axles, bodies, etc.; and third, the final assembly of the vehicle. Not all stages are combined within the auto industry itself. In the U.S.A., 20 to 25 percent of the parts come from industries outside the automobile industry, and another 25 to 40 percent come from suppliers of parts and components. The rest of the value added is accounted for by the automobile industry in a more narrow sense (Behrman, 1972: 140).

The final assembly operation is more labor intensive than the manufacturing of components. This stage accounts for about 45 percent of the total labor input in the industry, but only for about 18 percent of the capital inputs. The manufacturing of the motor, chassis, and suspension requires only 33 percent of the labor and almost 50 percent of the capital. The body manufacturing takes around 22 percent of the labor input and 33 percent of the capital (Behrman, 1972: 141).

The selected factory forms part of a conglomerate dominating the sector and having a total equity capital investment of over 50,000,000 pesos (1971). Within the conglomerate a considerable degree of vertical integration has been achieved. The company started after World War II as a shop manufacturing trailers, and expanded to its present size in less than two decades. The assembly division, producing jeeps and pickups, vans, trucks and trailers, and tractors and buses, is served by four enterprises, each with independent legal status, that belong to the parts division. This latter division covers the first two stages of automobile production. It produces the chassis, bodies, and most of the component parts, except for the engines that are entirely imported. The parts division also supplies accessories to automobile plants in other parts of the country.

The assembly division employed 1,777 people (1971), 540 employees and 1,270 workers, and it represents a very labor intensive part of the conglomerate. The study has concentrated on the workers in the assembly plant, because, here, the distinctive technology of the industry has been most clearly expressed. This technology has been conditioned by the standardization of the final product, but even more so by the standardization of the individual parts and components that are put together to form the completed product (cf. Blauner, 1964: 90 ff).

This process, during which the parts are combined into a final product, takes place along an assembly line that takes the cars past the stations of the workers. This is, in fact, the final stage of production, and the other operations

---

[3] The total number of separate components of a car averages 3,000 (over 20,000 if each nut and bolt is counted separately). The materials range from iron and steel to plastics, cotton, copper, lead, zinc, glass, rubber, and various chemical-based products (Behrman, 1972: 140). A problem has been that the local suppliers of parts are by no means all locally owned. Some are affiliates of U.S. companies, and others are jointly owned with local investors (op cit.,: 57).

113

in the factory are geared to fill its need. Slightly less than 30 percent of the factory work force, works on the line itself.

The organization of the assembly line is somewhat removed from the extremely rationalized conveyor belt form of production that can be found in the large U.S. automobile plants. First, it has been organized on a much smaller scale. The output is not one car every minute, but a few jeeps, pick-ups, trucks, tractors and buses a day. The line, itself, is small and not very complicated. It consists of a rail on which the automobiles-to-be are pushed past the various stations. Second, the work process has been less subject to extreme subdivision, the jobs have been less fractionized. There still is a considerable amount of manual work done, in which each job includes a series of (standardized) operations within the specialization of the respective worker, and not just one single operation. Those tasks that are typical of extreme assembly line conditions, and that consist exclusively of the one-minute operation, are rather scarce. This situation is further exemplified by the fact that, in spring of 1971, the line was working below capacity due to a lack of *skilled* labor. Large-scale assembly operations, as can be found in the U.S. and European car factories, in most cases can be broken down into simple elementary tasks requiring few skills.[4]

The Monterrey line assembles what Friedmann has called a "social line," where the pace of work is less intense and the team element of the line has been more emphasized (Friedmann, 1950: 245). This type of assembly line should be distinguished from the "strain line" where the work is fast, tense, and nervous. The extent to which as assembly line shows social line characteristics appears, however, very much a function of the scale of operations in the respective plant. It follows that the assembly line in the Monterrey factory may lose most of its social line characteristics with any substantial increase in production.

The automobile industry, at least its assembly division, has been called a typically "modern" industry. This characterization has not been motivated by the presence of an elaborate, sophisticated machinery. The textile industry undoubtedly could be characterized as more "advanced" in that respect (cf. Blauner, 1964: 95). In the Monterrey assembly plant, the machinery is less complex and virtually limited to small sized power tools (drills, screwdrivers, welding, and soldering equipment, etc.) that are handled by the workers themselves. The basic manual operations, however, are standardized, due to the highly rationalized organization of work assignments. In these aspects of the organization of the production process, the main differences with the other types of technological structures are given (cf. Van Doorn, 1963: 32).

---

[4] Touraine defines the assembly line as "a type of work organization through which the various operations (of the production process) have been reduced to the same duration or to a multiple of that duration and are executed without interruption between them in a process continuing in time and space" (Touraine, 1955: 40). A good analysis of the effects of assembly-line technology in the automobile industry is offered by Turner et al. (1967).

The proportion of skilled workers in the factory was 31 percent; 44 percent were classified as semiskilled, 25 percent as unskilled. The semiskilled category contains not only medium-skilled personnel, but also the apprentices passing through a learning period. The unskilled category contains the operators who lack any kind of formal training, and have simple repetitive tasks. The division of labor in the factory is rather diversified, as exemplified by the system of job classification that includes 38 different categories, among them the general category of "operator," which stands for a wide variety of unskilled jobs.

The economic situation of the automobile industry is rather favorable. In the Mexican situation, it is still very much a growth industry experiencing a period of rapid expansion on a strongly protected internal market. The Monterrey company evolved from a small enterprise to a big industry in less than twenty years. In that period, it opened service and repair facilities in all parts of the republic and even expanded its operations to other Latin American nations. (Argentina, Chile, Peru, Paraguay and Guatemala). In this story of success, the only sour note was struck by the Borgward adventure, e.g. the effort to produce a 100 percent Mexican car using the old German Borgward car plant which had been dismantled and reinstalled in the Monterrey area.[5] The company was involved in the management of Borgward, and it had a minority financial interest in the plant. The effort, however, failed. Borgward went bankrupt after a period of operation of less than two years.

The company is virtually entirely Mexican owned and in essence it has remained a family enterprise. These is no foreign majority interest in any of the plants or subplants that form part of the conglomerate. In most Mexican industries the use of foreign technology almost automatically implies foreign financial interests in the companies concerned, following the rule that foreign firms will not transfer technology without having control of its use. The Monterrey enterprise has not followed this trend. It has preferred to dedicate great attention to the development of its own technology and to the training of its own technicians who supervise the application of technology to local needs and to buy technology and managerial assistance only if absolutely necessary.[6] The company was spending 12 percent of its monthly payroll on research (1971).[7]

2.4. The Chemical Plant

The application of continuous-process production technologies has grown rapidly in Mexico in recent decades. This growth has been identified, in

[5] Cf. "Origen, Nacimiento y Muerta de la Fábrica Automotriz Borgward." in: Oigamé, July 6, 1970.
[6] In the case of the Borgward plant, they enlisted the technical knowhow of the Spanish automobile firm Pegaso (Oigamé, July 6, 1970).
[7] This figure included the money spent on market research and similar activities. The technological research, however, accounted for the major portion of this item.

particular, with the expansion of the chemical industry, an expansion which in the 1960's has assumed "boom" characteristics. The differences between the industrial setting in which this technology has been implemented and the other settings are clearly marked (Blauner, 1964: 124 ff). The entire production process, here, has been regulated by automatic devices permitting a continuous flow in which the raw materials pass through various types of operations, and are transformed into different final products. The level of mechanization is very high, and the largely automated machine system has replaced most categories of manual workers. Those manual workers who continue to be employed fulfill job tasks that are different from those required under other technologies. They do not handle the product themselves, and it passes through a series of machine dominated operations. The workers only fulfill the tasks of checking the control instruments, occasionally adjusting a valve or other device regulating the flow of the materials, its temperature, pressure, or speed, insofar as this cannot be done automatically. A considerable number of workers also perform maintenance tasks on the elaborate machinery.

The chemical industry is a very capital intensive industry, and the investment per production worker is higher than in any other branch of manufacturing. The management of the selected plant estimated the investment per production worker at 300,000 pesos. The total capital investment amounted to 157 million pesos (1969). Its productivity in terms of the value added, is superior to those of production workers in the other industries. The skill distribution of the industry is higher than in the other three settings included in the study.[8]

The work force of the selected plant had 45 percent skilled workers, 35 percent semiskilled and 20 percent unskilled workers. Among all people employed, 15 percent were classified as medium-level technicians. The total number of employed numbered 1,316 people: 351 employees and 965 workers (1971). Given the present scarcity of certain categories of skilled labor in the Monterrey area, the management has become particularly interested in creating a permanent and stable work force. They have given considerable attention to the education and technical training of the personnel working in production and maintenance. This education and training work has been oriented to the acquisition of specific company needed skills. Programs serving wider educational goals have met management opposition.

The plant represents the mother plant of a conglomerate of chemical enterprises that form part of the Cuauthemoc group. This chemical branch started shortly after World War II, has experienced meteoric expansion since, and is now leading the sector on the regional as well as on the national level.

---

[8] The capital intensive nature of production is further illustrated by the considerable proportion of the monthly payroll spent on maintenance of the machinery, which varies among the subplants from 23 to 37 percent (compare: printing 4 percent, textiles 4 percent, automobiles 6 percent).

116

The conglomerate, itself, has a considerable degree of internal decentralization. It consists of three divisions that produce industrial chemicals, synthetic fibers and polyethelene, cellophane, and other transparent packing materials. In each division, several companies and subcompanies (each with independent legal status) are working. This study concerns the mother company which includes the following subcompanies:

(a) a plant producing heavy industrial chemicals, counting six subplants, each producing a different chemical;

(b) a plant producing rayon, and

(c) a plant producing polyethelene and cellophane.

The last two plants have been automated to a great extent. The work is mostly clean for all worker categories. The heavy-chemicals plants do have some dirty unskilled jobs where the bad smells, fumes, high temperatures and spillovers create a nuisance to those working close to the plant. Most of the work in both sectors, however, fits the category of the typical chemical operator: checking control panels and other automatic regulating devices. Little of it is physical or manual. The variety of tasks that are part of each job is considerably greater than in the textile and automobile industry. The presence of a large number of different plants and chemical production processes within one factory complex makes for a rather diversified work environment. This applies to the section of production as well as to the maintenance section. The number of workers per subplant is rather small (compare: the company has a total of 965 workers for the eight subplants and three shifts per 24 hours). Most of the production is run by work teams of modest size.

Blauner has pointed to the stability of employment in continuous process industries (Blauner, 1964: 128). His reasoning is that, in this type of industry, the volume of production is mainly determined by the technical capacity of the plant, and not that much by the number of workers that are needed to operate and maintain it. Fluctuations in production do not lead necessarily to fluctuations in the number of employed workers that has already been reduced by automation to the absolute minimum. In these settings, labor tends to become a fixed production cost, instead of a variable cost (Ibid.). This factor also plays in the Monterrey situation, but, of course, only in a general sense. Its relevance to the job security of the individual worker strongly depends on managerial decisions, a factor not mentioned by Blauner.

The economic future of the industry is very bright. The demand for chemicals on the internal market is rapidly expanding, and the Monterrey enterprise has a period of expansion ahead. A few years ago, the company amplified its operations, beginning the export of some of its products to Central and South America. The conglomerate has some foreign participation. The big synthetic fibers plant (not included in the investigation) has a participation of 40 percent Dutch capital (AKZO), tied in with Dutch technical assistance and the use of Dutch patents. The other plants, however, are genuinely Mexican-owned.

117

3. WORK EXPERIENCE AND WORKING CLASS PSYCHOLOGY: AN ANALYSIS[9] OF
SOME DETERMINANTS

3.1. *Introduction*

The study of intra- and interindustry variations in work experience and
working-class psychology is almost as old as the process of industrialization
itself. The thesis on the explanatory value of "industrial setting" with regard to
these differences has its roots in Marx's work itself. So have a number of other
variables that will be explored, next to those suggested by some more recent
studies of the labor movement in Latin America.

Most of the analysis will be quantitative, in particular in the case of those
variables and attributes that have an individual reference. Those factors that
move on the company level, such as the characteristics of the union, the
company labor policy and specific forms of entrepreneurial and/or official
control, will be explored through an analysis of a more qualitative nature.[10]

3.2. *The Influence of Industrial Setting*

Our core hypothesis concerning the influence of "industrial setting" more
specifically concerns the following:

The four industrial settings will show significant differences in work experience and working class psychology to the extent that:

(a)   The printers and chemical workers will show a less estranging work
experience and a weaker working class psychology than the textile workers
and automobile workers.

(b)   The automobile workers will show a more estranging work experience
and a stronger working-class psychology than the textile workers.

The direction of the relationship between industrial setting and the dependent variables flows the previous analysis of the concrete effects, by four types
of technological structure, on the characteristics of work, work environment,
and work conditions. Here, the subjective reflection of these effects upon the
individual workers is hypothesized to follow the same course.

Work experience: The various dimensions of work experience, except for
isolation, are most strongly represented among the textile workers. Next come
the automobile workers, the chemical workers and the printers in that order. A
considerable amount of variation between and within the industrial settings,

---

[9] In the text we will often refer to the orginal, more elaborate analysis of the material (Vellinga,
1975) on which the exposition in sections 3 and 4 is based.
[10] The discrepancies between the logic of reasoning here (linear) and the logic of argument in the
other chapters of the book (dialectic) are more apparant than real (the more if the dialectic is
primarily considered a heuristic category), and go back to contradictions inherent to any Marxist
inspired empirical research, that even Marx himself was not able to solve (cf. Bottomore, 1966).

TABLE 15: Relative importance of work experience dimensions, by four industrial settings.

work experience dimensions		industrial settings				
		printing	textiles	automobiles	chemicals	N
domination	1 (high)	13.0	30.0	9.0	20.0	77
	2	20.0	23.6	14.0	13.6	75
	3	24.0	30.0	39.0	34.6	134
	4 (low)	43.0	16.4	38.0	31.8	134
		100.0	100.0	100.0	100.0	420
fractioni- zation	1 (high)	7.0	20.0	22.0	14.5	67
	2	17.0	39.1	12.0	18.2	92
	3	41.0	28.2	41.0	37.3	154
	4 (low)	35.0	12.7	25.0	30.0	107
		100.0	100.0	100.0	100.0	420
isolation	1 (high)	32.0	15.5	34.0	34.5	121
	2	50.0	61.8	57.0	52.7	233
	3	18.0	21.8	9.0	12.8	65
	4 (low)	−	0.9	−	−	1
		100.0	100.0	100.0	100.0	420
distancia- tion	1 (high)	16.0	31.8	31.0	18.2	102
	2	28.0	30.9	26.0	31.8	123
	3	40.0	34.6	36.0	40.9	159
	4 (low)	16.0	2.7	7.0	9.1	36
		100.0	100.0	100.0	100.0	420
overall work ex- perience	1 (high)	4.0	16.4	11.0	8.2	42
	2	42.0	58.1	38.0	42.7	191
	3	53.0	25.5	51.0	49.1	186
	4 (low)	1.0	−	−	−	1
		100.0	100.0	100.0	100.0	420

however, does exist. Multiple discriminant analysis[11] has been used to investigate the pattern of these variations and test the corehypothesis.

Among the four work experience dimensions, only domination appears to be significantly related to industrial setting. Its presence is most pronounced among the textile workers. This may be related to the extensive modernization of the textile mill which has resulted in a much higher degree of mechanization, a faster work pace and, apparently, a greater physical and mental pressure upon those participating in the work process.

[11] The stepwise version (program BMD 07M) was used, treating the four industrial settings as four groups and investigating the relative contribution of each of the work experience and working-class psychology subindices to a discriminant function (cf. Cooley and Lohnes, 1971: 116-123). In this way the significance of the group separations on the basis of these variables could be determined.

119

Together the dimensions fail to predict the factor of industrial setting satisfactorily. Only among the textiles workers, substantial numbers (56.3 percent) were classified correctly.

In all four industrial settings together, the correctly classified count no more than 146 individuals or 34.7 percent.

Among the settings, machine tending technology is predicted best, followed by craft technology, assembly line technology and continuous process production. The number of incorrectly classified individuals, however, is rather high, expecially in the chemical plant. Furthermore, the direction of the relationship deviates from the predicted pattern. On the basis of the results of the analysis, the hypotheses can be rejected, as far as the relationship between industrial setting and work experience is concerned.

TABLE 16: Relative importance of the work experience dimensions predicting industrial setting

setting number	dimension entered	F value
1	domination	10.209*
2	fractionization	6.739
3	isolation	6.185
4	distanciation	2.215

* significant at the .05 level

TABLE 17: Percentages of the industrial settings classified correctly according to the four work experience dimensions*

a priori clas-sification	a posteriori classification									
	printing		textiles		automo-biles		chemicals			
	N	%	N	%	N	%	N	%	N	%
printing	39	39.0	21	21.0	27	27.0	13	13.0	100	100
textiles	14	12.7	62	56.3	21	19.1	13	11.9	110	100
automobiles	30	30.0	29	29.0	30	30.0	11	11.0	100	100
chemicals	35	31.8	32	29.1	28	25.5	15	13.6	110	100

* these dimensions are: domination, fractionization, isolation and distanciation

Working-class psychology: The presence of the working-class psychology dimensions, except for awareness, is also most pronounced among the textile workers. The printers, automobile workers, and the chemical workers follow in this order. The automobile workers form an interesting case. Their class identification and awareness are relatively "high," their quantitative and qualitative participation in the union are, however, exceptionally low. As will be shown later on, this phenomenon is related to the critical orientation of the automobile workers towards their *blanco* union, which has created a certain duality in their working-class psychology between the more classist dimensions (class identification and awareness) and the union participation dimensions.

120

TABLE 18: Relative importance of working-class psychology dimensions by four industrial settings

working-class psychology dimensions		industrial settings				N
		printing	textiles	automobiles	chemicals	
class identification	1 (high)	60.0	60.9	66.0	42.7	240
	2 (low)	40.0	39.1	34.0	57.3	180
	1 (high)	10.0	16.4	33.0	8.2	70
awareness	2	51.0	50.9	47.0	45.4	204
	3 (low)	39.0	32.7	20.0	46.4	146
quantitative union participation	1 (high)	31.6	23.6	6.4	9.9	58
	2	61.4	75.5	35.1	38.4	183
	3 (low)	7.0	0.9	58.5	51.7	107
qualitative union participation	1 (high)	29.8	20.7	9.5	16.2	61
	2	36.8	46.2	18.0	34.0	118
	3 (low)	33.4	33.1	72.5	49.8	169
overall working-class psychology	1 (high)	18.0	24.5	7.0	5.5	58
	2	33.0	63.7	65.0	41.8	214
	3 (low)	49.0	11.8	28.0	52.7	148

The tendency among the industrial settings to crystallize into four distinct groups as far as the working-class psychology of their workers is concerned, is rather weak. Among the four dimensions, quantitative union participation and awareness are significantly related to industrial setting. Together, they predict better than in the case of working experience, but still the results are not impressive. Among the textile and automobile workers more than half of the individuals are classified correctly, but the total number in all settings does not count more than 195, or 46 percent. The predicted pattern does not appear. The only striking result is that, in both cases (work experience and working-class psychology), machine tending technology is predicted best. The hypothesis has not been confirmed. Given the considerable proportion of individuals incorrectly classified, it can be concluded that working-class psychology is weakly related to industrial setting in the case of machine tending and assembly line technologies, and unrelated in the case of the craft industry and continuous process production.

TABLE 19: Relative importance of the working-class psychology dimensions predicting industrial setting

step number	dimensions entered	F value
1	quantitative union participation	42.655*
2	awareness	10.769**
3	qualitative union participation	8.135
4	class identification	2.667

* significant at the .01 level
**significant at the .05 level

TABLE 20: Proportion of the industrial settings classified correctly according to the four working-class psychology dimensions*

a priori clas-sification	a posteriori classification									
	printing		textiles		automo-biles		chemicals			
	N	%	N	%	N	%	N	%	N	%
printing	43	43.0	33	33.0	10	10.0	14	14.0	100	100
textiles	4	3.6	59	53.6	21	19.0	26	23.8	110	100
automobiles	6	6.0	21	21.0	54	54.0	19	19.0	100	100
chemicals	19	17.3	17	15.4	35	31.9	39	35.4	110	100

* these dimensions are: class identification, awareness, quantitative union participation, qualitative union participation

Work experience and working-class psychology: The proportions of correctly classified individuals increase substantially when the multiple effects of work experience and working-class psychology are taken into account. Together they apparently reflect the syndrome of factors represented by industrial setting better than when taken apart.

TABLE 21: Relative importance of the work experience and working-class psychology dimensions predicting industrial setting

step number	dimensions entered	F value
1	quantitative union participation	42.655*
2	awareness	10.769**
3	domination	8.660**
4	qualitative union participation	7.959
5	fractionization	4.065
6	class identification	3.104
7	distanciation	1.038
8	isolation	0.661

* significant at the .01 level
**significant at the .05 level

The partial analyses suggest that, except for machine-tending technology, the working-class psychology variables contribute most to this outcome, but still the results are not easy to interpret. The two syndromes may be related to each other, third factors may be involved that relate to either one of the syndromes and account for yet unknown interaction effects, or the concept of industrial setting may have "container" characteristics that result in the neutralization of variables with a potential contribution to the significance of group differences.

This relationship between work experience and working-class psychology will be further explored in paragraph 4.2. First, the impact of other variables, hypothesized to relate to intra- and interindustry differences in work experience and working-class psychology, will be dealt with.

TABLE 22: Percentages of the industrial settings classified correctly according to the work experience and working-class psychology dimensions*

a priori clas-sification	a posteriori classification									
	printing		textiles		automo-bile		chemicals			
	N	%	N	%	N	%	N	%	N	%
printing	59	59.0	26	26.0	6	6.0	9	9.0	100	100
textiles	5	4.5	75	68.2	12	10.9	18	16.4	110	100
automobiles	8	8.0	17	17.0	59	59.0	16	16.0	100	100
chemicals	22	20.0	22	20.0	23	20.9	43	39.1	110	100

* these dimensions are resp.: domination, fractionization, isolation, distanciation and class identification, awareness, quantitative union participation, qualitative union participation.

3.3. Skill

The relationship between skill and work experience has been explained before. In most industries, skilled work does escape the subdivision, repetitiveness, and standardization of operations that characterize so many of the semiskilled and unskilled jobs. Most of these jobs require some intelligence, dexterity, and responsibility, and thus may escape some of the estranging tendencies of modern industrial life. The possible relation between skill and work satisfaction has been confirmed in several investigations (cf. Wyatt and Marriott, 1956: 54). Among the unskilled, poorly paid sectors of the industrial labor force the estranging tendencies may be further reinforced by those other factors that in a way are low-skill specific (f.e. frustration of ambition, stagnant mobility, etc.) (Moore, 1954: 228).

"Skill" traditionally has been viewed as a factor that would affect the economic and social position of the workers, their outlook, and potential for militance. The attention of the classical authors, like Engels, Lenin and Michels, was focused on the tendency among the skilled workers to develop into exclusive, privileged groups that would take an inactive position within the general labor movement. This "labor aristocracy" would be an easy target for the employer's efforts to integrate the workers within his company (Lenin, 1943: 92; Michels, 1949: 292-295; Engels, 1958: 368-371).

In fact, skilled workers were in the forefront of the labor movement during the early period of industrialization. In Western Europe, and also in the United States, their craft unions and mutual aid societies took a vanguard position. With the growth of big industry and the emergence of the mass industrial unions, their dominant role began to weaken. Former craft union leaders continued, however, to function in leadership positions in the general labor movement.

In Mexico, skilled workers equally played a dominant role in the beginning phase of the labor movement. Their activities focused on the mutual aid and cooperative element in the movement. When these elements were replaced by mass organization, their role got more into the background.

123

The thesis that, within the working class, skilled workers would tend to support more conservative political positions, based on their superior socioeconomic status, inspired considerable comparative politicosociological research in the 1960's beginning with Lipset (1963: 230 ff). Some supported the thesis that the skilled are the basis of the more status quo oriented politics of the working class. Others, basing themselves mainly on data concerning German and Swedish workers (Segerstedt, 1954), called this proposition into question. The debate was not settled (cf. Miller and Riesman, 1961; Lipsitz, 1964 and 1965; Hamilton, 1965, 1965a and 1967). The scarce Latin American data offer some support to the first mentioned position (and thus to the classical thesis), ascribing relatively moderate political positions to skilled workers (Zeitlin, 1970: 91 ff). The basis for this phenomenon, however, needs a more systematic analysis, also against the background of the observation of Landsberger that Latin American organized labor, skilled and unskilled, in its totality shares such orientation (Landsberger, 1967: 264).

With regard to our study, the following hypotheses on the relationship between skill, work experience and working-class psychology can be formulated:

(a)   there is a significant relationship between degree of skill and work experience, controlling for the impact of industrial setting: that is, the more highly skilled the workers, the less estranging their work experience; and

(b)   there is a significant relationship between degree of skill and working class psychology, controlling for the impact of industrial setting: that is the more highly skilled the workers, the weaker their working-class psychology is going to be.

The analysis[12] shows indeed significant differences between the industrial settings in overall work experience and working-class psychology when the variable of skill is taken into account. In the case of the work experience syndrome, the main contributions are made by the domination and fractionization dimensions. The significance of the relationship between skill and working-class psychology, resides mainly with the variables of quantitative and qualitative union participation.

A further analysis of the respective tables (cf. Vellinga, 1975: 311 ff) shows the predicted direction of the relationship with work experience only present in the case of the automobile workers, and among highly skilled workers in the other settings. The prediction contained in the second hypothesis has to be rejected. The data actually point toward the opposite direction. Working-class psychology tends to increase in strength with skill, again with the exception of the highly skilled.

Those dimensions contributing most strongly to the significance of the relationship between skill and working-class psychology concern the quantity

---

[12] Using analysis of covariance (program BMD 04V), with "industrial setting" as a classificatory variable, the work experience and working-class psychology indices as dependent variables, and "skill" as independent variable.

124

TABLE 23: Skill, work experience and working-class psychology for all four industrial settings.

variable	F-value*
work experience	11.941***
domination	10.871***
fractionization	11.729***
isolation	3.899
distanciation	6.021
working-class psychology	19.603***
class identification	3.839
awareness	5.695
quantitative union participation	33.601**
qualitative union participation	19.603***

* degrees of freedom 3 and 415
**significant at the .01 level
***significant at the .05 level

and quality of union participation.[13] The dimensions that have a more "militant" reference carry little weight. These results do not necessarily indicate a deviation from the earlier mentioned pattern which defines skilled workers as a basis for more status quo oriented working-class politics, as opposed to the unskilled who are thought to be less moderate politically.

We refer here to the earlier exposition on the functioning and orientation of the Monterrey labor movement, and will elaborate on this subject later on.

3.4. Social Mobility and Satisfaction

The general prevalence of upward mobility among the workers of all settings is a striking phenomenon. Among the intergenerationally, intragenerationally and factory mobile, they represent 53.6, 75.2 and 83.1 percent respectively.[14] Downward mobility does occur among some workers in the settings. It concerns, however, relatively small numbers with middle or upper class origins (in total 3.2 percent; 96.8 percent of the respondents' fathers had jobs that also locate them within the working class). Most of the downward mobility has occurred within the working class itself, and it may include individuals who have not completed their careers yet.

A considerable proportion of this mobility represents an upward movement over a rather short distance.[15] Among the upward intergenerationally mobile,

[13] This may partially explain why the highly skilled category, which contains quite a number of *obreros de confianza* who are not unionized, present a decrease in working-class psychology.
[14] The extremely high proportions of upwardly mobile (factory mobility) among the textile workers relate to the specific composition of the factory population, which is rather homogeneous, has a traditional recruiting base, and contains a relatively greater proportion of "older" workers who have completed their careers (31.9 percent of the textile workers are in the age bracket of 41 to 60 years, compared to 14 percent of the printers, 12 percent of the automobile workers and 17.3 percent of the chemical workers).
[15] Given the indices used and the characteristics of the sample (e.g. limited to a worker population), the maximum distance covered by the upwardly mobile through intergenerational and intragenerational mobility was two steps, and through factory mobility five steps.

TABLE 24:   Intergenerational mobility, intragenerational mobility and factory mobility by four industrial settings*

| | | industrial settings | | | | |
mobility		printing	textiles	automobiles	chemicals	N
intergenera-	up	61.0	62.7	27.0	61.8	225
tional mobility	same	28.0	28.2	43.0	28.2	133
	down	11.0	9.1	30.0	10.0	62
		100.0	100.0	100.0	100.0	420
intragenera-	up	78.0	92.7	46.0	81.8	316
tional mobility	same	21.0	7.3	52.0	18.2	101
	down	1.0	0.0	2.0	0.0	3
		100.0	100.0	100.0	100.0	420
factory	up	76.0	98.2	75.0	81.8	349
mobility	same	23.0	1.8	25.0	18.2	70
	down	1.0	0.0	0.0	0.0	1
		100.0	100.0	100.0	100.0	420

* *Intergenerational mobility* represents the difference between the present job of the respondent and his father's last job. The stratification of jobs that has been used has been outlined in Appendix B.
Intragenerational mobility represents the difference between the present job of the respondent and his very first job, using the same stratification of jobs.
Factory mobility represents the difference between the present job of the respondent and his first job within the factory where he is actually employed. To this purpose skill a stratification of 6 ranks has been used.

54.0 percent of the printers, 44.9 percent of the textile workers, 74.0 percent of the automobile workers and 60.3 percent of the chemical workers climbed no more than one level. Among the upward intragenerationally mobile, these percentages were 55.2, 35.3, 39.1 and 60.0 respectively. Most of the upward factory mobile moved no more than one (printers: 22.8, textile workers; 12.3, automobile workers; 45.6 and chemical workers 22.4 percent) or two levels (43.8, 24.0, 21.2 and 35.5 percent respectively).

The impact of these mobility variables on the work experience and working-class psychology syndromes is being discussed in the following paragraphs.

Work experience: The relationship between social mobility factors and the reaction of workers to estranging aspects of the immediate working environment has received little attention among the students of alienation. Whether alienation among workers is related to upward social mobility and relative improvement in levels of living, to an absence of mobility, or to downward mobility and a corresponding relative worsening in work and/or life con-

126

ditions has basically remained unsettled. The issue is further complicated by the fact that, in general, upward social mobility may lead to satisfaction as well as to dissatisfaction and an awareness of blockage of further mobility chances, as a result of a shift in reference groups during the mobility process. The literature on the relationship between the subjective reaction to mobility chances and alienation is equally scanty. Research among Dutch workers indicates a positive relationship between lack of satisfaction over mobility perspectives within the company and alienation (Van Dyck and Van Oers, 1961: 56). These findings, however, have not been confirmed for other situations.

The process of economic development in Mexico has resulted in widespread upward social mobility. This movement has taken place over very short distances in the stratification system. Despite this limitation it performs, according to González Casanova, stabilizing functions with regard to the present socioeconomic structure, generating satisfaction and hope for further improvement (on an individual basis) in work conditions and levels of living (González Casanova, 1968: 185). In Monterrey, the process of industrialization has created a great number of new positions and considerable numbers of workers have achieved a modest degree of upward mobility, if only by getting a steady job as such. This will most certainly apply to the migrants form the surrounding rural areas (67.1 percent in our sample), and to those cases where father's job was located at the bottom of the occupational scale (80.0 percent in our sample). Amidst the general prevalence of upward mobility, the stagnant and downwardly mobile are most likely to develop feelings of dissatisfaction towards life and career. At the same time, they can be expected to develop a relatively greater sensitivity to the estranging tendencies of their working environment, which in our study would show in a positive relationship between stagnant and downward mobility (intragenerational, intergenerational and factory mobility) and the various dimensions of work experience.

The mobility variables were put to the test through a multiple regression analysis.[16] The results are presented in table 25. The combined effects of all variables explain only a rather limited proportion of the variance. In the case of the chemical workers, these effects account for close to one-fourth of the total variance. Among the workers in the other settings this proportion is even

---

[16] SPSS version; a number of other variables suggested by the literature as having a definite impact on work experience and/or working-class psychology were added to the analysis. The scores on the independent variables: inter- and intragenerational mobility, factory mobility and sector first job (agriculture/services/industry) were converted into dummy variables. This was done in order to allow for proper scaling of these variables (cf. Suits 1957: Draper and Smith, 1966: 134-141). The standardized betas, multiple R's and R^2's indicate, respectively, the amount of change in work experience and working-class psychology produced by a standardized change in each of the independent variables when all the other variables are controlled for, the combined effects of the variables and the total variation explained.

127

TABLE 25: Regressions of work experience dimensions on selected independent variables, by four industrial settings*

dependent variables per industrial setting	independent variables													MR	R²
	X2	X3	X4	X5	X6	X7	X8	X9	X10	X11	X12	X13	X14		
printing															
work experience	.31		.03		.03	.08		.12	-.10	.02	.05			.38	.14
domination	.10	-.10	.04		.11			.12	-.09	.10				.24	.06
fractionization		-.17	.14				.02	.03	.04	-.23	.03	-.12		.35	.12
isolation			.05	.16		.10		-.05	-.12	.06	.09	-.05		.28	.08
distanciation	.16		.01	.10		.02		.06	-.16	.11	-.02	.08		.30	.09
textiles															
work experience	.18		.11		-.07		-.11	.15	.09		.11	.12		.33	.11
domination		.07	.03		-.13		-.04	.13		.15	.11	.02		.23	.05
fractionization		.02	.12	-.04			-.22	.16	.20	.15	.07	.12		.35	.12
isolation	.14	.07		.04		.03		-.02	.02	.10	-.04			.20	.04
distanciation			.03	-.05		.11		.02	.24		.19	.04		.28	.08
automobiles															
work experience	-.25	-.33	-.18	-.36	-.24	.25	.28	.22	.10	-.22	-.15	-.07		.39	.15
domination	-.32	-.36	-.25	-.32	-.24	.18	.30	.19	.11	.05	.04	.17		.34	.12
fractionization	-.01	-.01	.19	.12	.11	.25		-.35	-.19	-.06	.13	.06		.40	.16

128

	X2	X3	X4	X5	X6	X7	X8	X9	X10	X11	X12	X13	X14		
isolation	.07	.20	.24	-.60	-.43	.53	.46	.02	-.14	-.06	.18	.06		.46	.21
distanciation	-.14	.11	-.07	-.08	.30	.08	-.19	-.17	-.18	.10				.41	.17
chemicals															
work experience	.05		-.15	-.16		-.13	.21	-.07	.16	-.21				.47	.22
domination		.12	-.12		.06	.10	.16	-.09		-.27				.40	.16
fractionization	.06	-.08		-.12		-.12	.29	-.27	-.02	.21	.07			.52	.27
isolation	.14	.04		.16	.04		.08	.02	-.13	-.08	-.10			.22	.05
distanciation	-.03	-.19			-.08		.20	.05	.17	.25	.12			.35	.12

* in the table all beta weights have been listed of those variables that showed a sufficient F- or tolerance level for further computation

Key:
X2 = upward intergenerational mobility
X3 = stable intergenerational mobility
X4 = downward intergenerational mobility
X5 = upward factory mobility
X6 = stable factory mobility
X6 = stable factory mobility
X7 = upward intragenerational mobility

X8 = stable intragenerational mobility
X9 = salary dissatisfaction
X10 = migrant background
X11 = agrarian job background
X12 = industrial job background
X13 = services job background
X14 = prosperity level

smaller. The beta weights of the mobility variables are almost all very low. Only among the automobile workers a weak impact is shown.

In general, the evidence does not support our hypothesis. Stagnant and downward mobility do not have a special impact on the work experience variables. Neither does upward mobility. Among the automobile workers, upward intragenerational mobility and factory mobility show a slight relationship to the isolation dimension. In addition, in three of the four industrial settings upward mobility belongs to the "best" predictors of overall work experience: upward intergenerational mobility (printing and textiles) and upward factory mobility (automobiles). As in the other cases the beta weights, however, are low and do not justify definitive conclusions.

Working-class psychology: The impact of social mobility on working-class psychology and related phenomena has been subject to contradictory hypotheses.

Marx predicted a politically conservative role for the downwardly mobile, whose recruiting base he located in the lower middle class. He related this phenomenon to their feelings of discontent resulting from a loss of status. In addition, their motives, ideas, and aspirations would continue to reflect their original class position and contradict dominant working-class values (Marx and Engels, 1965: 23).

This thesis has found some support in studies of class psychology and voting patterns. These studies have shown that the downwardly mobile, who have joined the working class, continue to express a class identification and a political stand that correspond to their former class backgrounds. In comparison with those having working-class origins, they are less likely to support leftist policies (Lipset and Bendix, 1959: 69; Centers, 1949: 179 ff). Contrary to these findings, Lopreato and Chafetz have hypothesized downward mobility into the lower classes to lead, under certain conditions, toward a class psychology of radical political content (Lopreato and Chafetz, 1970: 440-445).

The theses concerning the effects of upward mobility have been equally vague and inconclusive. Soares views upward mobility from the lowest strata as favorable to political expression of a radical content (Soares, 1965: 516-559). Upward mobility, he maintains, generates new expectations about improvements in socioeconomic position that are impossible to fulfill within the existing socioeconomic framework, and that intensify the feelings of relative deprivation. The resulting frustration on an individual level seeks explanation in the inherent unjust nature of the economic and social order, and expresses itself in leftist radical positions.

The least that can be concluded from these studies on the effects of the various kinds of mobility is that the phenomenon of social mobility in general is likely to undermine working-class solidarity. The fact that some rise while others fall may indeed have debilitating effects on labor unity, as Bendix and Lipset assert (Bendix and Lipset, 1959: 69). About the different political

130

orientations that are related to the various forms of mobility, and that very likely are expressions of differences in underlying class psychology, however, present research offers no unamimous results.

The starting point for the present investigation of the effects of the various forms of social mobility on working-class psychology has been taken in the originally Marxian ideas. Stagnant and downward mobility (inter-, intragenerational and factory mobility) will be hypothesized as negatively related to the various dimensions of working-class psychology. In dealing with this question, however, the other theses will also be explored.

The influence of the mobility variables on working-class psychology is not substantial. Among the printers, textile workers and chemical workers the virtual absence of any impact by the variables relating to the different forms of upward mobility is striking. Stagnant and downward mobility predominate among the variables in the final equation, but their contribution does not carry much weight. The "best" predictors, stagnant intragenerational mobility among the printers and stagnant factory mobility among the textile workers, have only a beta weight of .30 and .20 respectively.

The automobile workers form a slightly deviant case. The individual dimensions of the working-class psychology syndrome do show some reasonably high beta weights. The pattern of the effects of the mobility variables show, however, an interesting contradiction between the class identification/ awareness or more "militant" dimensions and the union participation or "status quo" variables. We will elaborate on this phenomenon later on.

Stagnant intragenerational mobility and stagnant factory mobility have some explanatory weight, especially with regard to class identification and quantitative and qualitative union participation. The beta weights, however, do not differ much from those pertaining to the upwardly mobile. Since, in this case, both figure as good predictors, it has to be assumed that the intragenerational mobility and factory mobility variables, as a whole, do not discriminate well with regard to the categories of the dependent variable. A similar phenomenon appears in the case of the intergenerational mobility variables as predictors of working-class psychology, again among the automobile workers.

The hypothesis has not been confirmed. In general, there appears to be little systematic impact by mobility variables on the various dimensions of working-class psychology, not in the predicted direction, nor in any other direction. This, in itself, is a very interesting result. In particular, the almost complete absence of a relationship between any kind of upward mobility and the working-class psychology syndrome among the printers, the textile workers and chemical workers, is a very relevant datum.

The subjective dimension: Until now, social mobility has been dealt with primarily as an objective phenomenon, that is the actual vertical movement of the workers up and down the occupational hierarchy has been studied. To this

131

TABLE 26: Regression of working-class psychology dimensions on selected independent variables, by four industrial settings*

dependent variables per industrial setting	independent variables													MR	R²
	X2	X3	X4	X5	X6	X7	X8	X9	X10	X11	X12	X13	X14		
printing															
working-class psychology			-.06				.30	.13	.25	-.21	.02		.02	.44	.19
class identification	.04	.12			.04	.07		.22	.02	-.30	-.11	-.22	-.30	.50	.25
awareness	.10		-.10		.09	.02		-.03	-.17	.09	.20	.15	.11	.30	.09
quantitative union participation		.08	.16		-.03	.35		-.12	-.27	.10	-.13	-.08	.02	.48	.23
qualitative union participation			.06	.04		.23		-.19	-.30	.18	-.07	-.02	-.08	.46	.21
textiles															
working-class psychology	-.05	.14	-.14		.20	.09	-.13	-.04	-.19	-.15	-.25	-.04	-.03	.41	.17
class identification		.05			-.07			.15	.03	-.10	-.11	-.05	-.12	.31	.10
awareness			-.16		.08		.09		-.04	-.19	-.25	-.11	-.04	.27	.07
quantitative union participation	.05	-.08			.03		-.03	-.02	-.09	-.05	-.13	-.15	.18	.27	.07
qualitative union participation		-.20	.02		.03		.03	-.11	-.23	.09	-.03	.03	.15	.35	.12
automobiles															
working-class psychology	-.30	-.28	-.20	-.07	.15	.19	.16	.12	-.01	.06	-.03	-.07	-.20	.28	.08
class identification	-.24	-.25	-.06	-.47	-.24	.95	.93	.22	.38	.01	-.09	-.21	-.22	.83	.68
awareness	.30	.13	.06	-.03	.02	.08	.36	-.13	.09	-.09	-.13	-.15	-.06	.41	.17

132

quantitative union participation	.30	.24	.12	-.58	-.67	.22	.41	-.19	-.10	-.02	.06	.21	.46	.21
qualitative union participation	.30	.24	.12	.63	.50	-.65	-.20	-.05	.05	.12	.08	.09	.48	.23

chemicals

working-class psychology	.05	.12	-.04	-.91	-.02		.16	.03	.19	.30	.16	-.07	.34	.12
class identification	-.08				.03	-.19	.16	.04	.08	.07	-.02	-.25	.38	.14
awareness		-.10	.04		.19	.05	.11	.20	.02	.17	.17		.35	.12
quantitative union participation			.11		.07	.01	-.09	-.06	-.03	-.15		.38	.48	.23
qualitative union participation	.05		.13		.04	.16	-.10	.08	-.09	-.20	-.05	.33	.48	.23

* in the tables all beta weights have been listed of those variables that showed a sufficient F- or tolerance level for further computation

Key:
X2 = upward intergenerational mobility
X3 = stable intergenerational mobility
X4 = downward intergenerational mobility
X5 = upward factory mobility
X6 = stable factory mobility
X7 = upward intragenerational mobility
X8 = stable intragenerational mobility
X9 = salary dissatisfaction
X10 = migrant background
X11 = agrarian job background
X12 = industrial job background
X13 = services job background
X14 = prosperity level

partial analysis the study of the subjective dimension will be added. This element has been mentioned before, where the attitudinal dimension was discussed that is assumed to accompany the objective movements between occupational strata. The specific relationship between these attitudes and the various forms of mobility, however, is not always very clear. In several cases the same attitudes have been hypothesized to relate to upward as well as downward mobility. Here the subject will be elaborated through several measures that form part of this subjective dimension and next to their linkages with social mobility, those with work experience and working-class psychology will be explored.

(a) *Plans for the future*: Among the workers, the mobility perspectives dominate their plans for the future. More than half, 56.5 percent, aspired to move further upwards, most of them within the company they were presently employed. A third, 34.7 percent, had the ambition to leave and start a business of their own. Only 8.8 percent planned to stay in the job they held at the time. There were no significant differences between the settings with regard to these future plans.

The numbers of workers who aspire to leave their present job and start a private business are surprisingly large. These aspirations may predominate among those workers who have a background of independent employment and experience a factory environment as too restrictive and confining. Their presence may also be related to a succesful penetration of petit bourgeois mobility aspirations among the workers. These and other plans are not primarily rooted in the workers' own social mobility and apparently result from the more general expectations generated by the development process in a wider sense. With the exception of the chemical workers,[18] they do not relate to work experience or working-class psychology either. Among these chemical workers, a growing emphasis on efforts to obtain better positions within the present company can be observed, together with a decrease in the estranging effects of work experience and also a weaker working-class psychology.

(b) *Aspirations with regard to the children*: The all pervasive mobility perspective is further exemplified by the job aspirations the workers cherish(ed) for their children (sons).

Among those who has sons, the great majority, 90.3 percent wanted or had wanted them to take different jobs from those the respondents themselves had. Asked to specify the kinds of jobs they had in mind, most workers, 73.3 percent, mentioned those jobs that, on the Mexican scene, typically represent middle class mobility aspirations: professionals, lawyers, doctors, etc. These preferences found an equally strong expression in all settings. Only 9.4 percent of the workers selected working-class professions.

---

[18] Work experience: $X^2 = 18.70$, 6 d.f., p = $<.01$
Working-class psychology: $X^2 = 40.23$, 6 d.f., p = $<.01$

134

Obviously, in most cases jobs were mentioned that are far beyond the workers reach. Apparently, they extrapolate from their own situations, without considering the conditions that indeed have created improvements through career mobility, while at the same time, however, severely limiting the extent of the upward movement. Optimism over the future course of the development process prevails. Half of the workers, 49.9 percent, estimated the possibilities for realization of the job aspirations they held for their sons as good to very good. Only 7.1 percent held a dim view of these possibilities.

In general, pure achievement criteria: "schooling" (70 percent), "initiative" (14.8 percent), and "hard work" (4.5 percent) predominate over ascriptive criteria: "family relations" (8.5 percent), "good personal relations" (8.3 percent), and "political influence" (1.9 percent) as the most important factors that according to the workers determine mobility. This selection, of course, will reflect the respondents own situations. In an environment where particularist proceedings prevail, especially in the selection of personnel on the medium levels, workers will resort to achievement criteria in the absence of control over any of the other factors that could determine their advancement through the occupational hierarchy.

(c) *Career and life satisfaction*: In this situation of generalized upward mobility, the comparison between past expectations concerning career achievements and the jobs that actually have been achieved has indeed generated disappointment for few.

Among the workers of all settings, 26.0 percent stated they had achieved less than expected. An almost equal proportion (26.7 percent) said that they had a job conforming to their expectations. The rest, 47.4 percent, maintained they had achieved more than expected.

The automobile workers are most dissatisfied over personal career mobility (48.0 percent); most satisfaction is found among the chemical workers (64.5 percent).

The phenomenon of relative deprivation has been measured through a number of items dealing with past, present and future life chances and in relative perspective, e.g. compared with "the average Mexican" whom the respondent was expected to take as his reference group. Together these items were assembled into a "life satisfaction" index.

The majority of workers identified as "average Mexicans," not better and not worse off than most others. The "relatively deprived" counted 29 percent. This category is most strongly represented among the automobile workers (42.0 percent). Those evaluating their life chances as relatively better counted only 16.4 percent. The chemical setting again counted most "satisfied" workers (20.0 percent).

On the basis of the literature discussed earlier, one would expect satisfaction with career and with life chances to coincide with a less estranging work experience and a weaker working-class psychology. In most cases, however, there is not even a significant relationship between these phenomena. Career satisfaction is significantly related to working-class psychology among the printers and to work experience among the chemical workers,[19] but that is it. The relationship between the workers' mobility and their career and life satisfaction is weak[20] and apparently more complex than one of straight determination. It probably should be viewed in a context of the wider effects generated by the dynamics of the development process.

3.5. Social Background

Here a number of variables will be discussed that concern the social background of the workers: (a) the workers' migratory background, (b) their early job experience, and (c) their education and educational mobility.

(a) *Migratory background*: Considerable numbers among the workers (67.1 percent) are of migrant origin. Most of them (76.3 percent) came from the rural areas of Nuevo León and the other North Mexican states of Coahuila, San Luis Potosí and Zacatecas. Many (58.5 percent) were born in small rural communities counting 5,000 inhabitants or less. The rest had city backgrounds, but very few (9.2 percent) came from big town environments (100,000 +).

Recent migrants do not account for large numbers among the workers. Only 9.2 percent had arrived less than five years ago. The great majority (80.2 percent) has settled in Monterrey before 1960.

(b) *Early job experience*: Many workers (37.9 percent) had started their careers directly in industry, 25.4 percent began in typical subproletarian occupations (services and small trade). The workers with artisan backgrounds count very few (3.6. percent).

Close to one third (30.5 percent) of the workers form a second generation of industrial workers, that is their fathers' last job was located in the manufacturing industry. This is one indication that the industrial labor force in these settings has come of age. Most of the fathers of the workers (96.8 percent) belong(ed) to the proletarian ranks. This applied to the workers in all settings. Fathers' occupation was mostly located at the very bottom of the occupational hierarchy (55.8 percent). Those having "nonproletarian" jobs counted small numbers.

Among most workers the number of years that have passed between first job and present job is substantial. Only slightly more than one-fourth entered the factory in recent times. Over half (50.3 percent) had been working already for a period of over ten years in the factory where they have their present jobs.

[19] X^2's are 20.66 and 15.71 respectively, 4 d.f., p = <.01
[20] Only among the automobile workers were career and life satisfaction (X^2's = 8.73 and 12.26, 4 d.f., p = <.05) and among the chemical workers life satisfaction (X^2 = 12.62, 2 d.f., p = <.01) significantly related to intragenerational mobility.

Apparently, a considerable proportion of the workers consitute a stable, sedentary industrial labor force, a phenomenon especially pronounced among the textile workers.

(c) *Education:* The (sub)proletarian backgrounds of the workers are reflected in the data on fathers' education. Most of them (74.3 percent) were either illiterate or had not completed primary school. Vere few (4.4 percent) received an eduation superior to primary school, not an abnormal phenomenon among this generation. The printers show a slightly superior background, but the differences with the workers from the other settings are not spectacular. The educational situation of the sons (our respondents) looks quite different. The category of workers without any education al all (2.4 percent) has virtually disappeared. Most workers did receive some kind of schooling, although those who did not complete primary school still count considerable numbers (30.5 percent). In this context, the textile workers represent the most "traditional" element: 52.8 percent had either no education at all or an incomplete primary education. This may relate to their age distribution (they count a greater number of "older" workers) and the socioeconomic characteristics of the company villages where they live. The printers continue the slightly superior levels of education of their fathers: 35.0 percent had secondary or superior education. In their education also, the high skill levels of the industry are reflected. Most of the workers (64.8 percent) achieved an eduaction superior to the one of their fathers. Only 8.1 percent suffered a downward educational mobility.

The impact of these factors on the work experience and working-class psychology syndromes will be discussed in the following paragraphs.

Work experience: The problems of migrant background (rural) and early job experience, commonly figure in the study of the processes of adaptation by migrants to urban life and to the norms of industrial labor (cf. Moore and Feldman, 1960; Moore, 1965; also Kerr, 1964: 333 ff). With regard to the problems of adaptation to industrial life, those elements of the industrial production process have been emphasized that contrast with rural work such as: the pace of work, its mostly subdivided and fragmented character and the lack of involvement with the entire act of production. Because of these obvious differences, rural migrants are thought to experience the estranging tendencies of modern industrial life more intensively. This relationship between rural migrant past and present work experience is, of course, more complex, will also be conditioned by the specific motives, goals, and aspirations the migrants may have, while moreover the length of the period that has elapsed since the actual migration took place, may influence the relationship in an unknown direction.

Here, the hypothesis that migrant background relates positively to the various dimensions of work experience, has been investigated, in addition to the impact of early job experience (first job) in agrarian production as opposed to a job background in the industrial or services sector. The results of the multiple regression analysis (cf. Table 25) show rather low beta weights for the variable "migrant background." The fact that for most migrants the actual migration is a phenomenon of a rather distant past may have contributed to an erosion of possible former differences between the native and the migrant populations as far as attitudes towards industrial work are concerned.

The influence of early job experience is small. It followed from the weak predictive value of "migrant background" that also the variable "agrarian job background" would not carry much weight: not all migrants were peasants (29.0 percent of the migrant segment has peasant status), but all peasants were migrants. However, industrial and services job background do not have much importance either.

The theses concerning the effects of education and educational mobility tie in with the earlier discussion of the effects of downward and stagnant mobility. Almost one-fourth of all workers had completed secondary school or received superior education. It has been mentioned earlier that especially the students leaving secondary school encounter serious difficulties in obtaining jobs that correspond to their expectations regarding income and social prestige. Many enter the industrial world where they are assigned to blue collar positions (Puenta Leyva, 1969: 39). In his study of a group of industrial workers in the Mexico City agglomeration, Kahl has pointed out that especially among the workers belonging to this category, strong feelings of relative deprivation and frustration about a perceived blockage of mobility perspectives occurred (Kahl, 1965: 222 ff). Given this situation one would expect education to be positively related to the various dimensions of work experience: the higher the educational level attained, the more estranging the work experience would be. However, chi-square analysis shows none of the relationships to be statistically significant (cf. Vellinga, 1975: 347). The hypothesis can be rejected.

Working-class psychology: The relationship between migrant background and working class-psychology has been subject to hypotheses that are not always consistent with each other. They share, however, as a common element the factor of frustrated aspirations which mediates the relationship between the two phenomena. This frustration is hypothesized as the result of the gap between past aspirations, e.g. aspirations that were cherished at the time of migration, and the hard realities of city life (Portes, 1971: 27). The hopes of substantial betterment in life conditions which made the migrants come to the city in the first place are destroyed by the incapacity of the economic structure to fullfill these hopes. Or, in Smith's terms, the levels of living that can be achieved fail to match up to the standards of living that have been developed (Smith, 1970: 224).

According to several studies, the exasperation flowing from this gap be-

138

tween standards and levels of living is most intense among the recent migrants who in most cases meet considerable problems securing a job (Cornelius, 1969; Nelson, 1969). Others, however, have shown this frustration to increase with length of residence in the city. Among recent migrants, according to Soares, initially a slight satisfaction prevails as a result of the fact that even their difficult situation in the city compares favorably with the rural misery they left behind (Soares, 1965). In the course of residence in the city, this satisfaction fades and is replaced by feelings of relative deprivation as the standards of comparison gradually shift from the rural past to the urban middle sector. These feelings of relative deprivation will be expressed in attitude complexes that form part of their class psychology.

Following Soares' thesis, it was hypothesized that migrant background would be positively related to working-class psychology. Inspection of Table 26 shows, however, insignificantly small beta weights for all four industrial settings. The hypothesis is certainly not substantiated.

The impact of early job background is not very conspicuous either. Neither agrarian, or industrial, or services job background carries much weight. As in the case of work experience, length of residence in the city may provide an explanation.

As far as the impact of education is concerned, one might expect, on the basis of the argumentation earlier presented, education to be negatively related to working-class psychology: the higher the educational level attained, the weaker the working-class psychology would be. The relationship between education and working-class psychology, however, shows a picture very similar to the one described before in the case of work experience. Only among the textile workers education relates significantly to overall working-class psychology ($X^2 = 15.78$, 8 d.f., p = <.05). The tendency for working-class psychology to decrease in strength with increasing level of education is too weak to support the prediction.

3.6. Bread and Butter

The complex of "bread and butter" variables contains (a) the information on personal and family income, (b) the degree of dissatisfaction with family income, (c) the level of prosperity (as indicated by ownership of the house, characteristics of the house, utilities and possession of consumer durables). Before analyzing the impact of these objective and subjective dimensions of income on work experience and working-class psychology their specific definition among the workers will be indicated.

(a) *Personal and family income*: The income situation of the workers is exposed in the next table. The textile workers figure with the highest, and the automobile workers with the lowest personal income levels. The total number of workers who received personal incomes below federal standards (1,000

139

pesos a month for the Monterrey area in 1971) is relatively small: 4.5 percent. The average monthly personal income is around 1,900 pesos a month, and the average family income is 450 pesos higher. These compare favorably with the general (personal) income levels in the state of Nuevo León, and also with the income levels of the manufacturing industry in the same state.

TABLE 27: Personal and family income, by four industrial settings.

levels of personal and family income*	industrial settings				N
	printing	textiles	automobiles	chemicals	
<999: personal income	6.0	—	12.0	0.9	19
family income	5.0	—	5.0	—	10
1.000 - 1.499: personal income	37.0	32.7	46.0	51.8	176
family income	28.0	27.3	28.0	42.7	133
1.500 - 2.499: personal income	45.0	62.7	33.0	35.5	186
family income	45.0	50.0	43.0	33.6	180
2.500 - 4.999: personal income	12.0	4.6	9.0	11.8	39
family income	19.0	19.1	23.0	22.7	88
>5.000: personal income	—	—	—	—	—
family income	3.0	3.6	1.0	0.9	9
	100.0	100.0	100.0	100.0	420
	100.0	100.0	100.0	100.0	420

* in pesos per month; personal income equals the wages received from the company where the workers were employed at the time (before taxes), family income equals personal income plus the earnings of other family members in case the workers are family heads and principal wage earners.

The great masses of workers and industrial workers in the Monterrey area still receive income below federal standards. A considerable proportion of the workers in the four settings. however, are located in the middle income brackets (1,500 pesos and up). These latter incomes, it should be emphasized, are "high" only in a relative sense, that is against the background of the generally depressed wage levels in the Monterrey area.

(b) *Income (dis)satisfaction*: The average family ı come among the workers was 2,350 pesos a month. This leaves us an average per capita income of 356 pesos per month, given the size of the average family (6.6 persons). In the

140

TABLE 28: General income distribution and income distribution manufacturing industry in Nuevo León 1970, sample income distribution.

income levels	general income distribution Nuevo León*	income distribution manuf. industry Nuevo León*	sample income distribution
<999	58.8	44.6	4.5
1,000-1,499	19.7	28.7	41.9
1,500-2,499	11.8	15.8	44.3
2,500-4,999	6.1	6.7	9.3
>5,000	3.6	4.2	—
	100.0	100.0	100.0

* source: Censo 1970

previous discussion on the distribution of income in the Monterrey area (cf. Chapter IV, par. 2.3.), it was shown that 67 percent of the Monterrey population in 1965 lived below a normatively fixed level of minimum welfare. This level had been established using a number of indicators, which together could be translated into a monthly per capita income of 504 pesos. Assuming an average annual increase of the consumer's price index of 4 percent, this income would be 625 pesos per capita per month for 1971.[21] This would mean that most of the worker families in the settings received an income below the minimum welfare level that could be calculated at 4.125 pesos per month for the average 6.6 member family.

Most of these families, however, do not receive more than half of this amount. Yet, the fact that their incomes compare "favorably" in an environment where the terms of trade on the labor market traditionally have been adverse to the workers' side, has not missed its effects. Only a little less than one-fourth of the workers declared "dissatisfaction" with their family incomes: 2.1 percent said they suffered severe financial hardship, and 21.9 percent had difficulties making ends meet. The others presented some kind of "satisfaction": 58.1 percent declared they had no great financial problems, and 17.9 percent were even able to save part of their earnings. The chemical workers were most satisfied with their family incomes: 83.6 percent was without financial problems or even had accumulated savings. Their objective income situation, in pesos per month, however, was worse than among the workers in the other settings. This may illustrate the appeal of paternalist and reformist policies in a relatively low-income situation. The absence of such policies, may explain the presence of considerable dissatisfaction among the automobile workers (35.0 percent).

The relationship between income dissatisfaction and family income is only

[21] This percentage of 4 applies to the period of 1960-1965 (cf. Puenta Leyva, 1969: 20). It is unlikely to be less for any of the subsequent years due to inflation (4-5 percent in the 1960's, increasing to 20 percent in 1973-74).

significant among the textile workers ($X^2 = 17.02$, 9 d.f., $p = <0.5$ and the automobile workers ($X^2 = 24.06$, 13 d.f., $p = <.05$), which underlines the observation that variations in degree of satisfaction may exist with any given level of worker income and may find their primary explanation in other factors.

(c) *Level of prosperity*: a considerable proportion of the workers, 40 percent, owned their houses, about a third, 33.6 percent, rented, 13.3 percent lived with a family member who owned the house, and 13.1 percent had some other arrangement (cf. Chapter IV, par 3.2.3. for comparative material). The housing situation was most favorable among the chemical workers, due to the company policy in this area: 43.6 owned the house, while 27.3 percent were paying installments on homes provided by the company.

The workers' homes had an average of 2.6 rooms. The 1970 Nuevo León census indicates an average of 2.4 rooms for the entire state population. Half of the total number of houses, 50 percent, consisted of one- or two-room constructions, compared to 64 percent in the state (Censo 1970). The average number of bedrooms was 1.9, but a considerable number of dwellings, 22.4 percent had no separate sleeping quarters.

Some additional characteristics:

Presence of: (percentages)	Nuevo León[1]	Monterrey[1]	Sample
separate kitchen	78.3	78.5	87.4
running water (any kind)[2]	81.3	94.6	93.3
electricity	78.4	89.6	98.6
bathroom	50.0	64.4	81.4
gas/electricity for cooking purposes	67.8	78.2	61.9[3]
hot water	no inf.	no inf.	26.4
telephone	no inf.	no inf.	1.9

[1] the data for Nuevo León and Monterrey are from the 1970 Census, those for Monterrey refer to the City of Monterrey and not to the metropolitan area
[2] within the house or from a public tap
[3] this percentage refers to gas only

The data on the possession of consumer durables can be summarized as follows:

Possession of: (percentages)	Nuevo León[1]	Monterrey	Sample
radio	86.4	88.5	92.4
television	48.4	61.6	78.1
automobile	no inf.	no inf.	8.6
motorcycle	no inf.	no inf.	3.6
laundry machine	no inf.	no inf.	39.0
refrigerator	no inf.	no inf.	46.2

[1] Censo 1970

It appears that as far as housing and the possession of consumer durables is concerned (at least for those about which comparative data are available), the workers obviously do live in above average conditions. It should be emphasized again that these conditions may reflect a state of indebtedness to the employer and may not directly correlate with the buying power of their incomes.

The inter- and intraindustry differences show through the scores on the prosperity index for which housing items (kitchen, bathroom, hot water, gas) as well as consumer durables items (television, laundry machine, refrigerator) were used (for procedures, see Appendix A).

TABLE 29: Level of prosperity, by four industrial settings

| level of prosperity | industrial settings | | | | |
	printing	textiles	automobiles	chemicals	N
1 (high)	45.0	31.9	35.0	63.6	185
2	37.0	48.1	35.0	28.3	156
3 (low)	18.0	20.0	30.0	8.1	79
	100.0	100.0	100.0	100.0	420

The chemical workers are most well, the automobile workers are least well off, which ties in with our earlier comment on the variations in income (dis)satisfaction between the settings.

The status of these income-related variables has been dealt with before as part of our analysis of the dynamics of class. Classes tend to coincide with specific locations in the income structure, and many class struggles traditionally have concerned this class specificity of income. This is not a surprising phenomenon in a market economy where most of the things that workers and others seek can only be secured through cash transactions.

The reaction of the working class to these conditions, in the Marxian perspective, is viewed in connection with the general thesis concerning the relation between socioeconomic deprivation institutionalized in an existing societal order, and the tendency among the deprived to develop a class psychology directed towards elimination of the inequities through a radical change of this order. The deprivation, as Marx conceived it, does not always represent a *Verelendung*, pauperization in absolute terms. In many situations, it has to be understood in a relative sense.[22] What often counts, on the level of the individual worker, is the gap between the rewards he receives and those to which he feels he can reasonably aspire (Hyman, 1972: 89).

[22] Cf. *Wage Labour and Capital* in which Marx (1955: 94) shows an acute awareness of the phenomenon of relative deprivation.

143

Under a model of development following capitalist patterns, like in Mexico, the desires for material acquisitions and gratification among the members of the working class are easily stimulated, not only by the producers of mass consumption goods, but also by the pattern of conspicuous consumption of the upper and upper middle strata. In this context, it is reasonable, as we saw before, to assume considerable variations in degree of satisfaction with any given level of worker income, including the relatively highest ones (cf. Hyman, 1972: 118). For this reason wages are wanted for their own sake, or, rather, for the goods and services they can buy. In addition, however, income is one of the more important indicators of status. Contraditions between the actual income received and the subjective evaluations of status by the workers (translated into income terms) may generate frustration and conflict.

Thus the effects of "income" are not equivocal. Stagnant or decreasing real income, e.g. buying power, as well as increasing income that fails to meet the standard, may give rise to feelings of frustration and deprivation. This descrepancy between income levels and income standards mostly develops in a situation where the income fails to follow increases in productivity and profitability. It may also arise where workers relate their situations to the more general wage structure, compare with other workers, and keep a close watch on the remuneration for comparable jobs elsewhere.

Work experience: On the basis of the previous discussion, the specific impact of the "bread and butter" variables on work experience will be further explored. The following hypotheses will probe these relationships:
a.1. The workers' personal income levels will be inversely related to work experience; the higher the personal income level, the less estranging the work experience.
ɔ.1. Satisfaction or dissatisfaction with the general family income situation vill influence the workers' attitudes towards their work, to the extent that the more dissatisfied the workers, the more estranging their work experience will tend to be.
c.1. Relative prosperity, as measured by housing characteristics and the possession of consumer durables, will be inversely related to work experience; the higher the level of prosperity, the less estranging the work experience will tend to be.

ad a.1.- The relationship between personal income and the work experience dimensions is not significant, except for the printers. Among them, the significant relationship between the level of personal income and overall work-experience is supported by all dimensions except "domination." Inspection of the relevant tables shows that the direction of this relationship follows the predicted pattern. Among the automobile workers, income appears the be related to distanciation: the lack of involvement with and appreciation of the job appears to be relatively concentrated in the low income brackets. The relationship between income and isolation among the chemical workers may

144

TABLE 30: Personal income and work experience, by four industrial settings

work experience dimensions	printing		textiles		automobiles		chemicals		N
	X2	DF	X2	DF	X2	DF	X2	DF	
domination	14.12	9	6.59	6	8.75	9	9.35	9	
fractionization	25.88*	9	8.09	6	6.53	9	8.58	9	
isolation	13.30**	6	4.28	6	3.36	6	13.38**	6	
distanciation	38.56*	9	8.28	6	21.64**	9	14.72	9	
overall work experience	23.39*	9	3.03	4	5,12	6	10.03	6	

* significant at the .01 level
** significant at the .05 level

be related to the fact that the workers in the higher income brackets do live closely together (in the more expensive company housing), and consequently will score lower on the isolation dimension because of the better opportunities for contact with their colleagues in the neighbourhood.

ad b.1.- The effects of dissatisfaction with the family income situation have been investigated through a multiple regression analysis, the results of which have been summarized in Table 25. The impact on work experience is rather small. The relationship is strongest among the automobile and chemical workers, but even here the beta weights are only .22 and .21 respectively. The strongest contribution is made by the fractionization dimension, negatively in the case of the automobile workers, and positively among the chemical workers, which may relate to the wage structure of the respective industries or to differences in the characteristics of the work process. The beta weights, however, are really too small to attach much significance to them. The hypothesis has not been confirmed.

ad c.1.- The same conclusion can be drawn with regard to the hypothesized relationship between level of prosperity and work experience (cf. Table 25.) An interesting phenomenon, however, is the complete absence of even the slightest impact whatsoever. Among the workers in the various settings, the level of prosperity one has achieved has absolutely no influence on attitudes towards work. This phenomenon may find an explanation in the fact that this "prosperity" in most cases will be more apparent than real and reflect a state of indebtedness to the company.

Working-class psychology: With regard to the impact of "bread and butter" variables on working-class psychology, the following hypotheses can be formulated:

a.2. The workers' personal income level will be inversely related to working-class psychology: the higher the personal income level, the weaker the working-class psychology will tend to be.

b.2. Dissatisfaction with general family income will be positively related to

145

working-class psychology: the more dissatisfied the workers, the stronger their working-class psychology will tend to be.
c.2. Prosperity will be inversely related to working-class psychology: the higher the level of prosperity, the weaker the working class psychology will tend to be.

"Bread and butter" appears to have little influence on work experience. The situation is only slightly different in the case of working-class psychology.
ad a.2.- The relationship between personal income and overall working-class psychology is significant among workers in three of the four settings. Inspection of the tables showed a positive relationship among the textile and automobile workers, and a negative relationship among the chemical workers. in all cases, union participation, quantitative as well as qualitative, contributed most to the significance of the relationship.
ad b.2.- Dissatisfaction with general family income explains very little of the variation in the dimensions of the working-class psychology syndrome (cf. Table 26). It has a small but consistent impact on class identification, which suggests that discontent over income would tend to have people define themselves more in working-class terms. But, again, the beta weights are small. The hypothesis has to be rejected.

TABLE 31:   Personal income and working-class psychology, by four industrial settings.

working-class psychology dimensions	industrial settings							
	printing		textiles		automobiles		chemicals	
	X2	DF	X2	DF	X2	DF	X2	DF
class identification	10.33	6	9.63**	4	5.47	3	8.63**	3
awareness	3.44	6	.46	4	8.17	6	5.01	6
quant. union part.	15.86	9	75.23*	6	43.23*	9	56.88*	9
qual. union part.	18.63**	9	51.53*	6	40.70*	9	52.56*	9
overall working-class psychology	8.07	6	24.75*	4	14.03**	6	12.88**	6

*   significant at the .01 level
** significant at the .05 level

ad c.2.- The hypothesis concerning the effects of the level of prosperity on working-class psychology cannot be sustained either. The (weak) positive relationship between prosperity level and quantitative and qualitative union participation among the chemical workers may reflect the specific characteristics of their management oriented union in which those members supporting union activities leaning toward management interests are likely to reap most fruits from the *patrón's* paternalist and reformist endeavors.

The complex of "bread and butter" variables, dealing with very concrete basic issues concerning income and life conditions, does not affect work experience, nor working-class psychology in a substantial or unequivocal way as was predicted. The only factor having any importance at all appears to be personal income, which is related to variations in working-class psychology. Neither income dissatisfaction, nor level of prosperity shows any relationship to work experience or working-class psychology. It has to be concluded that, among the workers in the four settings the problem of relative deprivation, as manifested in "bread and butter" terms, does not play an important role, at least not in the hypothesized direction.

Among the workers 42.4 percent idenfified as *clase media*. In addition, it has been shown that among the Monterrey working class most of the respondents do have a privileged status despite the fact that most of them still live below the income level of minimum welfare. It seems that, despite the situation of relative privilege and an outward middle class identification, these middle classes in fact for most people concerned do not function as the reference groups from which their hopes and aspirations are derived, at least as far as "bread and butter" is concerned. A relatively small proportion of workers voice dissatisfaction with their situations: 12.4 percent stated that they have had less opportunities than the majority of Mexicans to get "the good things of life." In addition, only 3.6 percent maintained that their lives had been "bad" compared to "the average Mexican." The consciousness of relative privilege, rather than the feelings of relative deprivation, appears to condition the workers' thoughts on socioeconomic matters. Most workers apparently refer backwards towards the subproletarian and lower proletarian strata to which their fathers and they themselves have belonged. In this situation, fear of losing the little one has and sinking back into anonymous poverty is more likely to develop than feelings of deprivation relative to the middle and upper strata.

3.7. Conclusion

Those variables suggested by classic and modern theory as vital conditioning factors behind the work experience and working-class psychology syndromes appear to have a very weak influence or no influence at all among the workers of the four industrial settings. The factor "industrial setting" appears a significantly discriminating criterion as fas as variations in the two syndromes is concerned, but only so when their compound effects are taken into consideration. Neither the variables belonging to the social background-mobility-satisfaction complex, nor the "bread and butter" variables figure among the prime determining factors of variations in work experience and working-class psychology.

Skill appears to be the most important single factor capable of explaining differences in work experience and working-class psychology scores. Among the individual dimensions, this relationship concerns, in particular, domination and, in a lesser sense, fractionization, and further qualitative and quantitative union participation. Except for the automobile workers, the feeling of domination appears to increase with skill until the highest skill ranks, e.g. the supervisors and foremen, where a decrease sets in. Union participation, quantitative as well as qualitative, increases with skill, except again for the very highly skilled among whom union membership and, consequently, union participation is less.

Skill, of course, is a factor that is setting-specific (cf. Chapter V, par. 2). In fact, the relationship between skill and industrial setting is highly significant ($X^2 = 110.46$, 15 d.f., $p = <.01$). At the same time, it should be emphasized that industrial setting represents a conglomerate of factors, of which a specific skill distribution is only one. They should not be identified in the analysis.

The duality within the working-class psychology syndrome between, on the one hand, the quantity and quality of union participation, or the "conformist" dimensions, and, on the other hand, class identification and awareness or the "latent militant" dimensions is a very interesting phenomenon emerging from the analysis of the impact of skill and industrial setting. It can be observed that, in each setting, a distinct pattern is shown. The textile workers have relatively high working-class psychology scores, which are rooted, however, to a great extent in the quantity and quality of the participation in the "official" union. The automobile workers, on the other hand, show a relatively weak union participation. In their case, however, the "latent militant" dimensions are strongly developed.

The question becomes now how this "conformism" and "latent militancy" expresses itself, first, in the orientation towards the immediate structures the workers relate to. like unions and political parties, and second, in the orientation towards the wider political structure and towards issues that, within their frame of reference, can be labeled as "radical." Further the problem should be dealt with to what extent, and under what conditions, work experiences may serve as the point of departure for such orientations.

4. WORK EXPERIENCE AND WORKING-CLASS PSYCHOLOGY:
CONFORMITY, RESIGNATION AND LATENT MILITANCY

4.1. *Introduction*

The study of work experience, working-class psychology, and their determinants needs to be elaborated through an analysis of some additional factors that reflect more closely on the questions concerning the potential of the industrial working population as a dynamic factor in socioeconomic change. A first question to be dealt with obviously concerns the effects work experience may have on working-class psychology. The "generalization hypothesis" (cf. Chapter II, par. 3.1.) suggests a positive relationship between the two phenomena. Thus far, however, no tendency towards a correspondence between the two phenomena has emerged and the problem obviously needs some further exploration.

In addition, some other issues will be investigated that relate to working-class psychology, its specific composition, orientation and possible impact on the attitudes of the workers towards the structures that have been defined for their controlled mobilization. These issues are:

(a)   The importance of horizontal versus vertical linkages within the companies: the issue refers to the question of whether horizontal solidarity orientations prevail over solidarities cutting across class lines, and it forms, of course, an essential part of any discussion involving problems of class.

(b)   The role of the unions in the four industrial settings, and the orientations of the workers towards these organizations.

(c)   The attitudes of the workers towards official politics.

(d)   The phenomenon of political radicalism; its incidence, its determinants, and its relation to working-class psychology.

The analysis will be concluded with a discussion of its results in terms of alienation and class consciousness.

4.2. The Effects of Work Experience on Working-Class Psychology

The relationship between the two syndromes traditionally has been part of the above-mentioned "generalization hypothesis": estranging work conditions will have wider consequences in other spheres, and in particular result in a strongly developed working-class psychology. The analysis of the impact of "industrial setting" has shown some mutual interaction between both syndromes. In this interaction, the working-class psychology dimensions, except for the textile workers, appear to contribute most to the combined effects. Third factors may be involved, although the analysis of the other major independent variables also showed the absence of a significant impact on either work experience or working-class psychology. The problem of the relationship between the two phenomena and the specific characteristics of this relationship remains to be explored further.

As a first step, the relationship between each of the work experience and the working-class psychology dimensions has been tested separately for statistical significance in each of the industrial settings[23] (cf. Table 32). In most cases, the null hypothesis should be accepted. Reviewing the findings more closely, the following can be concluded:

(a)   The domination dimension does not relate significantly to any of the working-class psychology dimensions, with the exception of the automobile

[23] This conformed to the objectives of the study. It assured at the same time, given the size of the individual setting-samples, that statistical significance could be established rather accurately. Thus, one of the drawbacks of chi-square analysis could be eliminated, which concerns its use with large-size samples, and its tendency to produce "easy" significance in these cases due to its lack of refined discriminatory power. The direction of the relationships has been investigated through an inspection of the original tables.

TABLE 32: Work experience and working-class psychology, by four industrial settings

working-class psychology dimensions	work experience dimensions									
	domination		fractionization		isolation		distanciation		work experience	
	X2	DF	X2	DF	X2	DF	X2	DF	X2	DF
printing										
class identification	3.99	6	2.09	6	4.80	4	2.17	6	3.35	6
awareness	5.48	6	11.42	6	1.45	4	5.34	6	7.48	6
quantitative union participation	5.96	9	14.71	9	55.01*	6	7.57	9	13.74	9
qualitative union participation	14.00	9	17.98**	9	55.45*	6	5.08	9	11.85	9
overall working-class psychology	5.75	6	8.05	6	41.53*	4	3.95	6	12.88**	6
textiles:										
class identification	4.62	6	12.99**	6	2.45	6	4.42	6	3.01	4
awareness	6.40	6	1.32	6	5.41	6	6.26	6	9.71**	4
quantitative union participation	10.25	9	13.72	9	43.66*	9	12.74	9	3.38	6
qualitative union participation	11.73	9	11.70	9	44.51*	9	12.31	9	8.60	6
overall working-class psychology	2.85	6	12.06	6	19.71*	6	8.66	6	1.42	4
automobiles:										
class idententification	4.29	3	0.80	3	2.11	2	1.89	3	311	2
awareness	2.79	6	3.21	6	2.56	4	4.21	6	7.10	4
quantitative union participation	14.68	9	9.44	9	45.72*	6	23.27*	9	9.47	6
qualitative union participation	12.19	9	11.49	9	29.32*	6	17.35**	9	8.24	6
overall working-class psychology	12.70**	6	5.79	6	13.39*	4	5.27	6	4.64	4
chemicals:										
class identification	3.74	3	5.74	3	3.03	2	4.99	3	6.23**	2
awareness	7.11	6	4.36	6	2.09	4	5.29	6	14.46*	4
quantitative union participation	6.03	9	8.64	9	30.53*	6	13.94	9	6.25	6
qualitative union participation	3.86	9	9.66	9	31.13*	6	15.75	9	8.14	6
overall working-class psychology	8.39	6	10.75	6	13.04**	4	3.82	6	7.95	4

* significant at the .01 level

workers among whom it relates to overall working-class psychology. Inspection of the relevant table indicates an increase in domination to coincide with an increase in overall working-class psychology.

(b) There is virtually no impact by fractionization on any of the working-class psychology dimensions, except for qualitative union participation (printing) and class identification (textiles). In these two cases, an increase in fractionization appears to coincide with an increase in qualitative union particpation, and working-class identification respectively.

(c) There is a consistent significant relationship between isolation, the union participation dimensions and, through these, also, with overall working-class psychology. This relationship is not unexpected. It appears that those who are most cut off from the contact with their fellow workers on the job, also have below average union participation.

(d) Distanciation only relates significantly to union participation (quantitative and qualitative) among the automobile workers and, further, lacks any influence whatsoever.

(e) Overall work experience relates significantly to awareness (textiles and chemicals). Increases in estranging work experience appear to be accompanied by increases in awareness. The relationship with class identification among the chemical workers follows the same direction: the more estranging the work experience, the greater the tendency to identify in working-class terms. Overall work experience is only significantly related to overall working-class psychology in the case of the printers. Here the relationship follows the inverse pattern: the more estranging the work experience the weaker the working-class psychology.

It appears that the relationship between the two syndromes in general is a rather fragmentary one. Except for the constant impact of the isolation dimension, statistical significance has been established in a few single cases and further analysis does not seem warranted.

4.3. *Horizontal and Vertical Linkages*

The development of horizontal linkages, e.g. linkages directed towards those people sharing the same class position, forms the basis for communalization, a necessary precondition for the growth of class-based solidarities, and as such a most important part of the process of class formation. In the Marxian perspective, the emergence of these cohesive mechanisms on labor's side were facilitated by the growth of large scale industry. In the big industrial enterprises that replaced the small sized manufactures and artisan shops, the number of workers employed within the context of one industrial setting increased drastically. This concentration of large numbers of workers, as such, would generate an awareness of strength. Together with the improved objective possibilities for contacts and communication (in comparison with peasants, artisans and the like), this would facilitate the development of solidarities and other cohesive mechanisms resulting "in the ever expanding union of workers" (Marx and Engels, 1965: 21). At the same time, this situation would undercut the "divide and rule" strategy of the employer based on the existence of personal ties with individual workers.

In this perspective, which has inspired considerable research (cf. Kerr and Siegel, 1954; Hamilton, 1967; Lipset, 1963; Revans, 1956), the factor "size of plant" and its direct effects on the concentration of large numbers of workers sharing conditions of exploitation, takes a primary position.

It contains the implicit notion that this concentration will lead to an increase in frequency, range, and intensity of interaction and communication between the workers concerned with, as the ultimate result, a growing internal integration of the workers segment on the basis of common interests. Obviously, this connection cannot be assumed to be direct or automatic: an increased frequency in interaction may produce hostility as well as solidarity. In addition, the technological structure of the working environment, through its effects on the division of labor and the social organization within the plant may create structural barriers against the development of wide-scale contact in the working situation. This may interfere with a direct translation of a concentration of workers in time and space into the kind of interaction and communication that would promote the internal integration of the worker segment and give rise to solidary orientations.

These necessary preconditions for the growth of horizontal solidarities: social contact among fellow workers from the immediate working situation, have been studied among the Monterrey workers, next to a second indicator: the participation, with fellow workers, in organizations other than the company union.

4.3.1. Social contact among fellow workers: frequency and range

The frequency of the contact among fellow workers outside the plant is rather reduced. The total number of workers who are in daily contact with their work mates is, in general, rather small (17.6 percent). This category is most strongly represented among the textile workers and chemical workers (31.1 and 29.6 percent respectively). They live together in company villages and *colonias* and their objective possibilities for contact are best. Striking is the widespread absence of contact among the automobile workers: 39.8 percent never meet with fellow workers, and 45.3 percent only once a week or less. Among the printers little evidence can be found for the existence of a community of work mates as described by Lipset et al (1956) for this setting. Only 23.0 percent had daily contact, 52.5 percent met once a week or less with their fellow workers.

Most of the contacts with work mates involved workers with whom the respondents cooperated on a daily basis in the immediate working environment (89 percent). The textile and chemical workers probably for the same reasons mentioned above, form the categories that maintain contact most

152

intensively with those in the factory community who constitute their daily work companions (93.5 and 96.6 percent, respectively). These relations apparently are rather stable: in most individual contacts the same work mates or group of work mates are involved (76.1 percent). Among the printers, most contacts outside this category of workers are maintained (30.3 percent).

With regard to the frequency and range of social contacts among the workers of the four industrial settings, we can conclude that:

(a) Substantial numbers of workers either do not maintain contact with fellow workers outside the working environment, or meet on a very infrequent basis. Both categories include more than half of the total number of workers.

(b) Those workers who maintain rather frequent contact with their fellow workers mostly mingle with the same workers, and they represent, in most cases, companions in the daily work environment.

(c) Those contacts transcending the immediate working situation and that are directed towards fellow workers, who are not at the same time close work companions in the factory, appear to be relatively scarce.

The general paucity of the social contacts between the workers in the four industrial settings finds its correlate in their participation in organizations other than the company union. Nearly 80 percent among them are not involved in any organizational activity at all. More than half (55.2 percent) of those who do participate, do so through sports clubs, mostly the company soccer or baseball club. The others are distributed over "social clubs" (12.6 percent), political organizations (7.0 percent), and a variety of other clubs and organizations (25.2 percent). Most of the organizational involvement (75.8 percent) is with work mates. The absolute numbers of those participating are equally small in all four industrial settings (N = 87).

The readiness to assume positions of organizational responsibility may count as an indicator of the quality of participation. Among the organization members 27.5 percent (N = 24) met this criterion and declared to hold or to have held such position.

The general lack of involvement in social contacts with fellow workers may result from the emphasis on contacts within the extended family, which may limit the possibilities of the workers to maintain ample outside contacts. In many cases the "family isolationism" which has developed, leaves little room for contact with work companions, unless as among the textile and chemical workers, they live next door.

4.3.2. Vertical links: Some remarks on patronage and compadrazgo

The emergence of horizontal solidarities cementing labor unity presupposes the weakening of mechanisms oriented towards intergration along vertical lines. In this context, Engels refers to the destruction of "the last vestiges of the old system of benevolent paternalism between masters and men" (Engels, 1958: 137).

The analysis of the mechanisms of control utilized by Monterrey entre-

153

preneurs in their dealings with the working class has shown that these vertical linkages have not disappeared and, in some cases, have acquired new intensity and vigor. In all four industrial settings, the management has spared no pains to integrate the workers within the company and to involve them with the company effort, on unequal terms that is to say. This integration has assumed different forms in each of the settings, but the aims were the same. Behind the immediate goal of conflict prevention has lingered the long term objective of hampering the autonomous integration of labor on the basis of class interests, breaking emergent class solidarities, fractionizing labor unity.

In the small print shops, the paternalism based on the direct personal relationships between the shopowner and each of the workers has overshadowed the relationships between the workers themselves. In this environment, the relationship has lacked, however, the connotation of absolute power on the employer's side, and absolute dependence on labor's side. The relatively high skill level of the printers, combined with the general scarcity of skilled labor on the Monterrey labor market, has increased the workers' alternatives and has posed definite limits to the exercise of control by the *patrón*.

In the larger shops, these direct relationships are difficult to realize and, here, the *blanco* union serves as a mediator, integrating the worker in the company on terms that have been defined through management initiative.

A similar situation prevails in the other industrial settings, although the identification between union and management is not as close in the textile mill as in the automobile factory, or in the chemical plant. In all settings, the *patrón* has tried to create clientelist relationships with union leaders, foremen, or other workers who, given their structural positions, can function as intermediaries between workers and management (cf. *empleados de confianza*). Their solidarities with the lower levels are bought off through the distribution of favors and sinecures and changed towards loyalties and solidarities with the top. They are assigned the supervising and mediating functions in the management system of control. These tasks isolate them effectively from their fellow workers. At the same time, they are only delegated minor responsibilities that do not threaten the employer's interest in any way. Their major tasks do not exceed the implementation of management decisions. The authority and power over the workers are limited, and the distance to the top remains considerable despite their cooptation by the management. The "intermediaries" in these clientelistic structures often tend to combine their dependence on the *patrón*, for favors and rewards, with strong feelings of identification with this same *patrón* who is imitated also in his behavior towards the lower strata (cf. Freire, 1971).

The structures of control to which these vertical ties belong show, in a structural sense, a striking resemblance to the traditional domination systems that have characterized the Latin American rural areas since long (cf. Cotler, 1968). At the same time, they contain quite a few elements, in particular those related to the phenomenon of personalism, that form part of a Latin American cultural heritage in a wider sense. In this context, especially *compadrazgo*

154

or ritual kinship should be mentioned. This phenomenon traditionally has reinforced the vertical structural tendencies in Latin American society, to the extent that the pattern was followed to select the *compadres* or godparents of the newborn child from social strata superior to the one the parents belonged to (Gillin, 1966).

The incidence of these person-to-person linkages, crossing class boundaries among the workers in the four settings, has been investigated. At the same time, it was studied to what extent these ties served to link different positions in the occupational hierarchy within the factories where the workers were employed. This information will complement the picture of the importance of those vertical linkages and solidarities that may interfere with the development of horizontal solidarities. The workers were asked to describe the occupations of the *compadres* of their children at the time the respective *compadre* relationships were constituted. The answers suggest, as a very general conclusion, that the custom of selecting godparents from superior strata is not very widespread. Only 17.4 percent of all godparents did belong to the middle or upper strata of the occupational hierarchy. The others had working-class occupations. The proportion of *compadres* with middle- or upper-class jobs is relatively greatest among the early children. Among the first born children they count 19.0 percent; among the second born 19.4 percent. It descends gradually, however, with the later children to 5.5 percent among the tenth born. In fact a multiple regression analysis did show the occupation of the *compadre* (of the first, second . . . eleventh and more children) as a reasonably good predictor of the present job of the worker. The strength of this prediction increases with the number of children to the extent that, in the case of the children who are more recently born, the jobs of the *compadres* and the present jobs of the workers tend to converge.

Apparently the selection, in the case of the early as well as the later children, has taken place from similar strata in the occupational hierarchy. The slight status differences with regard to the *compadres* that initially existed probably have disappeared as a result of respondents' own career mobility. This thesis is further supported by the lack of a relationship between the job of the *compadre* and the first job of the worker. Mind, that the first job of the workers, with a few exceptions (mostly from the printing sector), was located on the very lowest stratum of the occupational hierarchy: 87.4 percent of the workers began their career here.

In a total of 20.3 percent of the cases, the *compadre* was selected from the personnel of the company where the respective workers were employed. This custom increases in importance with more recent children. Obviously, these differences are also conditioned by the number of years the respective workers have been employed by the factory and, consequently, the opportunity they have had to become integrated in the work community. The textile workers stand out in this type of *compadre* selection. They accounted for 44.6 percent of the cases in which a *compadre* was selected from within the factory (printing: 8.4 percent, automobiles: 18.2 percent, chemicals: 28.8 percent). These

job *compadre*	first job	present job
1 st child	—	.16
2 nd child	—	.15
3 rd child	—	.23
4 th child	.19	.24
5 th child	—	.32
6 th child	—	.22
7 th child	—	.20
8 th child	.13	.46
9 th child	.05	.34
10 th child	—	.53
11 th child and more (x)	—	.58
$_mR$	.13	.58
R^2	.02	.33

compadres all represented fellow workers, except one. The distribution of *compadres* over working-class and middle- or upper-class occupations for all industrial settings is shown in the next table.

TABLE 34: Job level *compadre* and location within or outside the factory where the respective respondent is presently employed.

	location job *compadres*		
level job *compadres*	within factory	outside factory	N
working class occupations			
low	4.2	13.0	169
medium	25.0	39.1	548
high	61.8	28.5	533
middle or upper class occupations	9.0	19.4	263
	100.0	100.0	1513

The relatively strong representation of *compadres* among the higher working-class occupations within the factory concerns to an important extent the textile workers. Among the workers in the four settings, *compadrazgo*, rather than crossing class lines, appears to create linkages of a horizontal nature and, in many cases, it may simply tie in with the emphasis on interaction within the extended family which we have noted before.

4.4. *The Workers and the Company Union*

In the previous paragraph several integrative mechanisms have been

156

reviewed: those underlying an integration along class lines and those cutting across those lines. Some concrete information on contact and communication has been provided for the discussion on the importance of horizontal versus vertical solidarities to which .ore attention will be devoted later on. First, however, the subject needs some further elaboration with regard to the participation, quantitative and qualitative, of the workers within their unions and their attitudes towards union activities, also in their relationship to working-class psychology, identification with official politics, and political radicalism. Despite the idiosyncracies of the Mexican labor movement that have been commented upon in earlier paragraphs, the point remains that, within the factory, the union as such constitutes the only framework that integrates the entire body of workers, excluding nonworkers. Despite official and entrepreneurial control mechanisms that have infiltrated its decision making process, and apart from the reservations the workers themselves may have towards their own union, it does offer a context within which workers do meet each other while confronting affairs related to their interests. In dealing with these questions concerning the union, first, a short exposition will be given of the labor management relations in the four settings.

4.4.1. *Labor and management in the four industrial settings*

The print shops: Printers traditionally have been the most literate and articulate of manual workers. In most Western industrial nations they have been in the forefront of the labor movement (Lipset *et al.*, 1956). In Mexico the printers were involved in the emerging labor movement in the capital city during the *Porfiriato*. In the last few years before the Revolution, the mutualist orientation in organized labor gave way to a more activist orientation on the basis of anarcho-syndicalist ideas. This change was realized under the influence of several groups of immigrants, together with local intellectuals of anarchist leanings. The results of their activities were most pronounced among various groups of artisans and the skilled workers in the Mexico City industries. Among them were the printers who, in 1909, founded the *Unión de Linotipistas Mexicanos* and shortly before the fall of Profirio Diaz in 1911 the *Union Tipográfica Mexicana*, later renamed to *Confederación de Artes Gráficas* but liquidated in 1915 (Araiza, 1964, vol. III; 9-13: De la Cerda Silva, 1961: 110). Although they participated in the movement, the printers did not play a vanguard role. This was done by the miners, railroad workers, and textile workers. The printers unions initially even had some difficulty associating themselves with the general labor movement.

At the present time the role of the printers unions is not conspicuous either. A problem in this branch of industry has been the predominance of the small sized shops. The degree of concentration of ownership is still relatively low. In the numerous small shops, a great proportion of the work force has not been unionized yet.

Among the workers of the print shops figuring in this study, 44 percent were

157

organized in a shop syndicate affiliated with the F.N.S.I. Only 13 percent were organized in the *Sindicato de Trabajadores de la Industria de Artes Gráficas* (STIAG), affiliated with the C.T.M., and 43 percent of the workers was not organized.

The textile mill: The textile workers in Mexico have a history of militancy. They led the unionization movement in the country and initiated the strikes that contributed to the ultimate downfall of the Porfirio Díaz regime (cf. Buve, 1972).

The union of the selected mill has a long history, but the incidence of activism or militant action has been rather low. The predecessor of the present union originated in the mutualist movement of the end of the 19th and the beginning of the 20th century. It belonged to the signers at the founding conferences of the C.R.O.M. on March 22, 1918 in nearby Saltillo (Rosendo Salazar, 1923: 22). In the 1930's the union joined with the C.T.M. and it presently belongs to the *Sindicato de Trabajadores de la Industria Textil y Similares de la Republica Mexicana* (STITSRM) again a C.T.M. affiliate.

The union organization consists of four sections, each division of the mill belonging to a different section. The company had a closed-shop policy. In fact, the union controlled the labor supply and presented the candidates for any opening that may occur. Within the factory, it exercised close supervision of the policies for promotion and conducted, together with a management representative, the time-task studies that formed the basis for the establishment of the production quotas, the corresponding pay scales and the system of bonus pay. In recent times the task of the union has revolved very much around the execution of the provisions of the new labor code and the explicit inclusion of these provisions in the collective contracts that are reviewed every two years.

Its orientation to labor-management relations has been no less formalistic and legalistic as in the case of the *sindicatos blancos*, but its tactics have differed. A certain distance has been maintained toward management and the close identification between union (leadership) and *patrón*, which has characterized most of the labor relations in the companies with F.N.S.I. or F.S.A. affiliated unions, is lacking. The workers have not been subjected directly to the paternalistic mechanisms of control by the company because the union has acted as a buffer. The company pays a fixed amount to the union for each affiliated member. Next, the union arranges the purchase and distribution of the *despensas familiares* or food packages to its members. It gives financial aid in case of sickness or of the death of a member of the worker family, and mediates other measures of support that form part of the collective contract, or are included in the social security package.

The automobile factory: Labor management relations until recently followed the traditional pattern of the Monterrey family enterprise. The company union was founded in 1956, and affiliated with the F.N.S.I. It was

158

strongly dominated by management until the end of the 1960's when a slightly more activist leadership took control. Until that time, the union officials had been handpicked by the management and promoted to the white collar ranks as a reward for "faithful service," after serving their period in office. Despite the breakdown of traditional paternalism and the rejection of *patrón*-worker relationships by the present union leadership as "a gimmick, only serving the interests of the *patrón* himself," the union has continued to operate close to the management. The new labor law, however, generated pressure from the membership. The number of workers, according to union officials, approaching the union for counsel and advice on problems related to work conditions increased rapidly at the end of the 1960's. This phenomenon forced more activist attitudes upon the leaders. They, consequently, put great emphasis on full compliance with the labor code, while proceeding, however, with great prudence and avoiding any kind of conflict that might have upset the relationship of "friendship and understanding" with the *patrón*.

At the time of the investigation, the union leadership acknowledged the existence of considerable tension among the rank and file due to the alleged failure of the company to improve its wage levels and general working conditions. Both were evaluated by them as "below average Monterrey standards." Part of the problem may reside in the fact that, after the breakdown of traditional paternalism, the control aspects were emphasized, while the range of small benefits for the workers that traditionally go with this kind of management labor relations were neglected. The automobile workers, unlike the workers of the other settings, had no company housing and did not receive food packages, clothing, and the like.

Within the factory, the primary union tasks concern the solution of frictional issues in the immediate working environment. On the section level of the factory, this task is fulfilled by the respective section delegate who hears the problem and tries to resolve it together with the respective supervisor, the worker(s), and representative of the company industrial relations department. If a compromise cannot be worked out, the issue is brought before the union Executive Committee. This committee is small, numbering four members. It is assisted by four additional committees, each dealing with a special problem area: union finances, legal affairs, organizational affairs and plant security.

The chemical plant: In this plant strong efforts have been made to integrate the worker into "the company family". The company forms part of the Cuauthemoc group which has conditioned labor management relations. Following the entrepreneurial ideology that has accompanied the paternalistic and reformist mechanisms of control, the Department of Industrial Relations has established a social work program directed towards the establishment of communities in which the workers and their families will obtain "levels of living that are superior to the present ones in the areas of health, culture, economics, work, ethics and social behavior."[24] In this effort, not only the

24 Internal communication, chemical plant.

workers themselves are involved. In addition their wives and children are drawn into the program through activities of an educational and recreational nature. This program, as the Department states, not only serves the interests of the company where it upgrades its labor force and furthers "good labor management relations," but also improves the life chances of the workers and their families and contributes to "the establishment of the truly social Christian order."[25]

The company union is affiliated with F.S.A. It has been firmly integrated in the company structure where it functions as a problem-solving institution, handling frictions and problems in the immediate working situation and, if necessary, mediating between the workers and the Department of Industrial Relations. The union has an Executive Committee of eight members, four additional committees, and delegates in all departments of the plant. Individual problems are dealt with on the departmental level between the respective delegate and the foreman. If the issue cannot be resolved, the Secretary of Conflicts of the Executive Committee comes in.

In all these proceedings the union, that is to say its present leadership, operates in close cooperation with management. There is little effort from their side to define a position that would maintain some distance towards the *patrón* and emphasize the characteristics of the union as an organization actively promoting workers' interests. During its entire existence of almost two decades, no collective labor conflicts leading to strikes have occurred. The apparent absence of tension, and/or discontent, other than on an individual scale, was attributed by the union leadership to a generalized satisfaction over the income and working conditions that had been negotiated for the collective contract and that, according to these leaders, were superior to most of the other companies in the area. This observation was, in part, confirmed by the investigation. The chemical workers indeed appeared to be most "satisfied" in comparison with the workers in the other settings. Their objective income situation, however, appeared to be worse then the others."[26]

4.4.2. The unions: membership, attendance and leadership

Membership: The three factories and four of the print shops adhered to closed-shop rules. In these settings only the *eventuales*, the workers on temporary contracts, and the *personal de confianza* do not belong to the union. Membership and affiliation are distributed as follows:

---

[25] Ibid.

[26] As an indication of a possible divergence between leaders and membership may count the strong opposition by the union members to a proposal of the leadership to cooperate with an inquiry into the social and economic conditions of the factory work force, organized by the Department of Industrial Relations. The result of this inquiry, that eventually was held despite the opposition, offered too many opportunities for control over the workers by management, according to the rank and file.

type of union	industrial settings				
	printing	textiles	automobiles	chemicals	N
C.T.M.	13.0	96.4	–	–	119
F.S.A.	–	–	–	82.6	91
F.N.S.I.	44.0	–	94.0	–	138
not affiliated	43.0	3.6	6.0	17.4	72
	100.0	100.0	100.0	100.0	420

These workers represent a rather stable membership. A great number have been union members for some time. Only 27.3 percent represent "recent" members of the union who had joined between one and five years ago, 39.6 percent had become union members in a period from six to ten years ago, 33.1 percent had already done so more than ten years ago.

Attendance: The union meetings are generally held once a month. The only exception is formed by a chapter of the C.T.M. printers union, which meets once a week. According to union statutes, attendance at meetings is obligatory for all members. The automobile workers union charges five pesos to each worker who fails to fulfill his duty to attend the meetings. The textile workers union charges three pesos for each "unjustified absence." In addition, the statutes assign to the leadership the authority to suspend union rights, such as food packages, financial aid in case of sickness or death, and other social welfare measures, to any worker who has failed to show at the meetings for more than three consecutive times. It is not known whether this authority frequently leads to action against delinquent workers. A fact is that 97.1 percent of the unionized textile workers do attend the monthly meetings. However, 17 percent of those attending do so "involuntarily," which may point to an existing fear of fines and/or suspensions (compare: printers 5.4 percent, automobile workers 11.2 percent, chemical workers 1.4 percent).

Striking is the poor participation of the automobile and chemical workers: only 39.3 and 42.8 percent, respectively, did attend the montly meetings; 24.5 and 20.9 percent, respectively, had never attented any meeting during their union membership (compare: printers 2.4 and textile workers 0.0 per cent). This phenomenon has its correlate in a rather skeptical attitude of the workers towards these unions. It comes as no surprise, then, that when asked to rate themselves with respect to their union activities, 70.2 percent of the automobile workers and 53.8 percent of the chemical workers classified as inactive union members (compare: printers 35.1 and textile workers 48.7 percent). This may well be related to the weak profile of these unions as genuine interest organizations, the prevalence of managerial initiative in union affairs, and the small maneuvering room for autonomous action.

Those printers who are unionized rate as the relatively most active union members. Their attendance of the meetings is rather high (95.2 percent attend each week or month) and largely voluntary. One explanation may reside with their superior educational level and skill distribution. In addition, the rather small size of the unions offers a real possibility for social contact among the workers and enables them to become personally involved in union affairs (cf. Lipset, 1956).

Leadership: An additional indicator of the intensity of involvement in printers unions is their participation in positions of responsibility. Among the members, 31.6 percent had been involved in leadership positions, and mostly in those of greater importance: secretary generals, and secretaries of the Executive Committees, rather than delegados. The proportion of union members involved in leadership positions was much less in the other settings: 24.5 percent (textiles), 10.6 percent (automobiles) and 17.6 percent (chemicals).

The Executive Committees of the *Mesas Directivas* of the union number from five to seven members, depending upon the range of functions that have been assumed by the unions. The automobile workers union has an Executive Committee of five: a Secretary General, and Secretaries of Conflicts, Organization and Publicity, Interior Affairs, and a Treasurer. The Executive Committee of the textile workers union numbers seven members: a Secretary General and Secretaries of Labor and Conflicts, Organization and Publicity, Technical and Industrial Affairs, Educational and Cultural Problems, Social Welfare, Finances, and Statistics.

Most of this participation in positions of organizational responsibility is of recent date, which justifies its use as an indicator of the intensity of present involvement in the union. Among all positions (N = 70), 91.4 percent had been occupied within the last decade (1961-1971), and more than two-thirds of these within the last five years (1966-1971). There are no substantial differences between the settings on this point.

In addition to the previous remarks, some other observations can be made with regard to the leadership situation:
(a)   The printers unions are more numerous and smaller in size; given the low incidence of *continuismo*, a relatively higher number of unionized printers will have the opportunity to receive leadership experience.
(b)   The textile workers union knows some *continuismo*; the Secretaries General of all four sections are union veterans who at the time of the research had already occupied these positions for an average of six years each.
(c)   The automobile workers union numbers relatively few ex-Secretaries General and Secretaries among its membership, due to the management policy (at least until 1971) to promote "faithful" union representatives who completed their terms to the ranks of the employees through *empadromiento*.
(d)   The chemical workers union has elections only every four years, contrary to the other unions in which all leaders are up for reelection every two

162

years. Due to frequent reelection and *empadronamiento*, relatively few ex-union leaders figure among the present membership.

Election to union office takes place by vote of the rank and file. Formally, the workers present *planillas*, lists of candidates for each position, all candidates requiring a minimum of 25 signatures of union members supporting the candidacy. In practice, there has been, especially in the automobile and chemical workers unions, a considerable amount of management maneuvering behind the scenes in order to get a *planilla* presented and elected that does not include "controversial" candidates.

This latter policy has been highly successfull until now, and it has helped to preserve a dependent labor movement. It is symptomatic that the union leaders do not occupy anything like a vanguard position, and do not distinguish themselves significantly from the rank and file on the variables indicating more "classist" of "militant" positions. The relationship between union position (leaders vs. nonleaders), and these variables for the unionized workers of all settings are as follows:

union position X	class identification	X^2	.11 (1 d.f.)
—	awareness	X^2	.99 (2 d.f.)
—	political radicalism	X^2	.17 (2 d.f.)

None of the relationship is statistically significant.

The Secretaries General (N = 5) figuring in the sample had held other union offices. The typical career in union affairs, as it emerged from the interviews with union leaders, starts through regular union meeting attendance. It is here that the potential leaders acquire their role of union activists through participation in attending, voting, and especially through speaking on the floor. Active intervention in union meetings was indicated by the respondents as the most important way of building a reputation and of getting further involved in union affairs.

This involvement typically includes election to the position of *delegado* as the first step. As a delegate, e.g. union representative on the section level of the factory, his main task is the solution of conflicts in the immediate working environment, together with the workers involved and the foreman or *mayordomo* who is responsible. In case the problem cannot be resolved, the delegate mediates its presentation before the Executive Committee.

The next step in the union career is membership on one of the auxiliary committees, as the *Comisión de Justicia, - de Hacienda, - de Vigilancia, - de Seguridad y Higiene*, etc., that function under the Executive Committee. Especially the "strategic" Secretaries: Internal Affairs, and Labor and Conflicts, offer ample opportunity for contacts with the rank and file as well as with the management. These constitute a good jumping-off board for the position of Secretary General.

4.4.3. *Attitudes of the workers towards their union*

The specific characteristics of Mexican organized labor in general, and of the union movement in Monterrey in particular, have been amply documented. Among these characteristics, the prevalence of official and entrepreneurial initiative and the suppression of any autonomous action that could have implication for the existing power relations in the industry, are striking aspects. Against the background of these phenomena, it appears essential to analyze, next to the objective data on union membership, attendance, and leadership, the subjective reflection of the rank and file on the functioning of their unions as interest organization, and on the possibility of exerting any influence in this respect.

The interviews showed a considerable distrust of union officials, and great skepticism with regard to the possibility of the rank and file to affect the decision making process. The great majority of workers (68.6 percent), declared they had little influence on the course of union affairs. Among the automobile and chemical workers, this category was especially numerous (74.6 and 70.4 percent, respectively). Their perception of the influence they can bring to bear on the course of union events clearly finds its correlate in the relatively low levels of quantitative and qualitative participation in the unions. The lesser importance of this category among the textile workers and the printers (63.3 and 46.8 percent, respectively) also conforms to the participation pattern outlined before.

Only 3.4 percent of the workers claimed they had much influence in union affairs, 28.0 percent stated they had some influence. In a situation where so many members of the rank and file perceive themselves at the margin of the major decision-making processes within the union, their ideas about the motives of those actually involved in decision making, and the nature of these decisions become rather important.

The majority of union members appeared to give the union leadership the benefit of the doubt as far as the first issue is concerned. Two-thirds of the unionized workers identified their leaders as men mainly interested in the well being of the rank and file. Especially the printers single out in this respect. Those who tends to think of their leaders as preoccupied with private power plays are most strongly represented among the automobile workers.

In relation to the second issue, the question should be asked to what extent the "good intentions" that, according to most respondents, characterize the union leadership, are reflected in the actual decisions made. Among the unionized respondents, a total of sixty percent still think this to be the case.

A considerable number of automobile and chemical workers, however, view the orientations of the actual decisions made by the union leaders as leaning towards management's side. The dependence of the respective unions as *sindicatos blancos* apparently has its place in the consciousness of the workers. This applies also to those textile workers who recognize their *sindicato rojo* as responding to official politics.

164

TABLE 36: Motives of union leaders according to the rank and file, by four industrial settings

	industrial settings				
motives of union leaders	printing	textiles	automobiles	chemicals	N
well being rank and file	80.7	71.7	55.3	67.0	235
private power plays	19.3	28.3	44.7	33.0	113
	100.0	100.0	100.0	100.0	348

TABLE 37: Orientations of actual decision-making by union leaders, according to the rank and file in four industrial settings

	industrial settings				
orientations	printing	textiles	automobiles	chemicals	N
towards the workers' side	78.9	69.8	44.6	52.7	209
towards official politics	5.3	21.7	3.2	–	29
towards management	15.8	8.5	52.2	47.3	110
	100.0	100.0	100.0	100.0	348

The information on the orientations towards union affairs, mentioned above, has been summarized in the index "union identification" in order to explore these orientations and related backgrounds factors.

These factors are: skill, work experience, working-class psychology, political preference, and identification with the wider political structure, and political radicalism.

Skill: Earlier, skill was shown to be one of the more important predictors of work experience and working-class psychology. In the case of working-class psychology, a positive relationship was shown to exist with quantitative and qualitative union participation as major contributing dimensions. This result suggests a significant and positive relationship between skill and union identification. The relationship is indeed significant among the union members in tree of the four settings:

printing X^2 13.66 (15 d.f.)
textiles X^2 21.52 (12 d.f.)**
automobiles X^2 37.40 (15 d.f.)*
chemicals X^2 44.55 (15 d.f.)*

* significant at the .01 level
** significant at the .05 level

The inspection of the respective tables (cf. Vellinga, 1975: 410) shows that the direction of the relationship between the two variables follows the predicted pattern: union identification will tend to augment in strength with increases in skill.

Work experience and working-class psychology: On the basis of the positive relationship between skill and working-class psychology, and between skill and union identification, working-class psychology should be expected to relate positively to union identification. Work experience may be expected to relate negatively to union identification through its isolation dimension.

The first prediction is carried out, the second one only partially. Inspection of the relevant tables (Ibid.) shows, that union identification tends to be higher when working-class psychology is stronger.

TABLE 38: Work experience, working-class psychology, and union identification, by four industrial settings

work experience and working-class psychology dimensions	industrial settings							
	printing		textiles		automobiles		chemicals	
	X2	DF	X2	DF	X2	DF	X2	DF
overall work experience	10.23	9	19.12**	6	7.63	6	6.21	6
domination	2.98	9	10.61	9	9.38	9	6.03	9
fractionization	8.20	9	16.62	9	13.91	9	7.82	9
isolation	26.11*	6	25.91	9	3.71	6	20.97*	6
distanciation	7.07	9	14.89	9	9.61	9	22.40*	9
overall working-class psychology	86.54*	6	31.86*	6	14.41**	6	27.71*	6
class identification	6.11	6	12.10	6	7.09	3	6.45	3
awareness	5.57	6	4.30	6	10.51	6	13.30**	6
quant. union part.	125.26*	9	114.03*	9	107.90*	9	134.78*	9
qual. union part.	111.60*	9	120.56*	9	123.58*	9	140.56*	9

* significant at the .01 level
** significant at the .05 level

In all settings, the union participation dimensions appear to contribute most to the significance of the relationship. The relationship to union identification follows the same pattern: union identification tends to become stronger with increasing union participation.

The relationship between awareness and union identification among the automobile and chemical workers follows a different course: an increase in awareness tends to be accompanied by a decrease in union identification. This phenomenon illustrates, again, the tension within the working-class psychology syndrome between the "classist" orientations (class identification and awareness) and the more "conformist" and "resigned" orientations underlying the union participation dimensions. This duality, as has been shown before, can be noted in particular among the automobile and chemical workers.

Work experience is indeed related to union identification through its isolation dimension. Those workers who are most cut off from contact with their work mates, as was observed earlier, have below average union participation. In addition appear to have a below average union identification. Apart from the isolation dimension, work experience in general, however, fails to influence substantially and consistently the attitudes of the workers towards their unions.

The relation to the wider political structure: The dependence of the unions upon official politics and the company management forms part of the consciousness of many workers. Among a strong minority of workers, an attitude has resulted towards the union organization and the role of its leaders ranging from skepticism to active distrust. To what extent this skepticism or distrust corresponds to similar orientations relating to the wider political structure, becomes obviously the next question, to be explored through the following issues:

(a)   The relationship between union identification and specific preferences with regard to political parties.

(b)   The relationship between union identification and the identification with official politics.

(c)   The relationship between union identification and political radicalism.

Regarding (a), there is a weak tendency for strong union identification to coincide with a preference for the official party. At the same time, union identification tends to be slightly weaker among those opting for the political opposition.

Even among the automobile and chemical workers, the preference for PAN tends to be superior among those workers whose union identification is relatively low, despite the fact that, in particular the chemical workers union, can be said to approach PAN positions.

TABLE 39:   Party preference and union identification for all four industrial settings

union identification	party preference			
	PRI	PAN	OTHER	N
1 (high)	23.9	17.0	11.9	75
2	50.5	40.4	45.2	168
3 (low)	25.6	42.6	42.9	105
	100.0	100.0	100.0	348

The relationship between union identification and party preference, however, remains weak and cannot shown to be statistically significant in any of the four settings.

Regarding (b), union identification and identification with official politics are weakly related. A tendency for decreasing union identification to coincide with a decreasing identification with official politics is present, but it is not very strongly expressed.

TABLE 40: Identification with official politics and union identification for all four industrial settings

union identification	identification with official politics			
	1 (high)	2	3 (low)	N
1 (high)	23.5	19.5	11.6	75
2	51.4	41.3	37.2	168
3 (low)	25.1	39.2	51.2	105
	100.0	100.0	100.0	348

Among the individual settings, only the automobile workers show a significant relationship between the phenomena concerned and also the most clear presence of the pattern mentioned above ($X^2 = 9.72$, 4 d.f., $p = <.05$).

In the other settings, this tendency is much more weakly expressed (chemicals), or virtually absent (printing and textiles).

Regarding (c), union identification and political radicalism are also weakly related. There is a tendency for those who are skeptical towards their union to take a more radical stand, but as in the cases mentioned above, this tendency is not very strong.

Among the individual settings, it is most pronounced with the chemical workers and, there, it may represent again a reaction against the strong management influence in the union. This setting is the only one in which the relationship is statistically significant ($X^2 = 10.45$, 4 d.f., $p = <.05$).

TABLE 41: Political radicalism and union identification for all four industrial settings

union identification	political radicalism			
	1 (high)	2	3 (low)	N
1 (high)	17.7	23.0	18.7	75
2	37.9	27.5	51.5	168
3 (low)	44.4	49.5	29.8	105
	100.0	100.0	100.0	348

168

Few of the relationships that refer to the three issues mentioned under (a), (b) and (c) can be proven to be statistically significant. Union identification, in general, does not relate clearly and unequivocally to either party preference, identification with official politics or political radicalism. Many workers who are critical of their unions do not project this criticism towards a wider political context. At the same time, however, it has also been shown that a sizable minority of workers combine their criticism of union affairs with estrangement from the PRI and official politics in general, and show a more positive position towards radical issues. This tendency is most pronounced among the automobile and chemical workers. In the next two paragraphs, these phenomena will be explored further.

4.5. The Workers and Official Politics

4.5.1. The cultural invasion of the working-class

The role of official politics with regard to the incorporation of the labor sector in structures that serve its neutralization as an autonomous and dynamic factor in social change has been amply documented. This process of integration and neutralization has been accompanied by ample revolutionary rhetoric. This rhetoric is a cultural legacy from the radical period of the Revolution, performs legitimizing functions, and has become part of the normative model of the political system with clearly "free-floating" characteristics. The lack of substantive policy measures that would fill the gap between ideology and reality, however, has not reduced its generalized application as a mechanism of cultural invasion of the working class, appearing in proclamations, speeches, and publications made by the *politicos* with working-class followings.

The declarations on national holidays, and especially on May 1st, made by representatives of organized labor and addressed to the State Governor and to the President of the Republic are a case in point. These constitute periodic affirmations of adherence to revolutionary ideals. "Revolutionary" carries here a double reference. In the statements,[27] frequently the class struggle terminology is used, but it is always related to the Mexican Revolutionary movement and, next to exhortations to increase proletarian strength in order to struggle with determination in the defense of labor interests, references can be found to concepts of "national unity," "national consciousness," the "common good," and the like.

The official labor movement and the unity party, PRI, are eulogized as the only effective means through which the emancipation of the proletariat can be realized. In this context, the praise is sound of the local and national protectors, the State Governor, and the President of the Republic, as "authentic

---

[27] Examples have been taken from *El Porvenir, El Heraldo,* and *El Norte,* May 1st, 1971.

revolutionaries," pleading the workers' cause in their struggle for an increase in levels of living. Invariably, the statements end with extensive declarations of support by the organized proletarian sectors for the government and its politicians.

Undoubtedly, this rhetoric may have infiltrated the consciousness of large numbers of workers, without a corresponding awareness of its manipulative intent. Yet, the fact that sizable proportions of workers show some skepticism with regard to the union and the role of the union leadership already indicates that these statements of organized labor's leadership cannot be attributed to the entire body of affiliated members in an unqualified way, as González Casanova does (González Casanova, 1968: 190).

The ideas of "common good" and "national unity" appear to have less than complete acceptance, especially among those workers who manifest a slightly more critical attitude towards the pretensions of entrepreneurs and political parties that they are dedicated to the promotion of working-class interests. More than half of the total number of respondents, 50.2 percent, concluded that the industrialists and businessmen primarily serve their own interests, as opposed to serving the interests of all Mexicans, 32.1 percent, or those of the working class, 17.6 percent.

In additionn 39.3 percent of the respondents maintained that the present political parties seldom or never attend to working-class problems in any adequate sense, next to 48.8 percent who assumed an occasional interest in these problems with them, while only 11.9 percent viewed working-class interests as always present among the political parties policies' primary objectives.

In this case, as well as in the previous one, the automobile workers stand out. Among them, 71.0 percent had a dim view of the activities of the entrepreneurial sector, which they viewed as primarily motivated by their own interests (cf. printers 43.0, textile workers 57.3 and chemical workers 30.9 percent); 49.0 percent was convinced the existing political parties seldom or never paid attention to working-class interests (cf. printers 38.0, textile workers 33.6, chemical workers 37.3 percent). The chemical workers' attitudes probably reflect the impact of entrepreneurial paternalism, and the textile workers will show most strongly the influence of official politics.

A similar pattern appears in the workers' reaction to government policies. While among the chemical workers and textile workers, 78.2 and 90.0 percent respectively, maintained that stable employment and adequate levels of living for all Mexicans were primary policy objectives, 65.0 percent of the automobile workers shared this opinion (cf. printers 82.0 percent). Among them, 35.0 percent felt that these issues were neglected with regard to the social class they considered themselves to belong to, a category only representing 10.0 percent among the textile workers (cf. printers 18.0, chemical workers 21.8 percent).

These opinions also affect the concrete political choices the workers make. Considerable numbers, 26.7 percent, show preference for political organi-

170

zations other than the all encompassing unity party, PRI. This political non-conformism is most pronounced among the automobile and chemical workers. Most of it is channeled through the opposition party, PAN, located on the right of the political spectrum. Surprising is the considerable preference shown for political organizations outside the established structure of official unity party and institutionalized opposition.

TABLE 42:   Political preferences, by four industrial settings

	industrial settings				
political preferences	printing	textiles	automobiles	chemicals	N
PRI	74.0	84.5	69.0	65.5	308
PAN	9.0	9.1	18.0	18.2	57
PPS	1.0	–	4.0	0.9	6
Others	16.0	6.4	9.0	15.4	49
	100.0	100.0	100.0	100.0	420

The data presented above obviously need some more elaboration. The conclusion, however, seems justified that at least some skepticism and nonconformance prevail and that the cultural invasion of the working class by employers and official politics apparently has been less than succesful. Those items that measure the identification of the respondent with the official political structure were assembled in an index (cf. Appendix A), and its relationship was probed with some strategic background factors.

4.5.2. *The identification with the official political structure*

Given the research problemn those categories of workers showing some skepsis with regard to official politics merit special interest. Their orientations have been studied, exploring the variations in identification with official politics through the following factors:
(a)   Skill, which on various earlier occasions was shown to account for basic differentiations in workers orientations and behavior.
(b)   The social mobility complex together with income, income dissatisfaction and the career- and life-satisfaction variables. This, in order to probe the relative deprivation dimension, and to further explore González Casanova's assertion that the dynamics of the process of economic development in Mexico, its effects with regard to social mobility, income, and their subjective consequences, account for the succesful way in which labor has been incorporated in the official political structures, a success, supposedly rooted in the wholeheartedly voluntary cooperation of the individual workers (González Casanova, 1968: 189 ff).

171

(c) Work experience and the working-class psychology variables.
(d) Political radicalism.

The outcome of the analysis of the relationships between "identification with official politics" and these variables are shown in Table 43. Striking results are: first, the lack of any relationship between the orientation towards the official political structure and a basic discriminating variable like skill; and, second, the absence of virtually any influence by the mobility/income/ (dis)satisfaction complex. Those factors that do relate to the dependent variable are located among the more "militant" variables, like "awareness" and "political radicalism."

TABLE 43: Identification with official politics and selected independent variables, by four industrial settings

| | industrial settings | | | | | | | |
| | printing | | textiles | | automobiles | | chemicals | |
independent variables	X2	DF	X2	DF	X2	DF	X2	DF
skill	7.78	10	4.35	8	8.73	10	12.93	10
income dissatisfaction	6.36	6	1927**	6	7.66	6	6.52	6
personal income	10.65	6	5.86	4	4.44	6	5.65	6
family income	12.16	8	6.61	6	11.51	8	6.94	6
intergen. mobility	2.81	4	4.73	4	5.00	4	5.77	4
intragen. mobility	1.34	4	1.16	2	6.21	4	10.92*	2
factory mobility	3.21	4	.27	2	.16	2	1.77	2
career satisfaction	3.96	4	4.55	4	5.70	4	6.22	4
life satisfaction	2.35	4	3.22	4	8.66	4	3.74	4
overall-work experience	5.77	6	3.25	4	4.58	4	7.58	4
domination	5.73	6	1.54	6	6.55	6	9.15	6
fractionization	9.02	6	10.38	6	2.31	6	11.24	6
isolation	3.54	4	4.44	6	2.17	4	.53	4
distanciation	3.37	6	3.92	6	7.47	6	5.53	6
overall working-class psy.	2.02	4	12.31**	4	3.40	4	6.40	4
class identification	.63	4	3.51	4	2.98	2	4.26	2
awareness	4.51	4	9.84**	4	12.65**	4	21.66*	4
quant. union part.	3.48	6	2.70	6	5.67	6	6.46	6
qual. union part.	4.86	6	4.11	6	8.63	6	4.59	6
political radicalism	16.97*	4	24.65*	4	3.29	4	11.31**	4

*   significant at the .01 level
** significant at the .05 level

An inspection of the tables (cf. Vellinga, 1975: 425) shows both the relationship with awareness and political radicalism to be of the inverse kind: when awareness cq. political radicalism increases, the identification with official politics tends to decrease. This tendency appears among the workers in each of the settings. Our findings suggest that those workers who possess some awareness of the nature of their economy, its exploitative characteristics, and the manipulative intent of the existing political parties, tend to take more radical political positions, apparently are less influenced by official rhetoric, and have a relatively weak identification with official politics (compare also Table 46).

In recent years, the official rhetoric has assumed full force as part of new efforts at controlled mobilization of the popular strata. After the increasing tensions between a rapidly changing economy and stagnating political structures had reached the boiling point in the late 1960's, this mechanism has been resorted to with increasing frequency and its safety valve functions have become more emphasized, especially since the presidential campaign of 1970.[28]

Behind an outwardly massive support for government policies, which largely has reflected the effectiveness of the mechanisms of controlled mobilization, lingers, as the data indicate, a certain degree of skepticism among those participating. In spring 1971, the Echeverría government had recently taken power and its *"México arriba y adelante"* apparently had not failed to impress the proletarian sectors. In that period, 86.7 percent of the workers in the four settings voiced active approval of government policies. They did so, however, following the patterns of persistent personalism in Mexican politics, by identifying government efforts with the president, Echeverria. This explains the considerable outward support for government policies, really reflecting identification with the person of the president or rather with his image of defender of working-class interests, which existed together with, and despite, the presence of critical attitudes towards the professional *politicos* and the formal political apparatus. In political practice, this criticism then is translated in political preference for parties other than the PRI. It, further, tends to coincide with an increased class awareness and more positive orientations towards radical issues.

4.6. The Workers and Political Radicalism

Among the basic discriminating issues on the political scene in the Mexican situation of 1971, the attitudes towards Cuba, the Cuban Revolution, and its leadership may count as a litmus test of radical political convictions.

In the preceding decade, the activities of the MLN (*Movimiento de Liberación Nacional*) had been widely publicized. This party had constituted itself on the radical left of the political spectrum with, as its most prominent leader, ex-president Lázaro Cárdenas. From the beginning, the movement propagandized solidarity and active support for Cuba, while advocating a radicalization of the process of socioeconomic change in Mexico, which was to draw its inspiration from the Cuban example. These issues received fresh impulse during the activities of the student worker movement of 1968.[29]

---

[28] Cf. "Luís Echeverria: Será el Mesías?", in *Oigamé*, II, 10, January 3, 1970.
[29] At the time of the project, Cuba received fresh attention in the Monterrey newspapers because of a visit by a Cuban baseball team to the city (cf. *El Porvenir*, May 12, 1971)

The respondents were asked to select from a list of six countries (Cuba, China-Mao, U.S.S.R., France, England, and the U.S.A.) the one whose government they felt most sympathy for and the one they felt most antipathy for. The answers to such questions obviously represents reflexes that are strongly conditioned by the mass communication media and, in particular, the press. The regional as well as the national newspapers appearing in the Monterrey area were all solidly hostile towards the Cuban example. In addition, some tensions had arisen, at the time, between the Mexican and Cuban governments which had been amply exposed in the communication media. Under those circumstances, a positive selection for Cuba is likely to reflect an underlying conviction rooted in an attitude which we have called "political radicalism."

Cuba drew most sympathy among 3.8 percent of the workers. The other socialist countries received the sympathy of only 1.7 percent. The U.S.A. pulled 83.6 percent of the sympathy vote. The U.S.S.R. and Cuba were the objects of most antipathy, respectively 42.6 and 39.2 percent.[30] The U.S.A. drew 5.7 percent. Asked to state their opinion on the Cuban revolutionary process as such, a more differentiated set of opinions emerges. The number of workers expressing favorable orientations towards the process, as such, remains small: 8.8 percent. However, those who are explicitly unfavorable inclined numbered less than half (48.1 percent), the other workers being not actively for nor explicitly against. The evaluations of the Cuban revolutionary leadership, Fidel Castro, included 5.7 percent favorable and 52.6 percent hostile responses. The printers and the automobile workers figure as most "radical," as far as both issues are concerned. Together, they account for most of the "favorable" answers, 67.5 and 83.3 percent, and least of the "hostile" answers, 41.1 and 41.2 percent, respectively.

The strongly favorable orientation towards the United States has, of course, strong links to the demonstration effects of American prosperity across the border. Many families have relatives "up North," and the frequent visits serve to emphasize the differences in levels of living to those who stayed behind. In fact, as we observed, an image of the United States as a country of "milk and honey" exists that shows some resemblance to the semimythical stories about life in the capital city that circulate around the provincial backwaters of Latin America (cf. also Solís Garza, 1971: 73 ff). An additional point is that the workers lacked the generalized critical attitude towards the U.S. influence in the economy that has become a part of the working-class subculture in many other Latin American nations. The role of U.S. companies in the process of economic development, as it appeared, was judged primarily on its contribution to the job supply and, on that basis, it was overwhelmingly evaluated

---

[30] The percentage for the U.S.S.R. may have been inflated as a result of a diplomatic incident around the alleged Russian support to urban guerilla groups which occurred at the time of research. "*La perfidia Rusa*" had been the subject of a hysterial press campaign. Cf. *El Porvenir*, March 20, 1971.

favorably, by 45.5 percent still with some reservations, by 23.1 percent even unconditionally. The other workers manifested critical orientations towards the U.S. economic influence, ranging from moderately, 15.0 percent, to strongly hostile, 16.4 percent. For most workers, however, a U.S. company is a source of steady jobs, how small the number and whatever the specific conditions may be, and already just for this reason has to be valued positively.[31] U.S. economic influence, in a wider sense, often falls outside their perspective of what the immediate basic factors are that condition the daily struggle to earn a living.

This perspective does not exclude the awareness that radical changes are somehow necessary in order to improve "the situation of the poor and deprived"; only 19.3 percent thought that such changes from the present situation were unnecessary. Most respondents, 51.2 percent, however, conceive of these changes within the existing structure, through government action. Those workers who do not share this perspective, and evaluate negatively the possibility to realize substantial socioeconomic change through official political structures amount to 19.5 percent. They often voiced a verbally aggressive skepticism with regard to the *politicos* and the governmental apparatus' inclination to handle the problems of poverty and unemployment.

TABLE 44: Political radicalism among workers of four industrial settings

political radicalism	industrial settings				
	printing	textiles	automobiles	chemicals	N
1 (high)	17.0	10.9	20.0	11.8	62
2	63.0	76.4	66.0	62.7	282
3 (low)	20.0	12.7	14.0	25.5	76
	100.0	100.0	100.0	100.0	420

The automobile workers score highest on overall political radicalism[32] but the numerical differences with the workers in the other settings are not spectacular.

In order to explore this phenomenon of political radicalism somewhat further, its relationship has been probed to a number of background factors. All have been disucssed before, in their relationship to working-class psychology. Parallel to this analysis, the relationship between these variables and political radicalism has been hypothesized to follow the same pattern as was predicted in the case of working-class psychology. Thus:

[31] U.S. economic interests in Mexico in recent years have focused on the capital-intensive sector that has helped little to alleviate the unemployment problem. It is not known to what extent the presence of the *maquiladores*, U.S.-owned labor-intensive industries founded in the Mexican border region because of the wage differentials with the U.S.A., has conditioned the responses of the workers.

[32] Cf. Appendix A for index construction.

(a) Skill, education, income satisfaction, personal income, family income, intergenerational mobility, intragenerational mobility, factory mobility, career satisfaction, life satisfaction have been hypothesized to relate significantly to political radicalism following the inverse pattern, e.g. increases in skill . . . life satisfaction, will tend to coincide with a decrease in political radicalism.
(b) Migrant background, work experience and working-class psychology have been hypothesized to relate significantly to political radicalism following the positive pattern.

Chi-square analysis has shown statistical significance in only a few isolated cases. Those relationships with political radicalism found to be significant, conform, as inspection of the relevant tables shows, to the predicted patterns with few exceptions.

Inversely related to political radicalism are: factory mobility (printing) and career satisfaction (printing and chemicals) following the hypothesized direction, and isolation (textiles) and quantitative union participation (chemicals) deviating from the pattern predicted for them.

Positively related to political radicalism are: migrant background (printing), education (chemicals), domination (chemicals), distanciation (automobiles), awareness (all settings), quantitative union participation (textiles). All these significant relationships, except for education, conformed to the hypothesized patterns. The relationships, however, are all incidental, and no clear consistent patterns emerge. Only "awareness" shows a consistent and strong relationship to political radicalism: an increasing awareness tends to coincide with increasing radicalism (cf. Vellinga, 1975: 436). This is not unexpected, given the analysis in the previous paragraph and the results with respect to the relationship between awareness, political radicalism, and identification with official politics.

Another interesting result concerns the role of career satisfaction. It appears that there is a general tendency for the politically radical to have a relatively lower career satisfaction. Thus a negative evaluation of one's own career mobility, against the background of the hopes and aspirations cherished before one started, tends to be accompanied by a more positive orientation towards radical issues. This relationship may lend some support to the relative deprivation-frustration hypothesis, although a wider analysis of the entire syndrome of career satisfaction and its determinants would be necessary to substantiate this point, also given the absence of a relationship to any of the mobility variables (cf. par 3.4.5.).

Few workers can be said to take politically radical position, Among the respondents they count no more than 14.8 percent. At the same time, however, the number of workers scoring "low" on political radicalism is also rather reduced. The radical issues only generated a hostile response among 15.7 percent of the workers. The greatest number of workers take moderate political stands. They are neither explicitly favorable inclined, nor explicitly hostile towards radical positions.

176

TABLE 45: Political radicalism and selected independent variables by four industrial settings

	industrial settings							
	printing		textiles		automobiles		chemicals	
independent variables	X2	DF	X2	DF	X2	DF	X2	DF
migrant background	6.86**	2	4.02	2	1.89	2	5.58	2
skill	9.65	10	5.22	8	5.16	10	12.48	10
education	6.40	8	6.62	8	13.45	8	13.82**	6
income dissatisfaction	3.08	6	8.10	6	1.43	6	4.90	6
personal income	8.83	6	4.98	4	2.87	6	5.53	6
family income	9.84	8	5.78	6	10.36	8	7.38	6
intergen. mobility	.96	4	6.14	4	4.44	4	5.59	4
intragen. mobility	4.60	4	1.96	2	1.14	4	5.02	2
factory mobility	12.84**	4	.63	2	.54	2	2.45	2
career satisfaction	10.57**	4	4.15	4	9.58**	4	14.79*	4
life satisfaction	7.53	4	3.80	4	7.14	4	5.81	4
overall-work experience	4.56	6	6.14	4	9.40	4	6.37	4
domination	5.48	6	4.06	6	10.83	6	13.13**	6
fractionization	3.64	6	2.43	6	3.32	6	6.48	6
isolation	4.59	4	15.80*	6	6.22	6	5.73	4
distanciation	6.35	6	1.44	6	13.01**	6	4.02	6
overall working-class psy.	6.54	4	6.82	4	1.12	4	4.53	4
class identification	4.30	4	1.08	4	3.89	4	2.13	2
awareness	10.37**	4	18.02*	4	13.46*	4	13.35*	4
quant. union part.	11.08	6	16.07**	6	2.46	6	12.97**	6
qual. union part.	10.76	6	15.22**	6	1.85	6	7.36	6

*   significant at the .01 level
** significant at the .05 level

As before, these outcomes refer to *individual* attitudes and the link with major societal processes certainly cannot be assumed to be automatic and direct. The fact that the number of individuals committed to a radical orientation is small does not mean that automatically the possibilities for radical change are nil. Even revolutionary processes, as history reveals, do not always require a majority of working-class individuals committed to a radical orientation.[33] Neither, however, would a majority of working-class individuals thus committed guarantee the realization of such changes. There would be, without doubt, a relationship between the presence of individuals with radical leanings and the emergence, development, and success of a movement for change embodying such orientations, but it would represent only one of the conditions that are behind its origin, growth, and ultimate success. Any attempt to extrapolate from the sums of the individual attitudes to the level of structural change would lead to unacceptable simplification and a disregard of those conditioning societal processes that have a certain reality of their own, and cannot be merely reduced to an added sum of variables with an individual reference.

177

The analysis on the micro level has been focused on the potential of the industrial workers as a dynamic factor in socioeconomic change, which on this level refers to a latent capacity stated in sums or proportions of individual attitudes. In terms of this potential, of course, not only the small number of workers who express radical opinions are important but also the large proportion of those who are taking moderate positions. The orientations of these individuals may only crystallize into more clearly defined positions in either direction, when confronted with concrete conflict issues, and possibly as part of the phenomena of collective behavior that serve to define their situations and force them to leave the neutral middle ground (cg. Killian, 1964). Their leanings are the active concern of entrepreneurs and of representatives of official politics whose efforts at active manipulation have not been without results. The actual situation of dependence, as has been shown, is located in the consciousness of a considerable number of these workers. In the face of overwhelming odds and confronted with power that cannot even be remotely controlled, theirs is a situation of resignation. They are participating in the process of development, less than most of them would have liked but more than most others of proletarian and subproletarian background do. In their evaluation of the situation, they receive "the possible" given "the circumstances." Their outward submission to these "circumstances" is shown in the reflection of official rhetoric which coexists however together with a weak identification with the political structures in which they have been integrated.

4.7. Conclusion

Reviewing the results of the analyses in this section, we can conclude that:
(a) Work experience, in a narrow sense, does not constitute a point of departure for action either way: militant or conformist. Its impact on working-class psychology is fragmentary and mainly directed at the union participation dimensions. It further does not relate significantly to the orientations the workers maintain towards the company union, or towards the official political structure; nor does it influence their leanings towards radical issues. As far as these phenomena are concerned, the "generalization hypothesis" has to be rejected.
(b) An important factor conditioning the response of the workers towards these issues seems to be located in a number of factors that form part of the work environment in a wider sense. In this context, the specific characteristics of the enterprise as a system of organization and control stand out, among which the pattern of industrial relations that has developed takes an important position. The union performs here a vital role. It has been firmly integrated in the enterprise as an essential part of the company mechanisms of conflict management. Management control over the functioning of the union organization is marked, notably in the chemical and automobile workers unions. The margins for critical debate within the union, questioning this

178

situation of dependence, are very small. Yet, this system of control is not ironclad, and some cracks appear.

(c)   The dependence of labor which is most visibly manifested in the manipulation of the union leaders by the management and the conformism of the rank and file, bought off through paternalist and reformist means, has a place in the consciousness of a considerable proportion of workers. The attitudes of disaffection or skepticism, of which the critical orientations towards the company union constitute an important part, show a tendency, most pronounced among the automobile workers, to crystallize into a pattern which could be called "latent militancy." The latently militant include those few workers who identify themselves clearly as part of the working class, show a relatively high degree of class awareness, have a critical attitude towards the union, have a certain degree of skepticism towards official politics, and relate positively to radical issues.

(d)   Next to the workers who share these orientations exists the broad mass of workers who take a middle of the road position. They show a certain awareness and critical orientation towards the structures that are behind their situation of dependence. Their attitude, however, is more one of moderation and resignation, aware on the one hand of *la situación*, or "the circumstances," and the overwhelming odds against the possibilities of translating more critical orientations into action, and, on the other hand, of the small advantages that come their way through paternalist or reformist means.

(e)   The remaining workers take conformist positions. They fully identify with the union organization and the official political structures, show a lack of working-class awareness, and hostility towards radical issues. These orientations may, in their strongest articulation, reflect the status of the enterprise in terms of its capacity to generate in the workers feelings of relative privilege, as for example, the chemical workers. These feelings, in turn, may lead the workers to accept the normative system of the enterprise and to intensify their desires to guarantee their privileges within the limits set by management. They are, in a way, the best adapted among the workers of the enterprise.

(f)   In order to give an impression of the relative importance of these three orientations,[34] Table 46 has been prepared.[35]

---

[33] This possibility was explictitly recognized by Lenin who incorporated the, according to him, inevitable numerical minority of the radically inclined in his theory of revolutionary organization (Lenin, 1969).

[34] This empirical typology shows some parallels with types of social consciousness developed by Touraine (1966).

[35] In this table, the scores on class identification, class awareness, union identification, identification with official politics, and political radicalism have been combined in a total score, with the only purpose to give some order of magnitude to those proportions of workers who showed a consistent pattern of scores on the variables mentioned. The items were equally weighted. The scores were assigned to the three equal-sized intervals located between the absolute maximum and the absolute minimum scores. Nonunion members (without union identification score) were first put in a separate order, but later added to the corresponding groups among the other workers when no deviant distribution was shown.

179

TABLE 46:   Latent militancy, resignation and conformism among the workers of four industrial settings

	industrial settings				
	printing	textiles	automobiles	chemicals	N
"latent militancy"	11.0	10.9	37.0	13.6	75
"resignation"	65.0	66.4	49.0	51.8	244
"conformism"	24.0	22.7	14.0	34.6	101
	100.0	100.0	100.0	100.0	420

Striking are the relatively large proportion of "latent militants" among the automobile workers and "conformists" among the chemical workers. This latter phenomenon, as has been pointed out earlier, is most probably related to the characteristics of the chemical plant as an industrial setting, and further reflects the success of paternalist and reformist company policies.

It has been emphasized, again, that these data refer to individual orientations. The study has approached these orientations in terms of "potential for action." The translation of this potential into autonomous action is another problem, although the analysis of the macro and meso level processes has clarified most of the structural factors conditioning such translation.

5. CONCLUSION: ALIENATION AND CLASS CONSCIOUSNESS

The study of work experience, working-class psychology and conditioning factors has produced some interesting results, highly relevant for the more general analysis of the Monterrey working class in terms of alienation and class consciousness.

5.1. Alienation

The organization of production on a societal level and its social and political correlates, as well as the organization of the process of commodity production itself, suggest the presence of a process of alienation in an objective sense. This process, however, in general has been only partially reflected in the attitudes of the individual workers toward their work. This may count as another illustration of the earlier mentioned problem of the relationship between structural conditions and subjective significance and as another warning against the assumption of an automatic and direct connection between the two (cf. also Smith, 1968: 86).

The core hypothesis which concerns a structural differentiation within modern industry as a consequence of differences in technological structure and correlated factors, and which assumes, due to these factors, certain in-

180

dustrial conditions as more conducive to a work experience in which alienative processes are reflected than others, has lacked sufficient evidence. We may conclude that on the level of concrete research, the question of what different aspects of the immediate working environment mean to the participants apparently has to be answered mainly outside the factor of technology as objective structure. As we have noticed, however, none of the alternative explanatory variables appears to have much significance either.

The orientation towards work that has been found in our study may be a function of the same resigned attitudes that figure in other areas. There is, however, another factor complex that should be considered and that, in our opinion, in the Monterrey situation interferes with the workings of all the others.

We allude to the existence of relative privilege among the workers in big industry in comparison with other segments of the industrial proletariat, the subproletariat, the rural proletariat, and to the corresponding awareness of such privilege. This factor may, in general, overshadow the workings of the process of class exploitation in the working environment, and it may intervene between this process and the attitudes toward the conditions of work.

It plays, of course, within the context of the specific pattern of capitalist development in Mexico and the characteristics of the labor market, where the supply by far exceeds the demand, a situation which consistently has undermined labor's power position.

Among the workers in the industrial settings that figured in our research, variations in remuneration, prosperity, mobility, and so on, occur but, as a collectivity, they are rather well off compared to the rest of the Monterrey industrial working population. Part of this, it should be recognized, is the result of paternalist and reformist policies. The fact that they have a job, receive steady wages and, consequently, can apply for all kinds of services under the social welfare program, already labels them as a privileged entity relative to those in service occupations or other subproletarian jobs, and certainly with regard to the rural proletariat in the surrounding areas which has formed the recruiting base for the greater part of the industrial worker population.

The conditions of factory work, as such, may represent an absence of control over the means of production, a break with creative workmanship, possibilities for involvement in the entire act of production, and the satisfaction of collective participation. However, those conditions left behind often have infrahuman features. The combination of fixed work/fixed income/fixed working days (eight hours) may further overshadow the incidence of class exploitation in the industrial work situation, and whatever other effects resulting from the subordination of large numbers of men to the discipline of factory work and to the autority of the employers. Bendix (1963: viii), in his treatise on work and authority in modern industry, raises this issue. Independently, Kahl (1965) mentions the same point in his study of a group of industrial workers near Mexico City, who also had been recruited from the

181

poorer sections of the countryside. Moore (1965), also on the basis of Mexican data, makes the general observation that whatever attitudinal barriers that may exist with regard to industrial labor, disappear against the background of extreme rural poverty. It is our impression that this factor complex also affects the phenomenon of class consciousness.

A final remark on the "generalization hypothesis". It was assumed, on the basis of the writings of Marx (1963), further substantiated by Seeman (1967), Barakat (1969) and Killian (1964), that changes in attitudes to work as a result of processes of alienation would affect the attitudes toward society and the socioeconomic structure, and notably those that form part of the working-class psychology. Reviewing the results of our study, that show a lack of impact by work attitudes on anything related to either this phenomenon or any of its correlates, it is our impression that the original "generalization hypothesis" should be reformulated. Class consciousness and the subjective experience of alienation are two phenomena that are related but in such a way that the development of class consciousness constitutes a necessary condition for the experience of alienation. Following this thesis, the attitudes toward work in which the subjective reaction toward alienative processes is reflected, should not be considered the prime generators of "classist" or "militant" attitudes. Rather, the classist or militant workers, operating from a situation in which class consciousness has been well developed, should be the first ones to experience alienation. In all other situation, the problems of work should be analyzed in terms of a lack of satisfaction or enjoyment as such. This hypothesis, which finds some support in Israel (1971: 252 ff), obviously has some consequences for the alienation discussion, but needs to be substantiated further.

5.2. Class Consciousness

The question of class consciousness points to the more basic problem of the stage of development of the process of class formation. This process appears to be still in the beginning phase. In terms of the earlier discussed model, it has not much advanced beyond the stage of the *Klasse an sich*.

On the ideological level, the action programs have tendend to be "trade unionist", and certainly not political-revolutionary. The basic objectives are mundane ones, short range, focused on limited issues as defined by the federal labor code and do not envision radical change to an alternative societal structure, not even as part of a long-term perspective. The existence of an extensive apparatus of control and manipulation, of which the dependent labor movement forms a part, and the emphasis on negotiation as the prevalent form of interest representation, prevent spontaneous as well as planned political-revolutionary action. This applies to the *blanco* as well as to the *rojo* union movement, although in the latter the ritual of the *emplazamiento de huelga* (strike threat) tries to respond to a different image.

The labor organizations, paradoxically, are not meant to facilitate autonomous labor mobilization, but to frustrate and prevent it. The organizations are weakly "ideologized," but, at least the *rojo* ones, highly politicized. The link between (*rojo*) labor on the one hand and the State and the political system on the other hand, is rather intimate. The effects of the counter ideology of the bourgeoisie are most strongly present in the *blanco* union movement which claims to be depoliticized, operates at the margin of the official political apparatus and responds strongly to initiatives from the Monterrey entrepreneurial sector.

Within the union movement, the behavior of the labor leaders follows the classic patterns, described by Robert Michels (1949) in his study of oligarchization in large-scale organizations. They operate separately from the members and are strongly oriented to personal advantage. The union between masses and the vanguard that Lenin envisioned is far from reality. Contradiction, rather than integration, typifies the relationship between leaders and the rank and file.

On the level of political parties, the interest representation is channelled through a unity party that pretends integration across class lines, and cannot provide the organizational context within which class-conscious action could find expression. The small numbers of revolutionary intellectuals, that in the Leninist scheme play a vital role in the elaboration of the ideology and schemes of action, are linked to various segments of the ruling elites. Their production remains limited to free-floating rhetoric, and they lack any roots in the labor movement. This is not only a Monterrey phenomenon, but applies to Mexico in general.

The political practice of the union movement revolves around the negotiations of the collective contract which take place every two years. Occasionally strike threats may occur, but they have a ritual significance mainly directed toward the rank and file, and may even conceal situations in which union leaders are bought off by management. The strict "trade unionist" approach in the setting of the goals of labor action is never deserted for other objectives.

These phenomena concerning the process of class formation of the industrial proletariat, and the manifestation of class consciousness on the levels of ideology, organization, and political practice, find a primary explanation in the idiosyncrasies of Monterrey patrimonial capitalism, as it has developed since the end of the last century and in its present strongly expansive nature.

It has been explained, before, how Monterrey appears to be one of the few places in Latin America where a national nondependent bourgeoisie has developed. This bourgeoisie represents a well integrated force, with a strong and dynamic economic base, a strong consciousness of interests, and a rather well-developed ideology. The tradition of family-dominated enterprises has persisted, and so has the characteristic organization of labor management relations. It has inspired the specific forms of paternalism we presently find in Monterrey. These are a continuation of the old traditional type of labor management that depended upon the personal relationship between the *patrón* and his workers to ensure the discipline and work performance needed

183

in the company. With the growth of large scale companies, this system, of course, could not be maintained in a strict sense. However, it was never superseded completely by the impersonal system of control, run through the "neutral" application of rules and elaborate controls as such, without which large companies in general may be difficult to manage. The elements of paternalism, personal relations, and personal arbitrariness, have remained characteristic of the relationship between workers and *patrón*.[36] They initially led to the violent repression of the unions, which given their horizontal orientation and characteristics of an interest organization, did not tie in with the emphasis on vertical ties integrating *patrón* and workers in the same framework of rights and duties. Subsequently, unions were organized in which the continued existence of these vertical linkages was guaranteed, be it that they were no longer directed at the individual workers but at the labor leaders who mediated the employer's influence and fulfilled a vital role in the execution of his carrot and stick policies. In this context, for example, the "closed-shop" clause did not represent the result of a hard fought union issue, but was "granted" by the *patrón* as part of his efforts to create a control apparatus that, in order to be effective had to encompass all workers concerned.

The internal differentiation of the working class has proceeded at a rapid rate. This is partly a consequence of the dynamics of the process of development itself, it is also a result of conscious efforts by the employers to create small labor aristocracies (*obreros de confianza*, etc.) and to promote individual social mobility often through the creation of an artificial "superstratification" within the companies. In combination with these efforts, they have tried to instill in the worker segment the hope of increasing their levels of living on an individual basis, together with the expectations that the problems they or their families may have can ultimately be resolved best, within the boundaries set by the government (federal labor code) and the employers, while conforming to the written (and unwritten) rules concerning the objectives and means of labor action.

This differentiation, as we have seen, had little effect within the segment of industrial workers figuring in our study. Apart from the factor "skill," its impact on work experience, working-class psychology, and related phenomena was minimal. It has, however, defined these workers all together as a privileged collectivity, more strongly conscious of the relative differences with the other worker segments than of those with other classes. In such a situation, it comes as no surprise that a sizable proportion of the workers identify as *clase media*, middle class.

These phenomena, again, have to be viewed against the background of two major conditions.
(a)   Labor's general market situation, which renders labor, and in particular

---

[36] See Bendix (1963: 55 ff) for a classic study of these traditional types of labor management relations.

184

the unskilled and semiskilled, a very weak power position facing the employers.

(b) The very dynamic characteristics of the companies involved. Through continuous growth and expansion, new positions are created, new possibilities arise, and the expectations of the workers are fed for continued mobility on an individual basis.

The above mentioned factors help to explain the fact that the actual existence of great differences in wealth between classes does not necessarily and automatically correspond to a political consciousness and a political class struggle. The continued expansion of the economic sector plays an important role in the continuation of the situation. Only with the appearence of long-term stagnation or deep recession, a more or less drastic change may occur when rising expectations are clearly frustrated (cf. Davies, 1962: 5 ff). But, even then, the occurence of spontaneous action seems more likely than other action forms that would testify to the presence of a higher degree of political consciousness. We will elaborate on this proposition and on the possibilities for alternative courses of action in the final chapter.

CHAPTER VI
ECONOMIC DEVELOPMENT AND THE
DYNAMICS OF CLASS: SOME FINAL REMARKS

When reviewing the results of the analyses on the macro, meso and micro levels, several points come to our attention. These concern not only the explanation and evaluation of Mexican economic and sociopolitical reality, but also raise some theoretical issues.

In terms of our theoretical perspective one could make the very general observation that the functioning of the Mexican socioeconomic system shows a contradiction between the level of development of productive forces and the nature of the relations of production. The analysis in Chapter III has made this point clear. We have pointed, among others, at the inefficient use of existing resources, the problem of unemployment and at the lack of political will with the elite to implement those reforms that would amplify the internal demand. Continuing on this rather general level, we could say that in this contradiction between changing productive forces and the evidently stagnating nature of the relation of production, the "objective" conditions are given for a process of change that in particular should concern the relations of production. In our study we have shown that this tension up till now has not produced the processes of social mobilitzation that would show a presence of the "subjective" conditions for such changes. A class-conscious proletariat has not come into being yet. As we have explained before, phenomena of class consciousness and political-revolutionary action orientations are not only the product of continuous experiences by the worker in productive life but also depend on the interpretation of this experience by organized groups over a long period of time. In case a dualism exists between the two, a dialectical progress of class consciousness, as indicated by Marx, will not occur. In Mexico those roads leading to a redistribution of power and income towards the working class have been blocked by the bourgeoisie, including labor's own organizing power. Next to the impotence of the production sector to meet the desires and expectations of the general working population for an improvement in levels of living, we find social mobility on an individual basis. This individual mobility, apart from its important ideological function, plays down the stagnating nature of these socioeconomic structures for those participating, by changing individual subproletarians to proletarians, promoting unskilled workers to the ranks of the skilled and by integrating labor and peasant leaders into the bourgeoisie.

The Mexican Revolution originally had a nationalistic anti-imperialistic overtone and further eliminated the semifeudalistic features of the relations of production in the country. Since 1940 this Revolution has known its restorative phase. The emphasis has shifted more and more to a neocapitalist development strategy, led by a complex economic and political elite. It has produced a rather unbalanced growth process directed at a few "growth poles" among which Monterrey figures as the most important one. This process of growth has been very dynamic, but has not proceeded without tensions and fluctuations and in social respect it has demanded a high toll. The political apparatus has become very elaborate. It has exerted stern control, discouraged the ambitions of the popular strata for an autonomous participation in national political decision making and prevented those conflicts feeding further expectations.

This strategy has been actively supported by Mexico's northern neighbor who in recent decades has intertwined its interests more and more with those of national capitalists and whose omnipresence in the economy has limited the possibilities of alternative strategies. To this condition we should add the unity, internal cohesion, group consciousness and self-confidence of the national economic and political elite itself. Next to the belief in its "historical calling" and in the legitimacy of its power and privileges, it has preeminently acces to the mechanisms of control and manipulation that handle any possible challenge either in a "negative" repressive or in a "positive" cooptive or paternalistic way. The functioning of these mechanisms of control obviously has been facilitated by the weakness of the popular organizations, the dependent nature of the processes of mobilization of which they resulted, their internal contradictions, the formation of relatively privileged groups of support within the working class. These organizations' participation in national decision making has followed patterns dictated from above.

Within this strategy, the ideology has served as a safety valve. The ideological offensive directed at the popular strata has utilized revolutionary phraseology suggesting radical solutions to the problem of underdevelopment while emphasizing that the potentialities of the "regular" struggle through the existing sociopolitical structures have not been exhausted yet.

As yet, this strategy has met a considerable degree of success. Especially during the government of Echeverría (1970-1976) these safety valve functions of the politico-ideological system became more and more pronounced. Within the government itself they meant a change of "style" that, despite a few reforms, left the political structure basically unchanged. In this they took the place of those substantial reforms that would have challenged the private sector and started a process of redistribution of power and income.

Paradoxically, this ideological offensive not only raised charges of demagoguery on the left, but also managed to arouse the private sector's hostility.[1] This latter development became particularly pronounced in the case of the

---

[1] Cf. *Latin America, A Weekly Political and Economic Report,* vol. IX, 12, March 21, 1975.

Monterrey entrepreneurs. This sector's traditional suspicions with regard to federal intention received a fresh impulse through the election of Echeverria in 1970. The president's intervention in Nuevo León politics in 1971 which led to the replacement of State governor Elizondo, spokesman for the entrepreneurial interests, his rhetorical call for a more socially oriented economy and his criticism of the private sector's "selfishness" and "conservatism," were all viewed as a deliberate attack on the rights of private enterprise and as the beginning of a development towards socialism. These feelings came to the boiling point after the killing, attributed to urban guerillas, in September 1971 of Eugenio Garza Sada, the patriarch of the family behind the Cuauthemoc interests.

The entrepreneurs' characteristics of a powerful, dynamic and successful, cohesive and self-conscious group which in recent years has left its "enclave" in the North and has diversified its interests to other areas of the Republic, have made them the natural spokesman for many Mexican businessmen. This leadership, accompanying their rise from regional to national prominence, has even been reinforced by the government's timid attempts in the last few years to implement a few reforms.[2] It should be emphasized that the hostility concerned in first instance Echeverría himself and his associates in the reformist sector of the P.R.I. and was less indicative of a schism within the bourgeoisie as a whole. All through 1973 and 1974 the challenges towards his policies intensified, in particular on account of his handling of the issue of inflation.[3] Government efforts to decrease the restiveness of the official unions by granting a compensation for the losses in real income (the cost of living had risen at an annual rate of close to 30 percent), clashed with the private sector's determination, under Monterrey leadership, to thwart any major economic or political decision taken against their opposition.

In reaction to a wave of strike threats in May 1974, relating to wage issues and involving 245 Monterrey establishments, the local *Cámara de Comercio* organized a one-day lockout closing over 6,000 commercial establishments. It announced further action against wage increases and prevailing labor unrest, including a threat to the government to stop the payment of federal taxes. The situation resembled the happenings during the Cárdenas period in the 1930's. The strike movement was carried mainly by *rojo* unions, a development not entirely unexpected, given the history of increasing strike frequencies under prolabor administrations. The call by C.T.M.'s *lider* Fidel Velázquez for a massive worker's reply to the events in Monterrey, should be viewed in the same light.[4] At the same time, the labor unrest was produced by a situation in which the combined effects of economic stagnation and inflation put the

---

[2] *Latin America, A Weekly Political and Economic Report*, vol. VIII, 28, July 19. 1974.
[3] See: *Latin America, A Weekly Political and Economic Report*, vol. VIII, 40, October 11, 1974.
[4] Velázquez remarked in this respect that action should be taken because Mexicans were living in the "epoch of LuízEchevarría, the epoch of revolution." Cf. *Latin America, A Weekly Political and Economic Report*, vol. VIII, 19, July 19, 1974.

sqeeze on the working class. Labor action was directed primarily towards income (compensation of losses by inflation), work conditions (a 40-hour work week) and did not touch more substantial, let alone politically radical issues yet, although the significance of these experiences of struggle, even if completely spontaneous, as part of the learning process that goes with class formation, cannot be underestimated. The real power base of the entrepreneurs, the big industrial settings dominated by the *blanco* union movement, has not been affected by this unrest as yet, although a continuing situation of stagnation might change this picture.

With regard to the feedback from our study to the general theoretical framework, some observations can be made. The main theoretical issues have been handled through the general tendency hypotheses that guided the study as part of the metatheoretical framework that inspired the formulation of the research paradigm. Additional issues have been explored through numerous lower-order hypotheses that relate to this paradigm and functioned on the empirical and operational theoretical levels.

Class analysis has been a very useful and fruitful tool of analysis in the study of the relationship between the economic and political structures. In the analysis of the clientelist structures that condition the role of labor in the socioeconomic process it has directed the attention to the dimensions of coercion and control that constitute those structures' essential features and make them function as instruments of class control. When reviewing these and other aspects of the dynamics of class in Mexican society, the deviations from the Marxian scheme appear to be located less in the idea of class conflict or class struggle as such, as well as in the patterns and issues of conflict, the conditioning factors and the ultimate objectives.

In Mexican society, the pattern of conflict has followed primarily one of a sectoral struggle, going back to the differences in interests between those connected with the process of urban-industrial development and those marginal to it, important segments of the urban-industrial working class being on the relatively privileged side of the fence. Within this context the short-term pactations in the political sphere have been organized.

What, however, would be the long-term perspective for emancipation of the working class through a replacement of this sectoral struggle by a struggle on class basis? A major precondition for this process, which obviously would entail the development of a working-class consciousness, would be the disappearance of the exceptional position of the regularly employed in the urban-industrial sector, as part of a general expansion of rural and urban employment, including the employment of those subproletarian segments that function as an "industrial reserve army." This would contribute to a basic homogenization of the working class and improve substantially labor's general bargaining position. Improvements in the employment situation are very likely to be followed by a gradual infiltration of wider, more "political issues in labor's action programs.

189

In the meantime labor will continue to emphasize trade-unionist issues, certainly in case the inflationary trend continues. This is likely to happen in a situation of continued emphasis on growth and inflationary spending by the government. This does not mean that periodic challenges to the mechanisms of controlled mobilization will not occur. They have been part of the Mexican labor scene for a long time as spontaneistic explosions of a long-term underlying trend towards autonomous popular participation in the political process. Their occurence illustrates again that the compliance of important segments of the working class with the existing political structures in largely "pragmatic", reflecting their consciousness of the balance of power in industry and in society.

This may apply in particular to those settings where the paternalist element in industrial relations has prevailed, as in Monterrey, how paradoxical this may seem. Earlier we have characterized Monterrey as an example of patrimonial-capitalist development. Mann (1973: 41 ff), in his comparative study of working-class consciousness, has indicated that the historical examples of politically-militant orientations in labor action have emerged in a number of countries where a purely capitalist ideology failed to achieve a hegemonic position and where employers were least willing to act within the narrowly capitalist frame of reference (France, Italy, Tsarist Russia, Wilhelmian Germany, Spain, Portugal). In those situations where the institutionalization of class conflict has been emphasized through compromise and market bargaining, working-class economistic and reformist tendencies are greatly strengthened. This would imply, that the employers in Monterrey, by hardening their attitudes, deepening their hostility towards any political reformism pretending more than piecemeal changes, and continuing to reject any labor organization operating independently from their initiative, may end up fomenting the very call for political participation and autonomous labor organization they are trying to avoid. Such development would be promoted, as we indicated before, by a reduction of the pressures on the labor market, wich would enable labor to operate from a position of greater strength while complicating the problems of control over labor by the employers. Given a continued predominance of patrimonial-capitalist patterns this obviously would have theoretical consequences. Marxist theory has, as we know, defended the proposition that the development of working-class consciousness will be directly related to the degree of capitalist maturity in a whole society.

The next issue concerns the ultimate objectives of such a development. In particular, the question remains if this working-class consciousness is likely to develop into a *revolutionary* force. The present dynamics of the Mexican situation, and in particular the process of large-scale industrialization, appears not to have produced the proletarian sector (yet?) that will assume a vanguard role with regard to a process of socioeconomic change which has the creation of a socialist society as its ultimate objective. This is not to say that Marx was not right in his emphasis on the major contradiction in capitalist society between the individual interests of capitalists and the collective interests of the working and consuming population. He was also correct in pointing out the working class' inherent tendency towards collective identity and organization. This all applies to the Mexican case. Yet this structurally generated conflict and the long-term tendency towards an autonomous organization of the working class need not necessarily discharge into a proletarian revolution. Apart from the internal balance of power on the Mexican political scene and the impact of the external factor (U.S. presence), which limit the political alternatives of working-class action, the working-class organizations themselves may structure the greater part of their concrete activities around an economism that will change the distribution of income and power but may not challenge the basic structure of capitalism.

There is another factor that should be brought in here. As we explained above, the present functioning of the political system includes an important and autonomous role of an ideology, emphasizing revolutionary language, instead of a bourgeois counterideology. The role of this ideology and its safety valve functions with regard to the tensions between productive forces and relations of production, underlines the relative autonomy of superstructural elements and the absence of a necessary parallelism between the economic and politico-ideological spheres, alluded to in the theoretical introduction. In Mexico, this "progressive" ideology may continue to cover succesfully patterns of basically neocapitalist development for a long time to come, without the emergence of the stark societal class confrontation which the Marxian model envisions. The Mexican proletariat may never develop into a *Klasse für sich* pursuing politico-revolutionary action programs if, again, next to a substantial reduction in under- and unemployment, the political structure would reduce its repressive orientation, and institutionalize instead class conflict through an emphasis on cooperation, compromise and bargaining with an independent labor movement. This may apply in particular to the Monterrey employers, who when they would continue to follow archaic paternalist patterns of labor management relations may find themselves creating more and more situations of labor unrest and confrontation. To them also Mann's observation (1973: 42) may apply:" the more employers behave as true capitalists, the securer will they rest in their beds."

APPENDIX A
THE INVESTIGATION AND ANALYSIS

During the investigation various data sources have been used. They range from census data, standardized interviews and a wide variety of written sources and documents to general-thematic interviews and observation, as part of a research strategy aiming at a combination of mutually supplementing data packages of a quantitative and qualitative nature. We will discuss in short our primary data sources.

1. Standardized Interviews

These data were gathered interviewing a sample of workers belonging to different industrial settings. Procedures and data were the following:

Population and sampling: The selection of the industries was made in two phases. On the basis of the definition of the four types of industrial setting to be included in the study and upon the advice of the staff of the *Centro de Investigaciones Económicas* at the *Universidad de Nuevo León* (C.I.E.), a number of industries were selected from the directory of industries in Nuevo León (Directorio Industrial, 1968-1970).

These included: textile mills (2), automobile/tractor assembly plants (3), iron and steel mills (2), a metal wares factory, chemical plants (4), a cigarette and tobacco factory, a brewery, print shops (3) and a wood furniture factory.

These factories were visited and observations were made of the work process. Some basic data were secured on investment, number of workers and employees and the skill and age distribution of the worker population. Those industrial settings that were rather heterogeneous as far as technological arrangements were concerned, and that showed mixture and coexistence of different technologies, were progressively excluded from the sample. Four industrial settings were left: a textile mill, an automobile factory, a chemical plant, and several print shops, an outcome supporting the rationale behind Blauner's selection (Blauner, 1964). In the case of the printing industry, all shops were selected from the directory with a declared capital investment of 500,001 pesos or more. This limit was set arbitrarily in order to exclude the traditional small shops. All selected shops were visited. Ultimately eight shops were chosen, each with an investment superior to 1,000,000 pesos.

The objective of the empirical study was the comparison between various subgroups of the industrial proletariat, that is between those working in distinctive industrial settings, and not the description of the distribution of some general characteristics among this population. Given this point of departure, a sample had to be defined that would allow generalization to that part of the subgroup population working in a setting considered most typical for the industrial arrangements to which the subgroup population as a whole was being subjected.

The population for our study was defined as: male workers from 21-60 years of age, who had been working for one year or more in the selected industries and who, within these industries, were participating in the actual production process, e.g. were dealing with production machinery (chauffeurs, porters, etc. were excluded). The actualization date for the data was set at March 1st, 1971.

Female workers were excluded. They constituted a very limited proportion of the labor force, whose deviant characteristics could not be adequately specified. Only the chemical industry employed female workers and, there, they counted not more than 4 percent of the work force. Those male workers of 60 years and older, and those of 20 years and younger, were excluded for reasons flowing from the definition of the research problem, suggesting the selection of steady workers and the exclusion of those who had entered the labor market recently or were close to leaving it. In addition, the rather homogeneous age cohort that resulted allowed a full study of the variables that according to the literature carry explanatory weight with regard to variations in work experience and working-class psychology.

Only workers were selected who had worked for at least one year in the factory where they were employed. This assured the inclusion in the sample of only those laborers who most probably did develop some stable opinions and attitudes towards the work in this specific factory.

The selection of workers participating in the actual production process further guaranteed the inclusion of only workers who were subject to the specific technological arrangements of the selected industries. At the same time, they belonged to that part of the working class actually dealing with machines and that was ascribed by Marx a leading role in processes of social and economic change.

The process of sampling has not proceeded uniformly in each of the settings. Because of the uncooperative attitude of the management of some companies, the sampling strategy had to be adapted.

Only in the case of the printshops did the management allow the drawing of a simple random sample from the personnel files, using a table of random numbers. Those workers who did not conform to the selection criteria were replaced, continuing the procedure with random numbers. To this purpose, before each interview, questions were asked on the period of work in the factory, age and type of work.

In the case of the textile mill, the sample was drawn from the union membership files, which included all potential members of the sample be-

193

cause of the factory's closed shop policy. The small number of workers who had been promoted to the category of *personal de confianza* and consequently had left the union, were added to the total file from which a simple random sample was drawn, using the same procedure as in the case of the printshops.

The selection of the chemical and automobile workers followed the model of a quota sampling plan, a viable and pragmatic alternative to the other procedures that, despite the possible violations of some canons of methodological purism, has produced good results (cf. Kish, 1965: 564). "Skill" was chosen as quota control. Next to "industrial setting," it was considered the most useful stratification factor that would separate the population into strata differing in work experience and working-class psychology. The actual analysis has proven this assumption to be right. The known skill distribution in both factories referred, however, to the entire body of workers, including those of 20 years and under, those over 60 (this category is extremely small and can be neglected), those working less than a year in the factory and those working outside the actual production process. Those of 20 years old and under counted 10 percent of the total number of workers in the chemical plant, and 20.7 percent of those in the automobile factory. Many of them must have belonged to the *eventuales* or other categories working less than a year in the factory, and most of them will have belonged to the ranks of the unskilled. Consequently, the semiskilled and skilled categories had to be slightly oversampled in order to compensate for this bias and avoid complicated weighting procedures. The results are the following. Among the chemical workers the population counted 80 percent skilled and semiskilled, the sample: 84.6 percent. Among the automobile workers the population counted 75 percent skilled and semiskilled, the sample: 81 percent.

In the case of the chemical workers, the quotas were filled from the *colonias*, where the workers lived more or less concentrated. In the case of the automobile workers, this type of concentration occurred on a much smaller scale. The interviewers joined the buses in which the workers left the factory after each shift, and held a small inquiry among them asking for name and address, age, job and time of work in the factory. This way a pool of workers was assembled from which the quotas were completed. An interviewers manual, containing a list of jobs in the respective factories together with the corresponding classification: skilled, semiskilled and unskilled, facilitated the selection of the cases. This way, the sampling error which normally arises in quota sampling because interviewers will differ in the samples they select to meet the quota requirements was reduced.

The sample size initially was established at 440, or 110 for each subgroup. The ultimate size of the sample was 420. The print shops and the automobile factory each accounted for 100, and the textile mill and the chemical plant for 110 respondents each. In the case of the print shops, the 100 members of the subsample were distributed over the eight selected shops in proportion to the size of the work force in each of them: $\frac{n1}{N} \times 100 \ldots\ldots\ldots \frac{n8}{N} \times 100$.

194

Size of the sample and subsample were primarily determined by the anti-cipated requirements of the analysis.

The fieldwork: The standardized interviews were done by four groups of interviewers, experienced through participation in C.I.E. investigations. After the pretest, each group interviewed the workers of one specific industrial setting (printing, textiles, automobiles and chemicals). The completed inter-views were reported to the respective group coordinators, who checked for blanks and inconsistencies. Each week, the interviewers reported directly the experiences and difficulties they had encountered. After termination of the group jobs, the coordinators reinterviewed a random selection of 10 percent of all completed interviews, using a short questionnaire that repeated a few of the questions from the original schedule. Some sixty interviews showing persistent inconsistencies were checked by the author personally. Fourteen interviews were ultimately rejected. The interviews took place in the homes of the respondents. The questions were read to them in such a way that, while sitting at a table together, the respondents could both see and hear them. A content and wording was used that made administration possible to a low-income, low-education population. Only items were included that related to the respondents' concrete living and working situation, and that could be assumed to form part of their frame of reference. The interviews took between forty-five minutes and one hour and a quarter to complete. The number of refusals was minimal (N = 5). In general, the workers were receptive and friendly, with a certain eagerness to talk about their work and its problems.

The data: Information has been collected on a wide range of variables and atributes, assembled in the following codebook:

items
001:   case number (001-420)
002:   card number (1 = deck 1, 2 = deck 2)
003:   industrial setting (1 = printing, 2 = textiles, 3 = automobiles, 4 = chemicals)
004:   size of community of birth, based on the census-stated size at the time of migration to Monterrey (1 = 4,999 and less; 2 = 5,000-19,999; 3 = 20,000-99,999; 4 = 100,000 and more; 5 = abroad).
005:   state of birth (1 = Nuevo León, 2 = Coahuila, 3 = San Luis Potosí, 4 = Zacatecas, 5 = other and abroad)
006:   year of last arrival in Monterrey, grouped (1 = 1966-1970, 2 = 1961-1965, 3 = 1956-1960, 4 = 1951-1955, 5 = 1946-1950, 6 = 1941-1945, 7 = 1931-1940, 8 = 1930 and before)
007:   age on March 1st, 1971 (21-60)
008:   age, grouped (1 = 21-30, 2 = 31-40, 3 = 41-50, 4 = 51-60)
009:   marital status (1 = single, 2 = married, 3 = separated/divorced, 4 = widowed, 5 = *unión libre*)

195

010: number of (life) children (00-19)
011, 013, 015, 017, 019, 021, 023, 025, 027, 029, 031: job level *compadre* 1st born, resp. 2nd, 3rd, 4th, 5th, 6th, 7th, 8th, 9th, 10th, n th born (life) child (1-7, cf. Appendix B; for 11th and more child the average job level *compadre* was computed)
012, 014, 016, 018, 020, 022, 024, 026, 028, 030, 032: employed by same factory where respondent is presently employed? (1 = yes, 2 = no)
033: level present job respondent (1-7, cf. Appendix B)
034: level last job respondent's father (1-7, cf. Appendix B)
035: intergenerational mobility (1 = up, 2 = stable, 3 = down).
036: degree of upward intergenerational mobility, item 035, category 1 (1 = steps, 2 = 1 step)
037: education respondent (1 = no education, 2 = incomplete *primaria*, 3 = completed *primaria*, 4 = *secundaria* or *preparatoria*, 5 = higher education)
038: education respondent's father (coding as 037)
039: educational mobility (1 = up, 2 = stable, 3 = down)
040: level first job respondent (1-7, cf. Appendix B)
041: intragenerational mobility (1 = up, 2 = stable, 3 = down)
042: degree of upward intragenerational mobility; item 041, category 1 (1 = 2 steps, 2 = 1 step)
043: economic sector first job (1 = agriculture, 2 = mining, 3 = manufacturing industry, 4 = construction, 5 = electricity and water, 6 = commerce, 7 = transport and communication, 8 = services, 9 = artesan trade)
044: second generation of workers in the manufacturing industry (1 = yes, 2 = no)
045: skill level first job in present factory (1-6, using each setting's internal stratification of skill)
046: skill level present job (coding as 045)
047: factory mobility (1 = up, 2 = stable, 3 = down)
048: degree of upward factory mobility, item 047, category 1 (1 = 5 steps-5 = 1 step)
049: number of years of employment in present factory (1 = 1-5, 2 = 6-10, 3 = 11-15, 4 = 16-20, 5 = over 20 years)
050: present job located on the assembly line automobile factory; item 003, category 3 (1 = yes, 2 = no)
051: house ownership (1 = respondent is owner, 2 = family member is owner, 3 = rented, 4 = other)
052: number of rooms in the house (1-9)
053: number of rooms used as sleeping rooms (1-9)
054: presence of kitchen (1 = yes, 2 = no)
055: presence of electricity (1 = yes, 2 = no)
056: presence of running water (1 = yes, 2 = no)
057: presence of toilet (1 = yes, 2 = no)

058: presence of hot water (1 = yes, 2 = no)
059: presence of gas for cooking purposes (1 = yes, 2 = no)
060: presence of telephone (1 = yes, 2 = no)
061: ownership of automobile (1 = yes, 2 = no)
062: ownership of television (1 = yes, 2 = no)
063: ownership of radio (1 = yes, 2 = no)
064: ownership of motorcycle or moped (1 = yes, 2 = no)
065: ownership of laundry machine (1 = yes, 2 = no)
066: ownership of refrigerator (1 = yes, 2 = no)
067: prosperity index (1 = high, 2 = medium, 3 = low)
068: monthly *personal* income, totalling all (net) incomes from job(s) held or other activities; in case of variable income the average of the last three months was taken (1 = 199 and less, 2 = 200-499, 3 = 500-999, 4 = 1000-1499, 5 = 1500-2499, 6 = 2500-4999, 7 = 5000-9999, 8 = 10.000 pesos and more
069: monthly *family* income, totalling all (net) incomes from job(s) held or other activities by all family members, including respondent (coding as 068)
070: income (dis)satisfaction, based on monthly family income (1 = suffer severe financial hardship, 2 = have difficulties making ends meet, 3 = have no great financial problems, 4 = can save part of income)
071: periods of unemployment within the last two years (1 = yes, 2 = no)
072: possibility of unemployment within the next six months (1 = yes, 2 = no)
073: pace of work too fast (1 = yes, 2 = no)
074: too tired after a day's work (1 = yes, 2 = no)
075: possibility to leave job for more or less half an hour without replacement (1 = no, 2 = yes)
076: possibility to apply own ideas in work (1 = no, 2 = yes)
077: index domination (1 = high, 2 = medium, 3 = low, 4 = none)
078: job perceived as essential for company's production effort (1 = no,
079: intrinsic quality of job to generate feelings of satisfaction or accomplishment (1 = no, 2 = yes)
080: job perceived as essential for company's production effort (1 = no, 2 = yes)
081: job is monotonous and routine like (1 = yes, 2 = no)
082: index fractionization (1 = high, 2 = medium, 3 = low, 4 = none)
083: frequency of contact with work mates, outside the working situation (1 = never, 2 = monthly, 3 = weekly, 4 = daily)
084: daily work companions from the working environment are involved in these contacts item 083, categories 2-4 (1 = yes, 2 = no)
085: same workmates are constantly involved in these contacts or are others also included? item 083, categories 2-4 (1 = same workmates, 2 = others)
086: affiliation with any club or organization, other than the company

197

	union (1 = sportsclub, 2 = social clubs, 3 = cultural organizations, 4 = trade organizations, 5 = political organizations, 6 = others, 7 = none)
087:	workmates belong to same organization(s); item 086, categories 1-6 (1 = yes, 2 = no)
088:	occupied position of organizational responsibility; item 086, categories 1-6 (1 = yes, 2 = no)
089:	index isolation (1 = high, 2 = medium, 3 = low, 4 = none)
090:	job requires concentration (1 = no, 2 = yes)
091:	job monotonous or changeful (1 = monotonous, 2 = changeful)
092:	job preference in case a new start in life could be made (1 = preference for job, other than present job, 2 = preference for present job)
093:	level preferred job; item 092, category 1 (1-7, cf. Appendix B)
094:	freetime preferred over working hours (1 = yes, 2 = no)
095:	index distanciation (1 = high, 2 = medium, 3 = low, 4 = none)
096:	index overall work experience (1 = high, 2 = medium, 3 = low, 4 = none)
097:	concrete future plans (1 = start an independent business, 2 = a better position in an other company, 3 = a better position in the present company, 4 = stay in present job)
098:	job aspirations for son(s) of respondent (1 = preference for job different from respondent's job, 2 = preference for same job as respondent)
099:	level job aspirations for son(s) of respondent; item 098, category 1 (1-7, cf. Appendix B)
100:	appraisal of future chances to realize such level of job aspirations; item 98, category 1 (1 = very good, 2 = good, 3 = fair, 4 = bad, 5 = very bad)
101:	comparison between past expectations concerning career achievement and present job (1 = achieved less than expected, 2 = achievement conforms to past expectations, 3 = achieved more than expected)
102:	most important factor in career advancement (1 = belong to a rich family, 2 = good personal relations, 3 = political influence, 4 = hard work, 5 = initiative, 6 = studies and training)
103:	evaluation of past life chances, compared to "the average Mexican" (1 = bad, 2 = medium, 3 = good)
104:	assessment of present chances to obtain "the good things in life", compared to "the average Mexican" (1 = bad, 2 = medium, 3 = good)
105:	appraisal of future comparative life chances (1 = bad, 2 = medium, 3 = good)
106:	index life satisfaction (1 = low, 2 = medium, 3 = high)
107:	class identification, on the basis of self-location in the class structure (1 = working class terms, 2 = middle class terms, 3 = other)
108:	U.S. influence in the Mexican economy, does it benefit or harm the process of development (1 = strongly hostile: nationalization of existing U.S. companies, while preventing new investments; 2 =

moderately hostile: stop future expansion of U.S. investments; 3 = moderately positive: permit selectively new U.S. investments; 4 = strongly positive: unlimited support for U.S. presence in the economy)

109: differences in interests between rich and poor (1 = yes, 2 = no)
110: best solutions for problems of poor and deprived offered by whom; item 109, category 1 (1 = the poor and deprived themselves, 2 = all together, 3 = the rich)
111: interests served by industrialists and businessmen (1 = primarily serve their own interests, 2 = serve the interests of all Mexicans, 3 = primarily serve working-class interests)
112: present political parties attend to working-class problems (1 = seldom or never, 2 = now and then, 3 = always)
113: index awareness (1 = high, 2 = medium, 3 = low)
114: membership union (1 = yes, 2 = no)
115: kind of union (1 = CTM, 2 = FSA, 3 = FNSI)
116: period of affiliation (1 = over 20 years, 2 = 16-20, 3 = 11-15, 4 = 6-10, 5 = 1-5 years)
117: frequency of union meetings (1 = weekly, 2 = monthly, 3 = yearly, 4 = never)
118: frequency of assistence to union meetings (1 = weekly, 2 = monthly, 3 = yearly, 4 = never)
119: voluntary assistance (1 = yes, 2 = no)
120: self evaluation of union activities (1 = very active, 2 = active, 3 = not active)
121: position(s) of responsibility in the union (1 = yes, 2 = no)
122: highest union position occupied; item 121, category 1 (1 = secretary general, 2 = secretary, 3 = delegate)
123: period in which highest position was occupied (1 = 1966-1970, 2 = 1961-1965, 3 = 1956-1960, 4 = 1951-1955, 5 = 1950 and before)
124: index quantitative union participation (1 = high, 2 = medium, 3 = low)
125: index qualitative union participation (1 = high, 2 = medium, 3 = low)
126: index overall working-class psychology (1 = high, 2 = medium, 3 = low)
127: influence in union affairs; item 114, category 1 (1 = much influence, 2 = some influence, 3 = little influence)
128: motives of union leaders; item 114, category 1 (1 = well being rank and file, 2 = private power plays)
129: orientations of actual decision making by union leaders; item 114, category 1 (1 = towards the workers side, 2 = towards official politics, 3 = towards management)
130: index union identification (1 = high, 2 = medium, 3 = low
131: political preference (1 = PRI, 2 = PAN, 3 = PPS, 4 = other)
132: general evaluation of present government policies (1 = positive 2 = negative)

133: positive evaluations of government policies, main reasons stated (1 = new federal labor code, 2 = solution of peasant problems, 3 = solution of worker problems, 4 = solution of worker and peasant problems, 5 = work for "Mexico" in general, 6 = identification with Echeverría)

134: negative evaluations of government policies, main reasons stated (1 = high prices and taxes, 2 = anti-worker policies, 3 = anti-peasant policies, 4 = government corruption, 5 = antigovernment, general)

135: government should be supported unconditionally by working class (1 = yes, 2 = no)

136: objectives of government policies: stable employment and adequate levels of living for all Mexicans, or lack of concern for these issues with regard to social class respondent belongs to (1 = government policies serve all Mexicans, 2 = government policies neglect the problems of respondent's class)

137: index identification with official politics (1 = high, 2 = medium, 3 = low)

138: which government most sympathetic (1 = Cuba, 2 = China (Mao), 3 = USSR, 4 = France, 5 = England, 6 = USA)

139: which government most antipathetic (1 = USA, 2 = England, 3 = France, 4 = USSR, 5 = China (Mao), 6 = Cuba)

140: opinions on the Cuban Revolution (1 = favorable, 2 = neutral, 3 = unfavorable)

141: opinions on Fidel Castro (1 = favorable, 2 = neutral, 3 = unfavorable)

142: need for massive changes in Mexico to improve the situation of the poor and deprived (1 = yes, 2 = no)

143: the government will carry out such changes; item 142, category 1 (1 = no, 2 = yes)

144: index political radicalism (1 = high, 2 = medium, 3 = low)

Measures: For most of the variables referring to any specific action involving an element of opinion or attitude, a set of items was assembled into a small scale or index and a scale or index score was computed for each respondent. These indices were:

(a) A "prosperity" index, using items 054-066, which refer to characteristics of the house, utilities and the ownership of consumer durables. They were factor-analyzed; the respondents were assigned scores, multiplying the coding with the relevant itemloading, and put in rank order. Only those items were used with a principal axis factor loading of .30 or more: item 054 (.31), 057 (.55), 058 (.54), 059 (.49), 062 (.45), 065 (.50) and 066 (.60). The distance between lowest and highest possible scores was divided into three equal parts (high-medium-low), the respondents were assigned their appropriate values, which were punched on the IBM card.

(b) A "life-satisfaction" index (Kahl, 1968: 93), using the responses to items 103, 104 and 105. The same procedure was used as above. The loadings were: item 103 (.51), 104 (.59) and 105 (.60).

200

(c) An "identification with the union" index, using the responses to items 127, 128 and 129. The same procedure was used. The loadings were: item 127 (.94), 128 (.72) and 129 (.93).

(d) An "identification with official politics" index, using the responses to items 131, 132, 135 and 136. The same procedure was used as before. Item 131 was rejected for inclusion (loading .20). The other loadings were: item 132 (.57), 135 (.62) and 136 (.57)

(e) A "political radicalism" index, based on the responses to items 138, 139, 140, 141 and 143. The same procedure was used. The loadings were: item 138/139 combined in one variable (.43), item 140 (.84), 141 (.85) and 143 (.90).

(f) The various indices of the work experience syndrome were handled differently. Each was constructed, weighting all items equally. The indices were:

"Domination", using the responses to items 073, 074, 075 and 076;
"Fractionization": items 078, 079, 080, 081;
"Isolation": items 083, 084, 085, 086 and 087;
"Distanciation": items 090, 091, 092 and 094.

The four subindices were combined into an overall work experience index in the same way, e.g. weighting the scores equally, computing a total score for each respondent, and assigning them to one of the four intervals obtained by dividing the range between the minimum and maximum possible score into four equal-distant groups.

(g) The dimensions of working-class psychology were handled similarly. The items were indicators for variables that form part of the general theoretical discussion around class consciousness and class-psychology. Given the involvement of standard concepts, the proceeding were here also of a more theoretical-logical nature. The indices were:

"Class identification", using the responses to item 107;
"Awareness": items 108, 109, 111 and 112;
"Union membership" item 114;
"Quantitative and qualitative union participation", two indices constructed on the basis of the responses to items 117, 118, 119, 120, 121, 122, 123.

The overall index of working-class psychology was constructed, combining the subindices' scores which, for this purpose were equally weighted. The respondents were put in rank order on the basis of their total scores, and assigned to one of the three groups obtained by dividing the range between the absolute maximum and the absolute minimum scores into three equal-distant intervals.

Analysis: Next to nonparametric statistics, an extensive use has been made of parametric statistics (factor analysis, multiple discriminant analysis, analysis of covariance, multiple regression analysis). This, although some of the preconditions for their use could not entirely be satisfied.

The criterion of random sampling was met in two of the four settings. In the other two, a carefully controlled quota sample was drawn.

The criterion of interval level of measurement has been approached through an ordinal scale with metric characteristics. Equal intervals were assumed through assigning numbers to ordinal data and through the use of dummy variables.

It was felt that a strict adherence to the ordinal level of measurement would have led to an extensive loss of information. This more pragmatic approach, which finds support in Labovitz (1967) and Boyle (1970), does not deny that the power and elegance of the methods used imposes stringent requirements on the empirical measurements of the variables that are used. It realizes at the same time, however, that an excessive formalism on this point (cf. Wilson, 1971) would force most of present day sociological research into oblivion.

2. Written Sources

These sources have been manifold. The more important ones are:

(a) *Newspapers and periodicals*: for the years 1970-1971 the dailies *El Porvenir* and *El Norte* (Monterrey) and *El Heraldo*, *Novedades* and *Excelsior* (Mexico, D.F.) were consulted, further the weeklies *Oigamé* and *El Ciudadano* (Monterrey) and *¿Por Qué?*, *Sucesos, Siempre* (Mexico, D.F.). In addition the periodicals published by the industrial departments of leading Monterrey companies were consulted, mostly on a monthly basis.

(b) *"Official" publications*: the *Junta Estatal de Censos* of Nuevo León proportioned the necessary census data. Organizations like *Centro Patronal, Cámara de la Industria de Transformación* and COFIDE proportioned general data on the evolution of management labor relations. From the relevant industries annual reports were obtained, next to company memoranda concerning the departments of industrial relations. From the unions, statutes, rules and regulations were obtained in addition to some internal memoranda concerning the functioning of the unions.

(c) *Other secondary sources*: the wide range of C.I.E. publications and research materials dealing with socioeconomic problems in Monterrey, Nuevo León and Northern Mexico in general, was consulted.

3. Additional Interviews

In addition to the standardized interviews a number of fourty-eight focused intervies were conducted with:

(a) Representatives of employer organizations: *Centro Patronal, Cámara de la Industria de Transformación*, COFIDE.

(b) Representatives of organized labor on the state federation level: C.R.O.C., C.T.M., C.G.T., F.N.S.I., F.S.A.

(c) A number of persons who, given their positions, possessed special information pertaining to specific aspects of the study. These were: local industrialists, politicians, university professors, and journalists.

(d) The directors of the industrial relations departments in three of the four

202

enterprises (textiles, automobiles, chemicals), and the managers of five of the eight print shops.
(e) The union leaders of the selected enterprises.
These more qualitative interviews were of the thematic type. They were organized around a number of topics relating to: Monterrey labor history, characteristics of the industrial bourgeoisie, labor management relations, the role of organized labor, entrepreneurial paternalism and control, the internal structure of the labor unions and union leadership patterns.

4. *Observation*

The initial plan for the study was elaborated in Mexico in 1968. In 1970 the groundwork was laid. The four important industrial growthpoles Mexico (D.F.), Puebla (Puebla), Guadalajara (Jalisco) and Monterrey (Nuevo León) were visited. Some basic information on the process of industrialization in the areas was secured through the local *Cámaras de la Industria de Trans-formación* (in Puebla: the *Comisión de Promoción Industrial*) and in each area several factories were visited. The certain "specialness" of Monterrey in the more general picture of Mexican industrial development was confirmed through own observation. In Monterrey a pilot study was done in order to determine the more detailed outline of the project and prepare the structure of the interview schedules. All through this phase and during the actual research in 1971, observations were made of the work process in numerous factories, life in the working-class *colonías*, recreational activities among the working population in the four settings.

APPENDIX B
OCCUPATIONAL HIERARCHY[1]

Level 1:   farm worker, member of *ejido*, peasant,[2] unskilled miner, assistant industrial operator, porter, watchman, soldier, janitor, domestic personnel, street vendor, etc.

Level 2:   peasant, skilled miner, machine operator, noncommissioned army personnel, truck drivers, bus drivers, etc., storekeeper (*tienda de abarrotes*), stand owner (*estanquillo*), etc.

Level 3:   farmer, skilled worker or artisan, foreman in industry, driver with own vehicle, owner of small business or workshop (when he himself works in the shop and employs no more than two persons), etc.

Level 4:   farmer, section head in factory, salesman in big store, business agent, clerk, primary-school teacher, owner of small business or workshop (with three to five persons employed), etc.

Level 5:   farmer, secondary and prep-school teacher, technician, office head, etc.

Level 6:   farmer, university graduate (salaried), owner or manager of medium-sized enterprise (with six to forty-nine persons employed), etc.

Level 7:   owner or manager of large enterprise (with fifty or more persons employed), self-employed university graduate, etc.

[1] *Source*: Balán, 1967: 188-189.
[2] The peasants and "farmers" have been located on the various levels according to the size of holding, the number of persons employed and the type of agriculture: from the owners of 1 to 10 hectares who mainly practice subsistence farming with traditional crops (corn, beans, etc.) and are located on level 1 to the owner of more than 200 hectares and over 50 people employed who have been located on level 7.

204

BIBLIOGRAPHY

AGUILAR M., ALONSO. "El Proceso de Acumulación de Capital," in México: Riqueza y Miseria. Alonso Aguilar M. and Fernando Carmona. Mexico D.F.: Editorial Nuestro Tiempo, 1970a.

AGUILAR M., ALONSO. "Problemas y Perspectivas de un Cambio Radical," in El Milagro Mexicano. Fernando Carmona, et al. Mexico D.F.: Editorial Nuestro Tiempo, 1970b.

ALISKY, MARVIN. Government of the Mexican State of Nuevo León. Tempe: CLAS Arizona State University, 1971.

ALTHUSSER, LOUIS. Pour Marx. Paris: François Maspéro, 1965.

ALTHUSSER, L. "Teoria, Práctica Teórica y Formación Teórica. Ideología y Lucha Ideológica," Casa de las Americas, 34. La Habana: Febrero de 1966.

ANDERSON, BO and COCKCROFT, JAMES D. "Control and Cooptation in Mexican Politics." in Dependence and Underdevelopment: Latin America's Political Economy. James D. Cockcroft et al. Garden City: Doubleday, 1972.

ARON, RAYMOND. Main Currents in Sociological Thought. New York: Doubleday, 1968, Vol. 1.

ASHBY, JOE C. Organized Labor and the Mexican Revolution under Lázaro Cardenas. Chapel Hill: The University of North Carolina Press, 1967.

BALÁN· JORGE et al. Movilidad Social, Migración y Fecundidad en Monterrey Metropolitana. Monterrey N.L.: Centro de Investigaciones Económicas de la Universidad de Nuevo León, 1967.

BALÁN, JORGE. "Are Farmers' Sons Handicapped in the City?" Rural Sociology, 33, 2 (1968), 160-174.

BARAKAT, HALIM. "Alienation: a Process of Encounter between Utopia and Reality." British Journal of Sociology, XXII, 1, (1969), 1-10.

BARKIN, DAVID. "Mexico's Albatross: the United States Economy." Latin American Perspectives, II, 2 (1975), 64-80.

BASURTO, JORGE. "Obstáculos al Cambio en el Movimiento Obrero," in El Perfil de México en 1980, Vol. 3. Jorge Martinez Rios et al. Mexico D.F.: Siglo XXI Editores, 1972.

BEHRMAN, JACK N. The Role of International Companies in Latin American Integration: Autos and Petrochemicals. Lexington, Mass.: D.C. Heath, 1972.

BENDIX, REINHARD. Work and Authority in Industry: Ideologies of Management in the Course of Industrialization. New York: Harper & Row, 1963.

BLALOCK, HUBERT M. Social Statistics. New York: McGrawHill Book Company, 1960.

BLAUNER, ROBERT. Alienation and Freedom. Chicago: University of Chicago Press, 1964.

BONILLA, FRANK. "The Urban Worker," in Change and Continuity in Latin America. Ed. John J. Johnson. Stanford University Press, 1964.

BOTTOMORE, T.B. "Karl Marx, Sociologist or Marxist," Science and Society, 30, 1 (1966), 11-24.

BOYLE, RICHARD P. "Path Analysis and Ordinal Data." American Journal of Sociology, 75, 4 (1970), 461-480.

BRANDENBURG, FRANK. The Making of Modern Mexico. Englewood Cliffs, N.J.: Prentice-Hall, 1964.

BRIDGES, JULIAN C. The Population of Mexico: Its Composition and Changes. PhD. Thesis, University of Florida, 1973.

BUENO, GERARDO M. "La Industria Siderúrgica y la Industria Automotriz," in El Perfil de México en 1980, Vol. 2. Mexico D.F.: Siglo XXI Editores, 1972.

BUVE, R.TH.J. "Protesta de Obreros y Campesinos durante el Porfiriato," in Boletin de Estudios Latinoamericanos, (1972), 1-20.

CAREAGA, GABRIEL. *Los Intelectuales y la Política en México*. Mexico D.F.: Editorial Extemporaneos, 1971.

CARMONA, FERNANDO. "La Política Económica," in *Mexico: Riqueza y Miseria*. Alonso Aguilar M. and Fernando Carmona. Mexico D.F.: Editorial Nuestro Tiempo, 1970a.

CARMONA, FERNANDO. "La Situación Económica," in *El Milagro Mexicano*. Fernando Carmona et al. Mexico D.F.: Editorial Nuestro Tiempo, 1970b.

CARRIÓN, JORGE. "La Corrupción en la Política," in *La Corrupción*. Rosario Castellanos et al. Mexico D.F.: Editorial Nuestro Tiempo, 1969.

CARRIÓN, JORGE. "Retablo de la Política 'a la Mexicana,'" in *El Milagro Mexicano*. Fernando Carmona et al. Mexico D.F.: Editorial Nuestro Tiempo, 1970.

Censo IX de Población y Vivienda 1970. Estado de Nuevo León. Monterrey N.L.: Junta Estatal de Censos en Nuevo León, 1970.

CENTERS, RICHARD. *The Psychology of Social Classes*. Princeton: Princeton University Press, 1949.

CHAPLIN, DAVID. *The Peruvian Industrial Labor Force*. Princeton, N.J.: Princeton University Press, 1967.

CLARK, MAJORIE RUTH. *Organized Labor in Mexico*. Chapel Hill: University of North Carolina Press, 1934.

CLINE, HOWARD F. *Mexico: Revolution to Evolution, 1949-1960*. London: Oxford University Press, 1962.

COCKCROFT, JAMES D. "Coercion and Ideology in Mexican Politics," in *Dependence and Underdevelopment: Latin America's Political Economy*. James D. Cockcroft et al. Garden City: Doubleday, 1972.

COLABELLA, S. "La Conciencia Obrera." *Revista Latinoamericana de Sociología*, III (Noviembre de 1967), 504-521.

Contrato Colectivo de Trabajo Obligatorio y Tarifas Mínimas Uniformes en la Industria Textil del Algodón y sus Mixturas 1950-1951. Consejo Nacional de Industriales para la Modernización Textil. Mexico D.F.: 1951.

COOLEY, WILLIAM W. and LOHNES, PAUL R. *Multivariate Data Analysis*. New York: John Wiley & Sons Inc., 1971.

CORNELIUS, W.A. "Urbanization as an Agent in Latin American Political Instability: the Case of Mexico." *American Political Science Review*, 63, 4 (1969), 833-857.

COSIO VILLEGAS, DANIEL. *El Sistema Político Mexicano: las Posibilidades de Cambio*. Mexico D.F.: Editorial Joaquin Mortiz, 1972.

COTLER, JULIO. "La Mecánica de la Dominación Interna y del Cambio Social en el Peru." in *Peru Problema I*. Jose Matos Mar et al. Lima: Fransisco Moncloa, 1968.

CREVENNA, THEO R. ed. *Materiales Para el Estudio de la Clase Media en America Latina*. Washington D.C.:. Unión Panamericana, 1950-1952, 6 vols.

DAHRENDORF, RALPH. "Karl Marx und die Theorie des Sozialen Wandels." in *Pfade aus Utopia: Arbeiten zur Theorie und Methode der Soziologie*. Hamburg: Piper Verlag, 1967.

DAHERENDORF, RALPH. *Class and Class Conflict in Industrial Society*. Stanford University Press, 1968.

DAVIDS, ANTHONY, "Alienation, Social Apperception and Ego Structure." *Journal of Consulting Psychology*, 19, 1 (1955), 21-27.

DAVIES, JAMES C. "Toward a Theory of Revolution." *American Sociological Review*, 27, 1 (1962), 5-19.

DEAN, DWIGHT G. "Alienation, its Meaning and Measurement." *American Sociological Review*, 26, 5 (1961), 753-758.

DE LA CERDA SILVA, ROBERTO. *El Movimiento Obrero en México*. Mexico D.F.: Instituto de Investigaciones Sociales UNAM, 1961.

DE LEÓN GARZA, MAXIMO. *Monterrey, un Vistazo a sus Entrañas*. Monterrey N.L.: 1968.

DE LEÓN GARZA, MAXIMO. *Grandeza de Monterrey. Respuesta a Don José P. Saldaña*. Monterrey, N.L.: Editorial Alfonso Reyes, 1970.

DEROSSI, FLAVIA. *The Mexican Entrepreneur*. Paris: Development Center O.E.C.D. Studies, 1971.

DE SCHWEINITZ, KARL. "On the Determinism of the Marxian System." *Social Research*, 29, 1 (1962), 37-49.

Directorio Industrial de Nuevo León 1968 y Anexo. Monterrey, Edición COFIDE-CAINTRA, 1968 y 1970.

DI TELLA, TORCUATO S. "Populismo y Reforma en America Latina." *Desarrollo Económico,* 4, 16 (1965).

DIXON, W.J. ed. *Biomedical Computer Programs.* Berkeley: University of California Press, 1970

DOMINGUEZ, JORGE E. *México: Prioridad en Asignación de Recursos Financieros en el Campo del Trabajo y Productividad de Recursos Humanos a la Luz del Presente Crecimiento Poblacional.* 24th Latin American Conference of the University of Florida, Februari, 1974.

DOS SANTOS, THEOTONIO. *Lucha de Clases y Dependencia en America Latina.* Medellin: La Oveja Negra, 1971.

DRAPER, NORMAN AND SMITH, HARRY. *Applied Regression Analysis.* New York: John Wiley & Sons Inc., 1966.

DUMONT, RENÉ. *Terres Vivantes.* Paris: Plon, 1961.

DURAND PONTE, VICTOR M. "México: Dependencia o Independencia en 1980," in *El Perfil de México en 1980,* Vol. 3. Jorge Martínez Rios *et al.* Mexico D.F.: Siglo XXI Editores, 1972.

ELDRIDGE, J.E.T. *Industrial Disputes.* London: Routledge & Kegan Paul, 1968.

ENGELS, FREDERICK. *The Origin of the Family, Private Property and the State.* New York: International Publishers, 1942 (edition of 1844).

ENGELS, FREDERICK. *The Conditions of the Working Class in England.* New York: MacMillan, 1958 (edition of 1845).

ENGELS, FREDERICK. *The Peasant War in Germany.* New York: International Publishers, 1966 (edition of 1870).

ENGELS, FREDERICK. *Anti-Dühring.* New York: International Publishers, 1970 (edition of 1878).

FERNANDEZ HURTADO, ERNESTO and NAVARRETE, ALFREDO. *Mexico's Recent Economic Growth.* Austin: University of Texas Press, 1967.

FEUER, LEWIS. "What is Alienation? The Career of a Concept," in *Sociology on Trial.* Eds. Maurice Stein and Arthur Vidich, Englewood Cliffs, N.J.: Prentice Hall, 1963.

FLYNN, PETER. *Class, Clientelism and Coercion: Some Mechanisms of Internal Dependency and Control.* CEDLA-Conference on Dependency in Latin America, Amsterdam, November 1973.

FLORES MAGÓN, RICARDO. *La Revolución Mexicana.* Mexico D.F.: Editorial Grijalbo, 1970.

FLORES OLEA, VICTOR. "Poder, Legitimidad y Política en Mexico," in *El Perfil de México en 1980,* Vol. 3. Jorge Martínez Rios *et al.* Mexico D.F. Siglo XXI Editores, 1972.

FREIRE, PAULO. *Pedagogía del Oprimido.* Lima: Universidad Nacional Mayor de San Marcos, 1971.

FREITHALER, WILLIAM O. *Mexico's Foreign Trade and Economic Development.* New York: Frederick A. Praeger, 1967.

FRIEDMANN, GEORGES. *Où va le Travail Humaine.* Paris: Gallimard, 1950.

FRIEDMANN, GEORGES. *The Anatomy of Work: Labor, Leisure and the Implications of Automation.* New York: Free Press, 1961.

FROMM, ERICH. *Marx's Concept of Man.* New York: Frederick Ungar, 1961.

GARCIA AYALA, RAMIRO. *Analisis Costo-Benificio de la Inversión en Capital Humano.* Tesis de Licenciatura, Universidad de Nuevo León, Facultad de Economía. Monterrey, N.L.: 1971.

GILL, MARIO. *Los Ferrocarrileros.* Mexico D.F.: Editorial Extemporáneos, 1971.

GILLIN, JOHN P. "The Middle Segments and Their Values," in *Latin American Politics: 24 Studies of the Contemporary Scene.* Ed. Roberto D. Tomasek. Garden City: Doubleday, 1966.

GLAZER, BARNEY G. and STRAUSS, ANSELM L. *The Discovery of Grounded Theory.* Chicago: Aldine, 1967.

GOLDMANN, LUCIEN. *The Human Sciences and Philosophy.* London: Jonathan Cape, 1969.

GOLDSMITH, RAYMOND W. *The Financial Development of Mexico.* Paris: OECD Development Center Studies, 1966.

GONZÁLEZ CASANOVA, PABLO. *La Democracia en México.* Mexico D.F.: ERA, 1967.

GONZÁLEZ CASANOVA, PABLO. "Enajenación y Conciencia de Clase en México," in *Ensayos Sobre las Clases Sociales en México.* Miguel Othón de Mendizábal *et al.* Mexico D.F.: Editorial Nuestro Tiempo, 1968.

207

GONZÁLEZ CASANOVA, PABLO. *Sociología de la Explotación*. Mexico D.F.: Siglo XXI Editores, 1969.
GONZÁLEZ NAVARRO, MOISÉS. "Mexico: the lop-sided Revolution," in *Obstacles to Change in Latin America*. Ed. Claudio Veliz. London: Oxford University Press, 1969.
GOODMAN, LOUIS WOLF. "The Unequal Distribution of Income in Latin America." in *Workers and Managers in Latin America*. Eds. Stanley M. Davies and Louis Wolf Goodman. Lexington, Mass., D.C. Heath and Company, 1972.
GOULDNER, ALVIN. *Wildcat Strike*. London: Routledge & Kegan Paul, 1955.
GUNDER FRANK, ANDRÉ. *Latin America: Underdevelopment or Revolution: Essays on the Development of Underdevelopment and the Immediate Enemy*. New York: Monthly Review Press, 1969.
GUNDER FRANK, ANDRÉ. *Lumpenburguesía: Lumpen Desarrollo, Dependencia, Clase y Politica en America Latina*. Santiago: Editorial Prensa Latinoamericana S.A., 1970.
HAGEN, E. E. *On the Theory of Social Change*. Homewood: Dorsey Press, 1962.
Hacia una Planeación de la Educación Media y Superior en Nuevo León. Vol. 1, Centro de Investigaciones Económicas de la Universidad de Nuevo León. Monterrey, N.L.: 1970.
HAJDA, JAN. "Alienation and the Integration of Student Intellectuals." *American Sociological Review*, 26, 5 (1961), 758-777.
HAMILTON, RICHARD F. "Affluence and the Worker: the West German Case." *American Journal of Sociology*, LXXI, 2 (1965a), 144-152.
HAMILTON, RICHARD. "Skill Level and Politics." *Public Opinion Quarterly*, XXIX, 3 (1965b), 390-399.
HAMILTON, RICHARD F. *Affluence and the French Worker*. Princeton: Princeton University Press, 1967.
HARNECKER, MARTA. *Los Conceptos Elementales del Materialismo Histórico*. Paris: Editorial Arnier Hnos., 1969.
HARNECKER, MARTA. *El Capital: Conceptos Fundamentales*. Santiago: Editorial Universitaria, 1971.
HUTCHINSON, BERTRAM. "The Patrón-Dependent Relationship in Brazil: a Preliminary Examination." *Sociologia Ruralis*, VI, 1 (1966), 3-30.
HYMAN, RICHARD. *Strikes*. London: Fontana, 1972.
IBARRA, DAVID. "Mercados, Desarrollo y Politica Económica: Perspectivas de la Economía de México" in *El Perfil de México en 1980*, Vol. 1. David Ibarra *et al*. Mexico D.F.: Editorial Grijalbo, 1970.
IGLESIAS, SEVERO. *Sindicalismo y Socialismo en México*. Mexico D.F.: Editorial Grijalbo, 1970.
ISRAEL, JOACHIM. "Remarques sur Quelques Problemes de la Théorie Marxiste des Classes." *L'Homme et la Société*, No. 15-18 (Janvier-Février-Mars, 1970), 269-294.
ISRAEL, JOACHIM. *Alienation: From Marx to Modern Sociology*. Boston: Allyn and Bacon, 1971.
JAGUARIBE, HELIO. *Economic and Political Development: A Theoretical Approach and a Brazilian Case Study*. Harvard: University Press, 1968.
JOHSON, KENNETH F. "Ideological Correlates of Right Wing Political Alienation in Mexico." *American Political Science Review*, 59, 3 (1965), 656-664.
KAHL, JOSEPH A. "Tres Tipos de Trabajadores Industriales Mexicanos," in *La Industrialización en America Latina*. Ed. Joseph A. Kahl. Mexico D.F.: Fondo de Cultura Económica, 1965.
KAHL, JOSEPH A. *The Measurement of Modernism: A Study of Values in Brazil and Mexico*. Austin: University of Texas Press, 1968.
KERR, C. and SIEGEL, A. "The Interindustry Propensity to Strike: An International Comparison," in *Industrial Conflict*. A. Kornhauser, *et al*. New York: McGraw-Hill Book Company, 1954.
KERR, C. *Labor and Management in Industrial Society*. Garden City N.Y.: Doubleday, 1964.
KILLIAN, LEWIS. "Social Movements," in *Handbook of Modern Sociology*. Ed. R.E.L. Faris. Chicago: Rand McNally, 1964.
KING, TIMOTHY. *Mexico: Industrialization and Trade Policies Since 1940*. London: Oxford University Press, 1970.
KISH, LESLIE. *Survey Sampling*. New York: John Wiley & Sons Inc., 1965.
KNOWLES, K.G.J.C. *Strikes: A Study in Industrial Conflict*. Oxford: Brasil Blackwell, 1952.
KRUIJT, DIRK and MENNO VELLINGA. "Klasse en Klassebewustzijn, Concepten en Paradigma's bij Klassieke Marxisten". *Sociologische Gids*, 24, 3 (1977).

KUHN, J.W. *Bargaining in Grievance Settlement.* New York: Columbia University Press, 1961.

LABASTIDA MARTÍN DEL CAMPO, JULIO. "Les Grupos Dominantes Frente a las Alternativas de Cambio," in *El Perfil de México en 1980,* Vol. 3. Jorge Martínez Rios *et al.* Mexico D.F.: Siglo XXI Editores, 1972.

LABOVITZ, SANFORD. "Some Observations on Measurement and Statistics." *Social Forces,* 46, 2 (1967), 151-159.

LA CASCIA, JOSEPH S. *Capital Formation and Economic Development in Mexico.* New York: Praeger, 1969.

LANDSBERGER, HENRY A. "The Labor Elite: Is It Revolutionary?," in *Elites in Latin America.* Eds. S.M. Lipset and Aldo Solari. New York: Oxford University Press, 1967.

LEFF, NATHANIEL. *Economic Policy-Making and Development in Brazil 1947-1964.* New York: 1968.

LEGGETT, JOHN C. *Class, Race and Labor: Working Class Consciousness in Detroit.* New York: Oxford University Press, 1968.

LEMARCHAND, RENÉ and LEGG, KEITH. "Political Clientelism and Development: A Preliminary Analysis." *Comparative Politics,* 4, 2 (1972), 149-178.

LENIN, V.I. *Selected Works,* Vol. X. New York, International Publishers, 1943.

LENIN, V.I. *What is to be Done.* New York: International Publishers, 1969 (edition of 1902).

LEWIS, OSCAR. *The Children of Sánchez.* London: Penguin 1964.

LEWIS, OSCAR. "Urbanization Without Breakdown," in *Contemporary Cultures and Societies of Latin America.* Dwight B. Heath *et al.* New York: Random House, 1965.

LIPSET, S.M. *Political Man: The Social Bases of Politics.* Garden City N.Y.: Doubleday, 1963.

LIPSET, S.M. "Values, Education and Entrepreneurship," in *Elites in Latin America.* Eds. S.M. Lipset and Aldo Solari. New York: Oxford University Press, 1967.

LIPSET, S.M. *et al. Union Democray.* New York: Garden City N.Y.: Doubleday, 1956.

LIPSET, S.M. and BENDIX, REINHARD. *Social Mobility in Industrial Society,* Berkeley: University of California Press, 1959.

LIPSITZ, LEWIS. "Working Class Authoritarianism: A Reevaluation." *American Sociological Review,* XXX, 1 (1965), 103-109.

LIPSITZ, LEWIS. "Work Life and Political Attitudes." *American Political Science Review,* LVIII, 6 (1964) 951-965.

LOPEZ APARICIO, ALFONSO. *El Movimiento Obrero en México: Antecendencia, Desarrollo y Tendencias.* Mexico D.F.: Editorial JUS, 1958.

LOPREATO, J. and CHAFETZ, J.S. "The Political Orientation of Skidders: A Middle-Range Theory." *American Sociological Review,* 35, 3 (1970), 440-445.

Los Pobres de Monterrey: Un Estudio Socio-Económico. Centro de Investigaciones Económicas de la Universidad de Nuevo León, 1964.

LUKÁCS, GEORG. *Historia y Conciencia de Clase.* La Habana: Instituto del Libro, 1970 (edition of 1923).

MANDEL, ERNEST. *Lenin en het Probleem van het Proletaries Klassebewustzijn.* Nijmegen: Socialistische Uitgeverij, 1970.

MANN, MICHAEL. *Consciousness and Action among the Western Working Class.* London, MacMillan, 1973.

MANNHEIM, KARL. *Essays on the Sociology of Culture.* London: Routledge & Kegan Paul, 1956.

MARASCIULO, EDWARD. *The Industrial Development of Monterrey, Mexico.* M.A. Thesis, University of Florida, 1952.

MARCUSE, HERBERT. *Reason and Revolution.* Boston: The Beacon Press, 1968.

MARTÍNEZ DE NAVARRETE, IFIGENIA. *La Distribución del Ingreso y el Desarollo Económico de México.* Mexico D.F.: Instituto de Investigaciones Económicas, UNAM, 1960.

MARTÍNEZ DE NAVARRETE, IFIGENIA. "La Distribución del Ingreso en México, Tendencias y Perspectivas," in *El Perfil de Mexico en 1980,* Vol. I. David Ibarra *et al.* Mexico D.F.: Siglo XXI Editores, 1970.

MARX, KARL. "Wage-Labour and Capital," in *Selected Works.* Moscow: Foreign Language Publishing House, 1955 (edition of 1849).

MARX, KARL. *Early Writings.* Trans. and Ed. T.B. Bottomore. New York: McGraw-Hill Book Company, 1963 (edition of 1844)

MARX, KARL. *Class Struggles in France 1848-1850*. New York: International Publishers, 1964 (edition of 1850).

MARX, KARL. *Capital: A Critique of Political Economy*. Ed. Frederick Engels. New York: International Publishers, 1967a, 3 vols (edition of 1867, 1885 and 1894).

MARX, KARL. *The Eighteenth Brumaire of Louis Bonaparte*. New York: International Publishers, 1967b (edition of 1852)

MARX, KARL. "The Civil War in France," in *The Civil War in France: The Paris Commune*. Karl Marx and V.I. Lenin. New York: International Publishers, 1969 (edition of 1871 and 1908).

MARX, KARL and ENGELS, FREDERICK. *The German Ideology*. New York: International Publishers, 1963 (edition of 1845-1846)

MARX, KARL and ENGELS, FREDERICK. "The Communist Manifesto" in *Essential Works of Marxism*. Ed. Arthur P. Mendel. New York: Bantam Books, 1965 (edition of 1848).

MARX, KARL and ENGELS FRIEDRICH. "Briefe 1842-1895." in *Marx-Engels Werke*, vol. XXVII-XXXIX. Berlin: Dietz Verlag, 1972-1974.

MAURO, FRÉDÉRIC. "Le Développement Economique de Monterrey (1890-1960)," in *Caravelle*, 2 (1964), 35-133.

MEDINA, IGNACIO and AGUILAR, RUBEN. *La Ideología del C.N.H.* Mexico D.F.: Editorial Heterodoxia, 1971.

MICHELS, R. *Political Parties*. Glencoe, Ill.: Free Press, 1949.

MICHELSEN TERRY, C.J. and OTÁLORA BAY, G. *Relaciones Industriales en México: Análisis de una Ocupación en Desarrollo*. Monterrey, N.L.: COMARI, 1970.

MILLER, DELBERT C. and FORM, WILLIAM H. *Industrial Sociology: The Sociology of Work Organizations*. New York: Harper & Row, 1964.

MILLER, S.M. and RIESMANN, FRANK. "Working Class Authoritarianism: A Critique of Lipset." *British Journal of Sociology*, XII, 2 (1961), 263-276.

MIZRUCHI, EPHRAIM H. "Alienation and Anomia," in *The New Sociology: Essays in Social Science and Social Theory in Honor of C. Wright Mills*. Ed. Irving L. Horowitz. New York: Oxford University Press, 1965.

MONTANO, GUILLERMO. "Los Problemas Sociales," in *El Milagro Mexicano*. Fernando Carmona *et al.* Mexico D.F.: Editorial Nuestro Tiempo, 1970.

MOORE WILBERT E. "Occupational Structure and Industrial Conflict,' in *Industrial Conflict*. A. Kornhauser *et al.* New York: McGraw-Hill Book Company, 1954.

MOORE, WILBERT E. *Industrialization and Labor: Social Aspects of Economic Development*. New York: Russell and Russell, 1965.

MOORE, WILBERT E. and FELDMAN, ARNOLD S. *Labor Commitment and Social Change in Developing Areas*. New York: Social Science Research Council, 1960.

MOSK, SANFORD A. *Industrial Revolution in Mexico*. Berkeley: University of California Press, 1950.

MUNOZ GARCÍA, HUMBERTO and ORLANDINA DE OLIVIERA, CLAUDIO S. "Migración y Marginalidad Ocupacional en la Ciudad de México," *El Perfil de México en 1980*, Vol. 3. Jorge Martínez Rios *et al.* Mexico D.F.: Siglo XXI Editores S.A., 1972.

NELSON, JOAN M. *Migrants, Urban Poverty and Instability in Developing Nations*. Cambridge: Harvard University Center for International Affairs, 1969.

NIE, NORMAN H. *et al.* *Statistical Package for the Social Sciences*. New York: McGraw-Hill Book Company, 1973.

O'BRIEN, P. "A Critique of Latin American Theories of Dependency." Amsterdam: CEDLA Conference on Dependency in Latin America, November 19-21, 1973.

Ocupación y Salarios en Monterrey Metropolitano. Centro de Investigaciones Económicas de la Universidad de Nuevo León. Monterrey, N.L.: 1965.

OLLMAN, BERTELL. "Marx's Use of Class." *American Journal of Sociology*, 73, 5 (1968), 573-580.

OSSOWSKI, STANISLAW. "Les Différents Aspects de la Classe Sociale chez Marx." *Cahiers Internationaux de Sociologie*, 24 (1958), 65-79.

OSSOWSKI, STANISLAW. *Class Structure in the Social Consciousness*. New York: The Free Press of Glencoe, 1963.

PADGETT, L. VINCENT. *The Mexican Political System*. Boston: Houghton Mifflin, 1966.

210

PADILLA ARAGÓN, ENRIQUE. *México: Desarrollo con Pobreza.* Mexico D.F.: Siglo XXI Editores, 1969.

PALERM VICH, ANGEL. "Factores Históricos de la Clase Media en México," in *Ensayos sobre las Clases Sociales en México.* Miguel Othón de Mendizábal. Mexico D.F.: Editorial Nuestro Tiempo, 1968.

PAPPENHEIM, FRITZ. *The Alienation of Modern Man.* New York: Monthly Review Press, 1959.

PETRAS, JAMES F. "Class Structure and its Effects on Political Development." *Social Research,* 36, 2 (1969), 206-230.

PETRAS, JAMES F. *Politics and Social Structure in Latin America.* New York: Monthly Review Press, 1970.

PETROVIC, GAJO. *Marx in the Mid-Twentieth Century.* Garden City, N.Y.: Doubleday, 1967.

PORTES, ALEJANDRO. "On the Logic of Post-Factum Explanations: The Hypothesis of Lower-Class Frustration as the Cause of Leftist Radicalism." *Social Forces,* 50, 1 (1971), 26-44.

POULANTZAS, NICOS. *Poder Político y Clases Sociales en el Estado Capitalista.* Mexico D.F.: Siglo XXI Editores, 1969.

POWELL, JOHN D. "Peasant Society and Clientelistic Politics," *American Political Science Review,* LXIV, 3 (1970), 411-425.

PUENTE LEYVA, JESUS. *El Problema de la Vivienda en Monterrey.* Centro de Investigaciones Económicas de la Universidad de Nuevo León, 1967.

PUENTE LEYVA, JESUS. *Distribución del Ingreso en un Area Urbana: El Caso de Monterrey.* Mexico D.F.: Siglo XXI Editores S.A., 1969.

QUIJANO, ANIBAL. *Polo Marginal de la Economía y Mano de Obra Marginada.* Lima: Programa de Ciencias Sociales de la Universidad Católica, 1971.

RATINOFF, LUIS. "The New Urban Groups: The Middle Classes," in *Elites in Latin America.* Es. S.M. Lipset and Aldo Solari. New York: Oxford University Press, 1967.

"RERUM NOVARUM en QUADRAGESIMO ANNO," in *Socialistische Documenten.* W. Banning and J. Barents. Amsterdam: N.V. de Arbeiderspers, 1952.

REVANS, R.W. "Industrial Morale and Size of Unit." *Political Quartely,* XXVII, 3 (1956), 264-280.

ROEL, SANTIAGO. *Apuntes Históricos de Nuevo León.* Monterrey, N.L.: 1954.

RUMMEL, R.J. "Understanding Factor Analysis." *Journal of Conflict Resolution,* XI, 4 (1967), 444-480.

SALAZAR, ROSENDO and ESCOBEDO, JOSÉ G. *Las Pugnas de la Gleba: Historia del Movimiento Social Mexicano.* Mexico D.F.: Editorial Arante, 1923.

SALDAÑA, JOSÉ P. *Apuntes Históricos sobre la Industrialización de Monterrey.* Monterrey, N.L.: Edición Centro Patronal, 1965.

SAYLES, LEONARD. *The Behavior of Industrial Work Groups.* New York: John Wiley & Sons Inc., 1958.

SCOTT, MARVIN B. "The Social Sources of Alienation," in *The New Sociology: Essays in Social Science and Social Theory in Honor of C. Wright Mills.* Ed. Irving L. Horowitz. New York: Oxford University Press, 1965.

SCOTT, ROBERT E. *Mexican Government in Transition.* Urbana: University of Illinois Press, 1959.

SEEMAN, MELVIN. "On the Meaning of Alienation." *American Sociological Review,* 24, 6 (1959), 783-791.

SEEMAN, MELVIN. "On the Personal Consequences of Alienation in Work." *American Sociological Review,* 32, 2 (1967), 273-286.

SEGERSTEDT, T.T. "An Investigation of Class Consciousness Among Office-Employees and Workers in Swedish Factories." *Transactions of the Second World Congress of Sociology,* III, 1954.

SHAW, FREDERICK J. *Poverty and Politics in Mexico City 1821-1853.* PhD Dissertation, University of Florida, 1977.

SIMPSON, GEORGE. "Alienation: Some Conceptual Developments in Present-day Sociology." *Mens en Maatschappij,* 43, 4 (1968), 309-330.

SINGER, MORRIS. *Growth, Equality and the Mexican Experience.* Austin: University of Texas Press, 1969.

SINGER, PAULO. *Desenvolvimento Econômico e Evaluçao Urbana.* Sao Paulo: Editora Nacional, 1974.

211

SMITH, MICHAEL A. "Process Technology and Powerlessness." *British Journal of Sociology*, 19, 1 (1968), 76-88.

SMITH, ROBERT FREEMAN. *Repression: Origins of Social Unrest in Mexico 1968*. New York: North American Congress on Latin America, 1968.

SMITH, T. LYNN. *Studies of Latin American Societies*. Garden City N.Y.: Doubleday, 1970.

SOARES, G.A.D. "Desarrollo Económico y Radicalismo Político," in *La Industrialización en America Latina*. Ed. Joseph A. Kahl. Mexico D.F.: Fondo de Cultura Económica, 1965.

SOLÍS, LEOPOLDO. *La Realidad Económica Mexicana: Retrovisión y Perspectivas*. Mexico D.F.: Siglo XXI Editores, 1970.

SOLÍS, GARZA, HERNAN. *Los Mexicanos del Norte*. Mexico D.F.: Editorial Nuestro Tiempo, 1971.

STAVENHAGEN, RODOLFO. *Las Clases Sociales en las Sociedades Agrarias*. Mexico D.F.: Siglo XXI Editores, 1969.

STAVENHAGEN, RODOLFO *et al*. *Neolatifundismo y Explotación: de Emiliano Zapata a Anderson Clayton & Co.* Mexico D.F.: Editorial Nuestro Tiempo, 1971.

SUITS, DANIEL B. "Use of Dummy Variables in Regression Equations." *Journal of the American Statistical Association*, 52 (December 1957), 548-551.

SUNKEL, OSVALDO. *Capitalismo Transnacional y Desintegración Nacional en America Latina*. Buenos Aires: Nueva Visión, 1972.

SUTCLIFFE, R.B. *Industry and Underdevelopment*. London: Addison-Wesley, 1971.

SZENTES, TAMAS. *The Political Economy of Underdevelopment*. Budapest: Akademiai Kiadó, 1976, 2nd ed.

TAVISS, IRENE. "Changes in the Form of Alienation: the 1900's versus the 1950's." *American Sociological Review*, 34 1 (1963), 46-57.

TIJERINA GARZA, ELIÉZER. *Análisis de Demanda de Productos Alimenticios: El Caso de Monterrey*. Monterrey N.L.: Centro de Investigaciones Económicas de la Universidad de Nuevo León, 1965.

TOURAINE, ALAIN and DANIEL PÉCAUT. "Working-Class Consciousness and Economic Development in Latin America." *Studies in Comparative International Development*, Vol. III, 4 (1967-1968), 71-84.

TOURAINE, ALAIN. *L'Evolution du Travail Ouvrier aux Usines Renault*. Paris: Centre National de la Recherche Scientifique, 1955.

TOURAINE, ALAIN. *La Conscience Ouvrière*. Paris: Editions du Seuil, 1966.

TURNER, H.A. *et al*. *Labour Relations in the Motor Industry*. London: George Allen and Unwin, 1967.

TRUEBA URBINA, ALBERTO and JORGE TRUEBA BARRERA. *Nueva Ley Federal del Trabajo*. Mexico D.F.: Editorial Porrua, 1970.

VAITSOS, G. "Strategic Choices in the Commercialization of Technology: the Point of View of the Developing Countries." *Social Science Journal*, XXV, 3 (1973).

VAN DOORN, J.A.A. *Sociale Ongelijkheid en Sociaal Beleid: Arbeiders en Employees in Onderneming en Maatschappij*. Utrecht, Bijleveld, 1963.

VAN DYCK, JULES and VAN OERS, MART. "Sur Quelques Dimensions Empiriques de l'Alienation." *Sociologie du Travail*, XI, 1 (Janviers-Mars 1961), 44-60.

VAUPEL, JAMES and CURHAN, JOAN. *The Making of a Multinational Enterprise*. Boston: Harvard University School of Business Administration, 1969.

VEBLEN, THORSTEIN. *The Instinct of Workmanship and the State of the Industrial Arts*. New York: W.W. Norton & Company, 1964.

VELLINGA, MENNO. *Economic Development and the Dynamics of Class: The case of Monterrey, Mexico*. Utrecht: Center for Comparative Socioeconomic Studies, 1975.

VERNON, RAYMOND. *The Dilemma of Mexico's Development*. Cambridge: Harvard University Press, 1963.

WERTHEIM, W.F. "Corruptie als Sociologisch Studie Object." in *Corruptie*. W.F. Wertheim and H.J. Brasz. Assen: Van Gorcum, 1961.

WHETTEN, NATHAN L. "El Surgimiento de una Clase Media en México." in *Ensayos Sobre las Clases Sociales en México*. Miguel Othón de Mendizábal *et al*. Mexico D.F., Editorial Nuestro Tiempo, 1978.

212

WILLIAMS, E.J. "Comparative Political Development: Latin America and Afro-Asia." *Comparative Studies in Society and History*, 2 (1969), 342-354.

WILSON, THOMAS P. "Critique of Ordinal Variables." *Social Forces*, 49, 3 (1971), 432-444.

WIONCZEK, MIGUEL. "La Inversión Extranjera Privada en México: Problemas y Perspectivas." *Comercio Exterior*, Vol. XX, 10 (1970), 816-824.

WIONCZEK, MIGUEL *et al. Crecimiento o Desarrollo Económico*. Mexico D.F.: Secretaria de Educación Pública, 1971, 2 vols.

WOLF, ERIC R. "Aspects of Group Relations in a Complex Society: Mexico." in *Contemporary Cultures and Societies of Latin America*. Eds. Dwight B. Heath and Richard N. Adams. New York: Random House, 1965.

WYATT, S. and MARRIOTT, R. *A Study of Attitudes to Factory Work*. Special Report of the Medical Research Council no. 292. London, 1956.

ZEITLIN, IRVING. *Marxism: a Re-Examination*. Princeton: D. Van Nostrand, 1967.

ZEITLIN, MAURICE. *Revolutionary Politics and the Cuban Working Class*. New York: Harper & Row, 1970.

ZOLBERG, ARISTIDE. *Creating Political Order: The Party States of West Africa*. Chicago: University of Chicago Press, 1967.

Newspapers and Magazines

El Norte (Monterrey, N.L.)
El Porvenir (Monterrey, N.L.)
El Heraldo (Mexico, D.F.)
Excelsior (Mexico, D.F.)
Novedades (Mexico, D.F.)
¿Por Que? (Mexico, D.F.)
Siempre (Mexico, D.F.)
Sucesos (Mexico, D.F.)
El Ciudadano (Monterrey, N.L.)
Oigamé (Monterrey, N.L.)
Latin America: A Weekly Political and Economic Report (London)